MW00715756

# WealthCare

## Power Principles To Help You
## Achieve Financial Security

# Jim Elder

WEALTHCARE
Power Principles To Help You Achieve Financial Security
Copyright© 2002 by Jim Elder

Editor: Kathryn Marion
Cover Design: Karen Saunders
Cover Photo: Joyce Jay

Additional copies of this book may be purchased for educational, business, or promotional use.

For information please write: ElderAdo Financial Publishing
1100 S. Townsend Ave., Montrose, CO 81401

*This publication is designed to provide accurate and authoritative information in regard to the subject matter covered. It is published with the understanding that the author is not engaged in rendering legal, or accounting advice. If financial advice is required, the services of a competent professional person should be sought.*

Printed in Canada

ISBN: 0-9722482-5-0

# Dedication

Thanks to...

Janet, my wife and best friend, who is a true "saver." To my daughters Jaimee and Jessica who bring joy to my life.

A special thanks to my Grandma Ruby (95 years young at this writing) who, by instruction and lifestyle, has taught me how to live a life of contentment and about the virtue of frugality. Not persuaded by worldly desires, she showed me that life is much more than material "things" that moth and rust can destroy.

# Table of Contents

# Introduction

The famous author F. Scott Fitzgerald once stated "the rich are different from you and me." But in reality, with few exceptions, the rich are no different from you and me. They just understand basic money management concepts. They know how to make money and most importantly, they know how to manage it.

So how are super millionaires different than you and me? According to a recent survey conducted by Thomas J. Stanley and William D. Danko, authors of *"The Millionaire Next Door"* here are the results from interviews of over 1,000 millionaires:

- They live far below their means, and have little or no debt. Most pay off their credit cards every month; 40% have no home mortgage at all.

- Millionaires are frugal; they prepare shopping lists, resole their shoes, and save a lot of money; but they are not misers.

- 97% are homeowners; they tend to live in fine homes in older neighborhoods. Only 27% have ever built their "dream home."

- 92% are married; only 2% are currently divorced. Millionaire couples have less than one-third the divorce rate of non-millionaire couples. The typical couple in the millionaire group has been married for 28 years, and has three children. Nearly 50% of the wives of the super-rich do not work outside the home.

- Most are one-generation millionaires who became wealthy as business owners or executives; most did not inherit their wealth.

- Almost all are well educated; 90% are college graduates and 52% hold advanced degrees; however, few graduated at the top of their class—most were "B" students. They learned two lessons from college: discipline and tenacity.

- Most live balanced lives; they are not workaholics; 93% listed socializing with family members as their #1 activity; 45% play golf.

- 52% attend church at least once a month; 37% consider themselves very religious.

- They share five basic ingredients to success: integrity, discipline, social skills, a supportive spouse, and hard work.

- They contribute heavily to charity, church and community activities (64%).

- Their #1 worry: taxes! Their average annual federal tax bill: $300,000. The top 1/10 of 1% of U.S. income earners pays 14.7% of all income taxes collected!

- Not one millionaire had anything nice to say about gambling.

Many non-millionaires wish to have wealth to live the "millionaire lifestyle." However, they would be surprised how true millionaires live—not the lavish lifestyles that Robin Leach exploits.

Most people with money problems believe they need to make more money to solve those problems, when in fact the solution usually lies in the management. Trimming back their lifestyle, rather than earning more is the solution in most cases.

Money is only a tool to help you get the things that you need and want. However, too many people allow money to control their lives instead of controlling money itself.

This book is designed to help the reader understand some basics of financial stewardship. As we go through this book, we will give you the tools and information necessary to excel in the area of finances.

# Chapter 1

---

# Setting Goals

The saying "If you aim at nothing, you will probably hit it" is true especially if you are living your life without goals. Too many people fail to take steps toward giving their life direction.

Goal setting is a very powerful technique that can yield strong returns in all areas of your life.

Just as a map shows you where you're traveling on a highway, so your goals are a map for the road you're traveling in life!

At its simplest level, the process of setting goals and targets allows you to choose where you want to go in life. By knowing precisely what you want to achieve, you know what you have to concentrate on and improve, and what is merely a distraction. Goal setting gives you long-term vision and short-term motivation. It focuses your acquisition of knowledge and helps you organize your resources.

Unlike the typical American that sets goals on New Years Day and drops them by February, a good goal setter follows through on an on-going basis.

By setting sharp, clearly-defined goals, you can measure and take pride in the achievement of those goals. You can see forward progress in what might previously have seemed a long, pointless grind.

## By Setting Goals You Can:

- Achieve more

- Improve performance

- Increase your motivation to achieve

- Increase pride and satisfaction in your achievements

- Improve your self-confidence

- Eliminate attitudes that hold you back and cause unhappiness.

## People Who Use Goal-Setting Effectively:

- Suffer less from stress and anxiety

- Concentrate better

- Show more self-confidence

- Perform better

- Are happier and more satisfied.

# The Importance of Setting Goals

With rare exceptions, nothing truly worthwhile in life happens by accident. Sure, you may win the lottery, but what are the odds? What if you could achieve everything you ever wanted without winning the lottery? What if it were as simple as deciding where you wanted to go and planning the route to get there? Well it is. Goal setting is the process of deciding where you want to go in life and then mapping out a series of steps to get you there.

Success is something we create for ourselves. Luck has nothing to do with it. All successful people set goals. Some may have a structured routine, others a "vision." Some may not even consciously set goals at all. But the process is the same. Successful people know what they want, determine the steps that will get them there and then they implement them.

By setting and achieving goals, you will use your time more productively, perform better and more efficiently than ever before. With every goal you achieve, your self-confidence will increase, motivating you to aim ever higher. If you have goals, you have purpose. If you have purpose, you have direction.

If you have direction, you do not waste a whole heap of time (such as a lifetime) on activities and things that will not get you where or what you want.

Think of it as setting out on a long journey to somewhere you have never been before. Would you even put the key in the ignition unless you had a destination in mind and a map to get you there? If you're heading out for a lazy Sunday drive, maybe you would. But if your destination is somewhere specific, no way. You'd just end up spinning your wheels.

Your life is the longest and most exciting adventure you will ever take. Make sure you have a map before you start out. You may decide to take some side trips along the way, but you'll at least reach your destination eventually. You may even find some shortcuts. But if you leave without a map at all, you may just waste the entire journey driving around in circles.

## Deciding Your Lifetime Goals

The first step in setting personal goals is to consider what you want to achieve in your lifetime—setting lifetime goals gives you the overall perspective that shapes all other aspects of your decision making.

To give a broad coverage of all important areas in your life, try to set goals in all of the following categories:

### Artistic
Do you want to achieve any artistic goals? Are there any skills that you should improve?

### Attitude
Is any part of your mind-set holding you back? Is there any part of the way you behave that upsets you? If so, set goals to improve or cure the problem, even if the goal is only to get help.

## Career

What level do you want to reach in your career? Are you doing what you enjoy? If not, what career would you enjoy?

## Education

Is there any knowledge you want to acquire in particular? A degree you want, or need, to learn? What information and skills will you need to achieve other goals?

## Family

Do you want to be a parent? If so, how are you going to be a good parent? How do you want to be seen by a partner or by members of your extended family? Are you spending enough quality time with your family?

## Financial

Have you been managing your money properly? Are you working on eliminating debt? How much do you want to earn by what stage in your life? Are you saving enough from your wages? Do you have a will or trust and proper insurance?

## Physical

Are there any athletic goals you want to achieve, or do you want good health deep into old age? Are you satisfied with your weight or appearance? Are you following a diet and exercise program? What steps are you going to take to achieve this?

## Pleasure

How do you want to enjoy yourself? Are you doing the things in life that you enjoy?

## Public Service

Do you want to make the world a better place by your existence? Is there anyone who has a need you can fulfill? Are there any local civic groups you may want to join?

## Social

Do you have any social ambitions? Are there people you would like to meet? Do you need to improve listening skills and manners?

## Spiritual

What church or organization should you join or get involved in? Do you set time aside for private meditation and prayer?

# Know What You Want

Remember the old adage, "be careful what you wish for, you may just get it"? Be careful what you choose for your goals because you will probably get it. The methodical process of goal setting will make it inevitable.

It is important to know what it is you want. The key word in the last sentence is "you." It is what you want that is important, not what others want for you or for themselves through you. If you don't want to achieve your goal, you certainly won't. Conversely, if you have a burning desire to achieve your goal, you surely will.

Begin defining your goals by writing a wish list. Don't censor yourself. Visualize yourself living your ideal life. Think of categories such as career, education, family, personal life, physical, spiritual, financial, social, pleasure, and attitude.

What is your highest ideal for each of these categories?

Write it down. Perhaps it is to be at the top of your profession. Perhaps to be self-employed. Maybe it's to earn a PhD by the time you're 45 or to marry and have a family. It might be to attain your ideal weight and be physically fit. It could be to have a small circle of very close friends or to earn enough money to retire at 50.

What kind of house do you want to live in? Where do you want to live? What type of car do you want to drive? What exciting destinations do you want to visit?

Paint a picture. Use sweeping strokes and bold color. There are no limits. You are the architect of your future. You are limited only by your imagination.

# Prioritize

Once you have decided your goals in these categories, assign a priority. Then review the goals and re-prioritize until you are satisfied that the goals and priorities you have set reflect the shape of the life you want to lead. Also ensure that the goals you have set are the goals that you, not your parents, spouse, family, or people around you, want them to be.

# How To Start To Achieve Your Lifetime Goals

## Start Long-Term And Work Backwards

Now that you have written down your wish list and understand the criteria for effective goals, it is time to begin translating your wish list into a goal plan.

Starting with your wish list, express each "wish" in terms of a long-term objective. For example, if one of your wishes is to retire at 50 because you are independently wealthy, your goal could read "I am independently wealthy and retire at age 50."

In some cases, a particular wish will be the equivalent of a lifetime goal. In others, it will be able to be achieved in a relatively short timeframe.

For long-term or "life-time" goals, you will need to work backwards, breaking your objective down into more manageable sub-goals. One approach is to take a lifetime goal (say a 25-year goal) and break it down into 10-year, five-year and one-year sub-goals.

The lifetime objective "to retire at age 50 because I am independently wealthy" could translate to a 10-year goal of "I am debt free and my business generated a net profit of one million dollars this year." You could then take this 10-year goal and set a five-year goal of "I have quit my job and I am earning $100,000 per year from my own business." Your one-year goal could be "I am researching home businesses so I can set up my own business next year."

It will be obvious that by starting long-term and working backwards, the idea is to break each intimidating objective down into manageable steps. The end result will be a daily "to-do" list. Before going too far with this, however, take a moment to think through what you will need to achieve those longer-term goals.

Think about what skills you will need to acquire and how to get them; what information and knowledge; what help, assistance and collaboration; what resources. Then try and anticipate obstacles and plan a way around them. Prepare for all foreseen contingencies. Once you have a clear idea of what you will need, you can build these things into your goal plan.

Once you have set your lifetime goals, now set a 25-year plan of smaller goals that should be achieved if you are to reach your lifetime plan. Then set a 5-year plan, 1-year plan, 6-month plan, and 1-month plan of progressively smaller goals that should be reached to achieve your lifetime goals.

## Create A Daily Task List

By this point you should have worked your way backwards to at least the one year mark. Now work back to the six-month mark. What do you need to do within the next six months to achieve your one-year goals?

When you've set your six-month goals, work backwards even further and set out your one-month goals. What do you need to do within the next month to achieve your six-month goals?

Finally, by continually working backwards in this way, you will eventually get to the point where you are writing out what you need to do TODAY to achieve your longer-term goals. In this way, long-term goals are broken down into small, manageable tasks that are done on a day-to-day basis. The process is an incremental one of small steps today leading you ever closer to achieving your life's desires.

Imagine not having a daily task list. What would you be doing instead? Going to the same old boring job day in, day out, pottering about, starting something and not finishing it? Going around in circles, watching too much TV?

With a daily task list, you can be sure that you're investing your time and energies in activities that will bring you long-term benefit. These activities will bring structure and purpose to your day and eliminate time wasters. Soon you will find yourself becoming discriminating in what you give your time to. You will ask yourself, "How does this bring me closer to my goal of x"? You will learn there is a certain satisfaction and sense of accomplishment in crossing off a task as completed.

You will feel secure in the knowledge that you are taking care of business and, of course, once you have taken care of business, you can take some guilt-free time for play.

Now set a daily to-do list of things that you should do today to achieve your lifetime goals. At this stage many goals may simply be to read books and gather information on the achievement of your goals so that you can improve the quality and realism of your goal-setting.

# Achieving Goals

Now once you have a daily task list you have in your hands the steps you need to take to reach your longer-term objectives. But along the road to your destination, you are going to encounter unexpected twists and turns—probably a pothole or two for good measure.

You may find you get bored doing the same things day after day. You are going to have setbacks and crises of confidence. These are all to be expected and are perfectly natural and normal. The trick, though, is not to let them derail you from your course. This is what separates the successes from the wanna-be's. There are five keys to staying on track: commitment, flexibility, discipline, determination, and persistence.

Designing a goal plan and sticking to it requires commitment. It requires commitment to yourself and to your values and ideals. Unless you are committed to improving your life, don't even bother starting with goal setting. It won't be worth the effort.

Remind yourself constantly of your objectives. Put up photographs that represent your goals in prominent places. Write the reasons you want to achieve a particular objective next to the objective in your goal plan. Read them every morning and evening.

If your reasons don't compel you to keep striving, then perhaps they are not good enough reasons. Maybe the objective is not something you want badly enough. If so, change it. Don't let your objectives lock you into a path you don't want to go down. Be flexible. Setting and achieving goals is a lifetime process. Over the course of a lifetime you will go through many changes. What was important to you ten years ago may not be a priority any more. If this happens to you, let it go. Set new objectives that are consistent with who you are today.

Many of the tasks you have to do on a daily basis to achieve your longer-term objectives will be laborious and may become boring. It is tempting when boredom sets in to do something different. Don't!

Discipline yourself to carry out those tasks every day even if you don't feel like it. An objective to lose 60 pounds is not going to be achieved overnight. It requires daily exercise and attention to diet. Bored with your exercise routine? Change your routine but exercise anyway. Exercise personal discipline. It is amazing what a difference the daily performance of seemingly minor tasks can make over a relatively short period of time.

When you suffer setbacks, and you will, grit your teeth and keep going. This is what separates the winners from the wanna-be's. Anyone can give up when the going gets tough. Most do, in fact. It is those who keep going in the face of setbacks who are ultimately victorious.

And finally, persistence, persistence, persistence! Never give up. Never ever let anyone else make you doubt whether you can achieve your goals. Your success is in your own hands. Reach out and take it!

Finally review your plans, and make sure they fit with the way you want to live your life.

## Staying On Course

Once you have decided your first goal plans, keep the process going by reviewing and updating your to-do list on a daily basis. Some people recommend doing this as the last thing done the day before—others as the first thing done in the morning. This is up to you. Periodically review your other plans and modify them to reflect your changing priorities.

## Setting Goals Effectively

The way in which you set goals strongly affects their effectiveness. The following broad guidelines apply to setting effective goals:

**Positive Statement:** Express your goals positively: "Execute this technique well" is a much better goal than "don't make this stupid mistake."

**Be Precise:** If you set a precise goal, putting in dates, times and amounts so achievement can be measured, then you know the exact goal to be achieved, and can take complete satisfaction from having completely achieved it.

**Set Priorities:** Where you have several goals, give each a priority. This helps you avoid feeling overwhelmed by too many goals, and helps to direct your attention to the most important ones.

**Keep Your Goals Personal:** Remember to make sure that they are YOUR goals and not what others think they should be.

**Write Goals Down:** Avoid confusion and give them more force. Place your written goals where you see them at least everyday to keep you mindful of your goals.

**Keep Operational Goals Small:** Keep the goals you are working towards immediately (i.e. in this session) small and achievable. If a goal is too large, it can seem that you are not making progress towards it. Keeping goals small and incremental gives more opportunities for reward. Today's goals should be derived from larger goals.

## Set Performance, Not Outcome Goals

This is very important. You should take care to set goals over which you have as much control as possible. There is nothing as disappointing as failing to achieve a personal goal for reasons beyond your control such as bad business environments, poor judging, bad weather, injury, or just plain bad luck. Goals based on outcomes are extremely vulnerable to failure because of things beyond your control.

If you base your goals on personal performance, or skills or knowledge to be acquired, then you can keep control over the achievement of your goals and draw satisfaction from them. For example, you might achieve a personal best time in a race, but still be disqualified as a result of a poor judging decision. If you had set an outcome goal of being in the top three, then this will be a defeat. If you set a performance goal of achieving a particular time, then you will have achieved the goal and can draw satisfaction and self-confidence from its achievement.

Another flaw is where outcome goals are based on the rewards of achieving something, whether these are financial or based on the recognition of colleagues. In early stages these will be highly motivating factors; however as they are achieved, the benefits of further achievement at the same level are reduced. You will become progressively less motivated.

## Set Specific Goals

Set specific measurable goals. If you achieve all conditions of a measurable goal, then you can be confident and comfortable in its achievement. If you consistently fail to meet a measurable goal, then you can adjust it or analyze the reason for failure and take appropriate action to improve skills.

Ask yourself "How much money will I need?" Or, "What day do I expect to reach this goal?"

General goals cannot be measured easily. The more specific the goal, the easier to monitor and measure.

## Set Realistic Goals

Goals may be set unrealistically high for the following reasons:

1. **Other people:** Other people (parents, media, society) can set unrealistic goals for you, based on what they want. Often this will be done in ignorance of your goals, desires and ambitions.

2. **Insufficient information:** If you do not have a clear, realistic understanding of what you are trying to achieve and of the skills and knowledge to be mastered, it is difficult to set effective and realistic goals.

3. **Always expecting your best performance:** Many people base their goals on their best performance, however long ago that was. This ignores the inevitable backsliding that can occur for good reasons, and ignores the factors that led to that best performance. It is better to set goals that raise your average performance and make it more consistent.

4. **Lack of respect for self:** If you do not respect your right to rest, relaxation, and pleasure in life, then you risk burnout.

## Setting Goals Too Low

Alternatively, goals can be set too low because of:

1. **Fear of failure:** If you are frightened of failure, you will not take the risks needed for optimum performance. As you apply goal setting and see the achievement of goals, your self-confidence should increase, helping you take bigger risks. Know that failure is a positive thing: it shows you areas where you can improve your skills and performance.

2. **Taking it too easy:** It is easy to take the reasons for not setting goals unrealistically high as an excuse to set them too low. If you're not prepared to stretch yourself and work hard, then you are extremely unlikely to achieve anything of any real worth.

## Setting Goals At The Right Level

Setting goals at the correct level is a skill that is acquired by practice. You should set goals so they are slightly out of your immediate grasp, but not so far that there is no hope of achieving them. No-one will put serious effort into achieving a goal that they believe is unrealistic. However, the belief that a goal is unrealistic may be incorrect. Such a belief can be changed by effective use of imagery.

Personal factors such as tiredness, other commitments and the need for rest, etc. should be taken into account when goals are set.

Now review the goals you have set, then measure them against the points above. Adjust them to meet the recommendations and then review them. You should now be able to see the importance of setting goals effectively.

## Thinking A Goal Through

When you are thinking about how to achieve goals, asking the following questions can help you focus on the sub-goals that lead to their achievement:

- What skills do I need to achieve this?

- What information and knowledge do I need?

- What help, assistance, or collaboration do I need?

- What resources do I need?

- What can block progress?

- Am I making any assumptions?

- Is there a better way of doing things?

# Reality Check

Ask yourself these questions:

- Is it really my goal?

- Is it morally right and fair?

- Are the short-range goals consistent with the long-range goals?

- Can I commit myself emotionally to complete the project?

- Can I visualize myself reaching this goal?

- Are you willing to take action and persevere?

# Summary For Effective Goals

Once you have a vision for your life, it is time to start crystallizing your dreams and expressing them in terms of specific objectives. Before beginning the work of actually setting objectives, goals, and supporting tasks, it is important to understand the criteria for setting effective goals.

First, use the present tense. Express the goal as if it has already been achieved and not as something that will only occur in the future. It is important to think of your goals in the present tense, as this is what registers with your subconscious.

If your subconscious believes it is not something that is to happen now, it will not work on it now. It will deal with it later, when the appropriate time comes. Of course, for a goal that is expressed in the future tense, the time never comes.

Make your goals specific. If they are fuzzy and ill-defined, you will not be able to internalize them in a way that will allow you to decide on precise actions to take to achieve them. Also, your subconscious won't perceive them clearly enough to act on them. Furthermore, you will not know when or if you have achieved them! An example of a specific goal is "I weigh 125 pounds," not "I will lose weight."

Make your goals realistic. Whatever you set as a goal must be within your power. While it should be challenging, it must be something that you can achieve as a result of your own efforts and not something that depends on someone else doing something. Example: "I am self-confident and project this attitude to others", not "I make Tom fall in love with me."

Make your goals challenging. While your goals must be realistic, they must also be challenging if you are to gain any real benefit from them. After all, if you merely set as a goal something you would have achieved anyway (such as that automatic raise next month), what have you really achieved?

One final thought: A goal is merely a dream with a deadline.

# Chapter 2

---

# Knowing Where You Are Financially

## Financial Inventory

Before you go any further, you need to figure out where you are today. In any journey, you'll never get where you want to go without knowing where you're starting, and where you want to go. The journey of financial planning has to begin somewhere and that is understanding your current financial situation.

Know where you stand financially. Take an inventory of your assets and liabilities. ASSETS include: cash on hand, checking and savings account(s), stocks and bonds, investment funds, cash value of term life insurance policies, market value of real estate, market value of personal property, and cash values of retirement funds, IRAs, separation pay, etc. LIABILITIES include: mortgage or rent payments, car payments, outstanding bills, loans, educational loans, credit card bills, etc. The difference between your total assets and your total liabilities is your NET WORTH. It tells you where you stand financially on the day it's computed. When computed monthly, it shows your progress, or lack of it, towards your financial goals. Keep a monthly financial inventory with supporting files and records.

You will need to take an "inventory" of your financial situation. This inventory is basically a "snapshot" of a short period of time which will evaluate your finances. The next day after you take your financial inventory, your inventory will change (ie, your car is one day older, your house may have appreciated more, or you may have purchased something since then). Therefore your financial situation is never static but dynamic, ever-changing day-to-day.

In order to complete your inventory, you will need to know the following:

**Your Current Income:** wages, tips, alimony, child support, investment income, interest, dividends, Social Security, etc.

**Your Current Expenses:** all items in your budget such as housing, food, clothes, automobile, insurance, education, medical, etc.

**Your Current Cash Flow:** take all your current income and subtract your current expenses. If your expenses are more than your income, you are in big trouble. Get help NOW!

**Your Current Assets:** house, automobiles, furniture, appliances, investments, savings, jewelry, coins, etc.

**Your Current Liabilities:** mortgage, auto loan, $2^{nd}$ mortgage, secured loans, credit cards, school loans, etc.

**Your Current Insurance Coverages:** homeowner's, automobile, umbrella, liability, renter's, health, life, disability, long-term care, business, etc.

**How Your Assets Are Titled:** individual, joint tenancy, joint with rights of survivorship, pay on death, etc.

**The Cost Basis Of Current Investments:** how much you paid for the investments.

**Your Current Tax Situation:** how much you have had withheld, how many exemptions you claim, or how much you pay in estimated taxes.

**Your Employer-Provided Benefits:** insurance, pensions, paid vacations, 401k plans, etc.

**Any Government Benefits Received:** Medicare, Medicaid, Social Security, pensions, etc.

**Your Current Estate Planning Arrangements:** wills, living trusts, power of attorney, family trust, executor, etc.

As you can see, you need to gather together a complete list of everything you have going on. You can't get a handle on what to do until you know what you have. You may have to dig through some old shoe boxes, safety deposit boxes, files, drawers and so on to find everything.

You may have to make some phone calls to get updated information on some things. You may have to call your accountant to get a copy of last year's tax return. You may have to call your insurance agent to find out what types of insurance coverage you have. You may have to guess on some items, because you cannot find the answer anywhere or get it from anyone. While you may not get 100% of this stuff together, getting as much as possible is better than doing nothing.

If you never do any financial planning; if you never take any actions to change what you're doing; if you never find out other options you have available to you, you should get a handle on where you are anyway.

Just going through the exercise of getting your stuff together, seeing what you have and don't have, and knowing where everything is, is worth it, in and of itself.

Having a grasp on what you've accumulated throughout the years is a great thing to know. You'll feel more organized, be more objective, and be in more control.

Remember, this isn't an exercise to criticize yourself, or to bring up things you might rather forget. It's simply the time to "take stock," to get an inventory, to see where you are today.

We promise you'll be glad you took the time to do this, no matter what you decide to do about the information you gather.

## BUDGET

|  | Monthly | Annual |
| --- | --- | --- |
| **HOUSING** | | |
| Mortgage/Rent | _____ | _____ |
| Property Taxes | _____ | _____ |
| Property Insurance | _____ | _____ |
| Association Fees | _____ | _____ |
| Maintenance | _____ | _____ |
| Landscaping | _____ | _____ |
| Gas & Electric | _____ | _____ |
| Water & Sewer, Trash | _____ | _____ |
| Telephone / Long Distance | _____ | _____ |
| Satellite / Cable TV | _____ | _____ |

**CHILD CARE**
Day Care
Child Support/Alimony        _____        _____

**TRANSPORTATION**
Car Payment #1
Car Payment #2               _____        _____
Car Insurance #1             _____        _____
Car Insurance #2             _____        _____
Car Maintenance (tires, oil, etc.)  _____   _____
Gasoline                     _____        _____
Licenses, Taxes              _____        _____

**FOOD**
Groceries
Lunches                      _____        _____
School Lunches               _____        _____
Take Out/Delivery            _____        _____
Dining Out                   _____        _____

**CLOTHING**
Dry Cleaning
New Clothes, Shoes, etc.     _____        _____
Jewelry, Watches, etc.       _____        _____
Laundry                      _____        _____

**VACATIONS**
Short-Term
Long-Term                    _____        _____

**HOME FURNISHINGS**
Couches, Tables, Beds
Decorations, Pictures        _____        _____
Appliances                   _____        _____

**PERSONAL CARE/CASH**
Allowances
Lottery Tickets              _____        _____
Pocket Money                 _____        _____
Health Club                  _____        _____
Beauty/Barber                _____        _____

**OFFICE / EMPLOYMENT**
Professional Dues
Stamps                       _____        _____
Bank Charges                 _____        _____
Computer Equipment           _____        _____
Office Supplies              _____        _____

**MEDICAL / DENTAL**
Vitamins & Supplements
Doctor Visits                _____        _____
Prescription Drugs           _____        _____

Dental (checkups, braces) _____ _____
Vision (glasses, contacts) _____ _____
Medical Equipment _____ _____

## EDUCATION
Private School Tuition _____ _____
Books, School Supplies _____ _____
College Education _____ _____

## DEBT REDUCTION
Credit Cards _____ _____
Student Loans _____ _____
$2^{nd}$ Mortgage _____ _____
Installment Debt _____ _____
Additional Principal to Mortgage _____ _____

## ENTERTAINMENT
Pet expenses _____ _____
Magazine Subscriptions _____ _____
Newspaper _____ _____
Tobacco Products _____ _____
Movie/Theater _____ _____
Baby-sitters _____ _____
Hobbies(skiing, hunting, etc.) _____ _____
Ball Games, Events, etc. _____ _____

## CHARITY / GIFTS
Charities _____ _____
Tithing _____ _____
Missionary Support _____ _____
Birthday Gifts _____ _____
Christmas Gifts _____ _____
Anniversary Gifts _____ _____
Mother's & Father's Day _____ _____

## INSURANCE
Life Insurance _____ _____
Disability Insurance _____ _____
Health Insurance _____ _____
Mortgage Insurance _____ _____
Long-Term Care Insurance _____ _____

## SAVINGS
(short)Emergency _____ _____
(mid)College Education _____ _____
(long)Retirement _____ _____

## TOTAL EXPENSES
_____ _____

**CASH FLOW = Income minus Expenses**

# MONTHLY INCOME

<table>
<tr><td><u>Client</u></td><td><u>Spouse</u></td></tr>
<tr><td>

**MISC. INCOME**
Interest _____
Dividends _____
Rental Income _____
Child Support _____
Alimony _____
**Total Misc Income (A)** _____

</td><td>

**MISC. INCOME**
Interest _____
Dividends _____
Rental Income _____
Child Support _____
Alimony _____
**Total Misc Income (A)** _____

</td></tr>
<tr><td>

**EMPLOYMENT INCOME**
Gross Wages _____
Bonus _____
Overtime _____
Self-Employment _____
**Total Employment (B)** _____

</td><td>

**EMPLOYMENT INCOME**
Gross Wages _____
Bonus _____
Overtime _____
Self-Employment _____
**Total Employment(B)** _____

</td></tr>
<tr><td>

**Total Gross Inc (A+B)** _____

</td><td>

**Total Gross Inc (A+B)** _____

</td></tr>
<tr><td>

**TAXES**
Federal Income Tax _____
S.S. OASDI _____
S.S. Medicare _____
State Income Tax _____
Self-Employment Tax _____
Local Tax _____
**Total Taxes (C)** _____

</td><td>

**TAXES**
Federal Income Tax _____
S.S. OASDI _____
S.S. Medicare _____
State Income Tax _____
Self-Employment Tax _____
Local Tax _____
**Total Taxes (C)** _____

</td></tr>
<tr><td>

**SAVINGS**
Retirement _____
E.S.O.P. _____
Thrift Plan _____
Savings Account _____
**Total Savings (D)** _____

</td><td>

**SAVINGS**
Retirement _____
E.S.O.P. _____
Thrift Plan _____
Savings Account _____
**Total Savings (D)** _____

</td></tr>
<tr><td>

**INSURANCE**
Health Insurance _____
Disability Insurance _____
Life Insurance _____
Accident Insurance _____
**Total Insurance (E)** _____

</td><td>

**INSURANCE**
Health Insurance _____
Disability Insurance _____
Life Insurance _____
Accident Insurance _____
**Total Insurance (E)** _____

</td></tr>
<tr><td>

**TOTAL NET INCOME** _____
**(A+B-C-D-E)**

</td><td>

**TOTAL NET INCOME** _____
**(A+B-C-D-E)**

</td></tr>
</table>

# INVENTORY OF ASSETS AND LIABILITIES

|  | **Market Value** | **Liability** |
|---|---|---|
| **Fixed Assets** | | |
| Savings Account #1 | _____ | _____ |
| Savings Account #2 | _____ | _____ |
| Checking Account #1 | _____ | _____ |
| Checking Account #2 | _____ | _____ |
| T-Bills, Money Market, CDs | _____ | _____ |
| Government, Municipal Bonds | _____ | _____ |
| Corporate Bonds | _____ | _____ |
| Life Insurance Cash Value | _____ | _____ |
| Fixed Annuities | _____ | _____ |
| IRA, Roth IRA, 401k | _____ | _____ |
| Corporate Qualified Plans | _____ | _____ |
| Other Fixed Assets | _____ | _____ |
| | | |
| **Variable Assets** | | |
| Residence | _____ | _____ |
| Second Home | _____ | _____ |
| Common Stock | _____ | _____ |
| Mutual Funds | _____ | _____ |
| Variable Life Insurance Cash | _____ | _____ |
| Variable Annuities | _____ | _____ |
| Real Property Income | _____ | _____ |
| Real Estate Partnerships | _____ | _____ |
| Business Interest | _____ | _____ |
| Art, Antiques, Stamps, Jewelry | _____ | _____ |
| Gold, Silver, Coins | _____ | _____ |
| Commodities, Options | _____ | _____ |
| IRA, Roth IRA, 401k | _____ | _____ |
| ESOP, Stock Options | _____ | _____ |
| Corporate Qualified Plans | _____ | _____ |
| Other Variable Assets | _____ | _____ |
| | | |
| **Assets In Personal Use** | | |
| Personal Property | _____ | _____ |
| Automobiles | _____ | _____ |
| Recreational Vehicles | _____ | _____ |
| Recreational Property | _____ | _____ |
| Other Loans Including Credit Card | _____ | _____ |
| | | |
| **Total** | _____ | _____ |

**Net Worth = Assets <u>minus</u> Liabilities**

## Life Insurance

**Policy Type    Owner        Beneficiary        Amount**

_____

_____

_____

_____

_____

## Disability Insurance

**Policy Type        Owner        Benefit Amount**

_____

_____

_____

_____

## Health Insurance

**Policy Type        Coverage        Limits**

_____

_____

_____

## Long Term Care Insurance

**Policy Type        Owner        Benefit Amount**

_____

_____

_____

# Chapter 3

## Managing Debt

The image of the debtor can be humorous, such as Popeye's friend Wimpy, who often pleads, "I'll gladly pay you Thursday for a hamburger today." But debt for Americans is no laughing matter. Between 55% and 69% of all American households carry credit card balances, and the average debt is more than $7,000.

Credit card companies have made running up that balance deceptively convenient. What's lost when you're on that spending spree is the realization that paying off your debt can be costly, in terms of both cash on hand and your overall financial health.

Credit card debt is the most cunning adversary to securing your financial future. Unfortunately, many college students obtain credit cards while still in school. Credit card companies use enticing promotions to lure consumers by increasing credit limits and offering pre-approval. All of these strategies attempt to develop the habit of spending now and paying later.

Many people don't realize how destructive this habit is, until their credit card payments become the largest part of their monthly budget. Credit card debt, as a percentage of income, has been on the rise for the past two decades. It may be difficult to break the habit of using credit cards; however, the reward is worth the effort. A debt-reduction strategy called **The Debt Eliminator** (explained later in this chapter) will enable you to completely pay off your credit card balances.

# Assessing Your Debt

How much debt is too much? The figure varies from person to person, but in general if more than 20% of your take-home pay goes to finance non-housing debt or if your rent or mortgage payments exceed 30% of your monthly take-home pay, you may be overextended.

Other signs of overextension include not knowing how much you owe, constantly paying the minimum balance due on credit cards (or worse, being unable to make the minimum payments), and borrowing from one lender to pay another.

If you find that you're overextended, don't panic. There are a number of steps you can follow to eliminate that debt and get yourself back on track. Working your way out of debt will, of course, require you to adjust your spending habits and perhaps be more judicious in your spending.

## Begin With a Budget

The first step in eliminating debt is to figure out where your money goes. This will enable you to see where your debt is coming from, and perhaps help you to free up some cash to put toward debt.

Track your expenses for one month by writing down what you spend. You might consider keeping your ATM withdrawal slip and writing each expense on it until the money is gone. Hang on to receipts from credit-card transactions and add them to the total.

At the end of the month, total up your expenses and break them down into two categories: Essential, including fixed expenses such as mortgage/rent, food and utilities, and Non-Essential, including entertainment and meals out. Analyze your expenses to see where your spending can be reduced. Perhaps you can cut back on food expenses by bringing lunch to work instead of eating out each day.

You might be able to reduce transportation costs by taking public transportation instead of parking your car at a pricey downtown garage. Even utility costs can be reduced by turning lights off, making fewer long-distance calls, or turning the thermostat down a few degrees in winter.

The goals are to reduce current spending so you won't need to add to your debt and to free up as much cash as possible to cut down existing debt.

## Smart Debt Management

Once you've got your budget settled, you can begin to attack your existing debt with the following steps:

### Transfer High-Rate Debt To Lower-Rate Cards

Consolidating credit card debts to a single, lower-rate card saves more than postage and paperwork. It also saves in interest costs over the life of the loan. Comparison shop for the best rates and beware of "teaser" rates that start low, at say, 6%, then jump to much higher rates after the introductory period ends.

If you can only find a card with a low introductory rate, maximize the value of that low-interest period. By paying off your balance aggressively, you will reduce the balance more quickly than you will when the rate goes up, because more of what you're paying each month actually gets applied to paying the balance rather than finance charges

You can also contact your current credit card companies to inquire about consolidation and lower rates. Competition in the industry is fierce, and many companies are willing to lower their rates to keep their customers. Even a percentage point or two can make a difference if you have a sizable balance.

### Consolidate Your Debt

If cash flow is a problem, then consider using the equity in your home to consolidate your debt to one bill. In most cases this will lower your monthly obligation. However, understand that the way the lender is able to lower your payment is by stretching out the time over which you make payments. For instance, if you have an auto loan for $599 per month for 5 years, you could refinance with a home equity loan for only $399 per month for ten years. Such a deal!

Most people fail to do the simple math and discover that the $399 payment would cost an additional $12,000 over the life of the loan.

Newspapers and television are full of advertisements urging you to apply for a home equity loan. Buyer beware.

If you are considering consolidating, find a reputable mortgage broker you can trust to help you wade through the maze.

## Borrow Only For Appreciating Items

The best use of debt is to finance things that will gain in value, such as a home or an education. Avoid using your credit card for concert tickets, clothing, vacation expenses, furniture or meals out. By the time the balance is gone, you'll have paid far more than the cost of these items and have nothing but memories to show for it.

## Pay Off Your Debt

Follow a system that reduces and eventually eliminates debt completely. One of the most successful methods is one we developed years ago called "The Debt Eliminator."

# Debt Eliminator

| Creditor Name | Interest Rate | Balance Due | # Payments Remaining | Min. Monthly Payment | Additional Payment Amount | Revised Payment (E+F) | Revised # of Pmts (C/G) |
|---|---|---|---|---|---|---|---|
| (A) | (B) | (C) | (D) | (E) | (F) | (G) | (H) |
| ABC | 18% | $300 | 10 | $40 | $50 | $90 | 4 |
| DEF | 21% | $500 | 12 | $50 | $90 | $140 | 3 (7) |
| XYZ | 21% | $700 | 12 | $60 | $140 | $200 | 2 (9) |
| CAR | 12% | $3,000 | 24 | $150 | $200 | $350 | 5 (14) |
| 2nd Mtg | 11% | $10,000 | 60 | $200 | $350 | $550 | 17 (31) |
| House | 8% | $80,000 | 360 | $600 | $550 | $1,150 | 90 (121) |
| | | | | | | | Paid-Off |

# The Debt Eliminator

The Debt Eliminator is designed to help you pay off your balances quickly and painlessly. This strategy is the same as if you tear down a pyramid. If you did this, where would you start? The most logical place is the tip, since the foundation is so enormous. You would begin at the top, removing one brick at a time until the entire pyramid is torn down. Thus, you will pay off your balances, one payment at a time.

There are four simple steps to follow:

## Step One:

The first step of this strategy involves writing down all outstanding debt balances in ascending order (smallest to largest). This is referred to as the Debt Pyramid.

## Step Two:

The second step of the strategy is to concentrate on completely paying off the lowest balance. By paying off the lowest credit card balance, the top of the debt pyramid is eliminated. In addition to the minimum monthly requirement, you should pay an additional amount above the minimum. For example, if the minimum monthly payment is $40 on the smallest balance, an additional $50 would make the total payment of $90. Pay this extra amount every month until the entire balance of the first card is paid off.

## Step Three:

Once the lowest card (the tip of the pyramid) is completely paid off, you will begin to concentrate on the second lowest bill. You can now use the $90 that was going toward the lowest balance card to help pay off the second lowest debt—add the $90 to the minimum payment of (in our example) $50 for a total payment of $140. The benefit of using this step is that the minimum payments are already allocated into your budget. Thus, no additional money is reallocated to pay off outstanding debt, except the $50 per month you found to help pay off that first, lowest balance debt.

## Step Four:

Continue using this strategy until all debt is completely paid off.

## Step Five:

Promise to never go in debt again. Do whatever you can to change your lifestyle in order to avoid the debt trap.

# Ideas To Stop Using Credit Cards

Once you begin conquering your credit card balances, the worst thing to do is begin using them again. Here are four ideas to follow to stop using plastic:

## Lock Up or Cut Up Any Credit Cards

One of the best ways to stop using credit cards is to not carry them. However, everyone should have access to at least one card in case of an emergency. There may be times when a large amount of money is needed immediately. For example, to purchase an airline ticket in a family emergency or rent a car. An innovative way to remind yourself of this is to tape a piece a paper on each card with the words: "FOR EMERGENCY USE ONLY."

## Get In The Habit Of Writing Checks

Writing checks offers two advantages: The first benefit is you can't make a purchase unless the money is in the account. This may eliminate frivolous spending. The other advantage is it will wean you out of the credit card habit and into a pay-as-you-go lifestyle.

## Use Debit Cards

A debit card is similar to a credit card with one distinct difference. Whenever you make a purchase, money is subtracted from your checking account. You cannot spend more than is in your account.

One additional note: never use debit cards for Internet purchases. Because if you need to cancel a purchase, a debit transaction is difficult to reverse as opposed to a credit card.

## Put a Reward System in Place

Every time a credit card is paid off, treat yourself to a long walk on the beach or a dinner out, but not a shopping spree to put you in more debt.

By following the Debt Reduction Pyramid Strategy, anyone can take control of and completely eliminate credit card debt.

# Chapter 4

---

# Becoming A Wise Money Manager

## Protect Your Assets

Most people think it will never happen to them. The thought of being sued and having everything taken away just doesn't seem like it will happen... it only happens to others.

Well this is the 21$^{st}$ century, and we are living in one of the biggest lawsuit-happy times ever. People are getting sued left and right, and many times we find that hard to believe.

Lawsuits are a fact of life that everyone needs to be aware of and prepare for. If you don't prepare and safeguard your assets from being confiscated from a lawsuit, you stand to lose everything.

Since the last thing we want to see is you being sued and left homeless and broke, we're going to pack this chapter with information about lawsuits and how you can protect yourself from being wiped out.

Unfortunately, there's no other way around the fact that lawsuits are a way of life in America. Lawsuits are becoming a household term. Our litigation explosion has caused attorneys, legislators, and the general public great concern.

In fact, the Department of Justice recently reported that there are over 100 million active lawsuits at any given time.

There is a new lawsuit filed every 30 seconds in America. Unfortunately, no one is immune to having a lawsuit filed against them. It can happen to anyone, anytime, anywhere.

Depending on your occupation and your life-style, the average American probably has a one in fifteen chance of being sued sometime in their lives.

Now, obviously doctors, attorneys, and other service professionals are more likely to be sued because of their chosen occupation, but that doesn't reduce or eliminate your chances. You are just as likely a target for getting sued as anyone else.

Although we can't do anything about protecting you from a lawsuit, we can help you protect your assets so if and when it happens, you won't lose everything you own. We'll be taking you through these strategies soon.

## Lawsuit Magnet

Do you really think you are impervious to a lawsuit? Let's think about this. How many times have you heard about someone you know getting sued because of an auto accident, a family dispute when a parent dies, a bad tenant, or even a disagreement with a neighbor.

For instance, we know a person who is suing his contractor, who was roofing his house. The homeowner fell through the roof and broke his leg. However, he managed to do this because he was up there at 9:00 at night, in the dark, inspecting the work. The homeowner was not acting out of reason, yet the roofing contractor will pay through the nose for this lawsuit.

Not only can even the frivolous lawsuits happen to you, they probably will happen to you. In this society, anything goes when it comes to suing one another.

You may not be defending yourself in a big case, and maybe not a case that's going to make newspaper headlines, but it may be a suit just the same. It will drag you into court, cost you a small fortune in legal fees, aggravate and disrupt your life, and generally be a major pain in the neck.

Even if you win a lawsuit, you lose. Most times, you may need to spend thousands of dollars to defend yourself even in the most frivolous of suits.

Let's say your neighbor came by your house to borrow a cup of milk. You oblige and later you get sued. Why? Because the neighbor got a touch of nausea, which is blamed on the milk. I know this is frightening, but it's reality. And as ridiculous as this may seem, a lousy cup of milk could end up costing you thousands in legal fees.

And to make matters worse, even your liability insurance does not cover you for all situations. So if your insurance doesn't pay, guess who does? You!

## Hot Coffee

We've all heard about how McDonald's was sued for $2.9 million for spilled coffee that was too hot. The woman who sued won, and even though she didn't get $2.9 million out of it, McDonald's had to spend tens of thousands of dollars to defend itself.

Not only that, it served as a huge reality check for others as to how greedy and lawsuit-happy our society has become. A poll indicated that most Americans thought this woman was wrong for filing the lawsuit, but who cares? She did it and came out with a nice sum of money.

Do you think our Founding Fathers ever thought that serving hot coffee would be such a travesty of justice?

Sooner or later, someone will sue because the ice cream is too cold, a pillow too soft, and if it hasn't happened already, someone will no doubt sue a hammer manufacturer because they hit their own thumb.

### Preventative Medicine

The best way of protecting yourself from a lawsuit is not to become a target. If you use a little preventative medicine, you can apply it to lawsuits as well.

If it looks like you have money and good insurance, you advertise that you are a good target for these con artists.

Just like you wouldn't walk around with expensive jewelry in a crime-ridden neighborhood or flash money in a subway, why advertise that you are an easy target?

Now, this doesn't mean that we shouldn't drive expensive cars, because we may get sued. It just means that people take the risk of lawsuits if they advertise their wealth. That's all there is to it. If your ego requires you to flash your status then you will also be putting a bulls eye out for being a lawsuit victim.

## What's Yours Is Mine

In case you aren't aware of this, let me explain how contingency lawyers make their money. They project what 1/3 to 1/2 of the final judgment will be, and then decide if they'll take the case or not, because that's what they'll get paid.

Contingency lawyers aren't exactly looking to sue the grandmother who is living on Social Security with only $50,000 in liability insurance. They want people with money.

It is very easy for these lawyers to determine how much money you actually have before deciding to take your case. Computer searches of your wealth go on all the time. Credit reports, medical records, financial transactions are very easy to get. They can tap into your personal and financial life with a few keystrokes on the computer using the Internet.

Your personal affairs are not considered private to them when it comes to seeing how much money they'll get out of you if they take your case. Attorneys first see what assets you possess and are available before they take a case.

And because of this, the general public often does not get a fair shake in hiring an attorney. If you've got money, you'll get a good one. If you don't, you probably won't.

To make matters worse, most people think their insurance coverage is enough, when it's not. Many times insurance doesn't cover what you think it would.

## How Much Is Enough?

We all make mistakes, and sometimes we goof up and are truly at fault. And yes, sometimes people are hurt or killed because of these mistakes.

And rightly so, those people or their family members need to file a suit and be compensated for the damages we may have caused.

But, what happens if we have an auto accident and kill a forty-year old executive who was making $300,000 a year? And has a wife and children? Do you think your $100,000 auto coverage will protect you? Do you think that the executive's wife would be pleased to only get a few hundred thousand dollars in life insurance, and maybe $100,000 from your auto coverage, and some Social Security payments for her kids?

It's doubtful. Remember, when people injure us, it's human nature to fight back and protect our own interests. So in this case, you'd get sued by the executive's wife for the loss of income that he would have made, the pain and suffering that the family went through, and potentially punitive damages for ruining his family's life. This could end up being a multi-million dollar lawsuit.

If your $100,000 pays out, where do you think the rest of the money will come from? Well, they'll start going after your home, your investments, and your other assets. Wherever you've got money socked away, they're sure to find it so they can take it away from you.

Are you beginning to see why you need all the protection you can get, when there are attorneys and the IRS looking over your shoulder at all times, waiting for an opportunity to take what you have?

# Ownership Of Assets

## Asset Titles

There are various ways to own your assets. How you own your assets can make or break your financial picture when you pass away or are involved in a lawsuit.

The states differ on how your assets will be protected, or not, if you are sued. For instance, in some states creditors cannot take possession of your house even if it's worth $2 million dollars. But, in some states, you'll lose your home no matter what it's worth, and only be able to protect $7,500 in value of the house. That's quite a difference.

One important appointment with your financial advisor will help you understand which assets are protected and which aren't. It varies from asset to asset and from state to state.

You've heard of "reading the fine print" before. Same goes with the "fine print" in your state laws, and in comparison to the federal laws. These rules are important to know, so you can set up your assets appropriately, to be located beyond the reach of attorneys if you're in a lawsuit.

## Which Ownership Title Is Best For You?

Married couples can own their assets in many different fashions. It can be joint tenancy, tenancy in common, credit shelter trusts, tenancy by the entireties; and there's also community property, exempt assets, and non-exempt assets.

There are a lot of options available. Which one is best for you? It all depends on your personal situation and how well you want to protect your assets. The most important question to ask yourself when deciding how to own your assets is, "How do you own your assets, and why?" The "why?" question is the hardest for most to answer. Most people will say they own everything in joint tenancy, but they can't tell you why. Some of the worst answers are, "Well, that's how we always owned it." Or, "That's what the bank told us to do." Or, "That's what mom and dad did."

Now, think about your own answer to the above question. Why do you own your assets the way you do? If you can't come up with a real good reason, you need to talk to your advisors to find out how you should own your assets and why, not only for creditor protection, but for tax reasons, too.

## Asset Protection

If you're involved in a lawsuit, frivolous or not, there are certain ways you can own your assets that can't be penetrated by creditors. Sometimes, it will work if you put your assets in your spouse's or children's names. We can't tell you specifically this will safeguard your assets or not, because again it depends on your state rules. It also depends on the claim against you and the type of assets you own.

The best advice is to get some good legal and financial planning advice. For instance, reassigning your assets to your spouse or children may not work, because there are some assets you are prohibited from transferring. And, you can't transfer your IRA or pension plan without paying a tax penalty for doing it.

You may not be ready to transfer your house or whatever to your children. With the new transfer laws, transferring assets can be dangerous and lead to unanticipated consequences.

There are a lot of questions, issues, and concerns to be addressed first. It's not painful, and it doesn't take a whole lot of time—but it has to be done. Once you can determine a) how you own your assets, b) why you own them that way, c) what the federal and state rules are, and d) how you personally want to ensure protection of your assets, then you can put together a bulletproof plan.

It is very easy for creditors to click a couple keys on the computer and learn everything they want to know about your financial status. This concerns some people, as it should. It kind of breaks the "right to privacy" notion we all want to believe in.

For any of you who are concerned about creditor protection, you can relax a bit; there are certain types of trusts and partnerships that can provide a buffer against certain types of suits and judgments. You can create your own barriers with some good maneuvers. In fact, if you seek the ultimate protection of your assets, some people create asset protection trusts in offshore countries.

In other countries, lawsuits are treated differently. So, if you have put your assets into trusts in these other countries, many of these jurisdictions don't even honor U.S. judgments. The theory is this: If you get sued and lose in the U.S., and your assets are titled in an offshore asset protection trust, the creditors won't ever be able to touch those assets.

However, this is a complex area of legal and financial planning. This issue should only be addressed with a competent trust attorney, who understands both the U.S. and foreign rules.

## Umbrella Insurance Policy

We strongly urge you to consider getting a minimum of a one-million-dollar Liability Umbrella policy that would cover you for lawsuits above the coverage you have on your homeowners and auto policies.

Most people only have $100,000 to $300,000 liability coverage, which will not be enough in most lawsuits. If you have only $300,000 of liability coverage, and lost a $1,000,000 suit, the insurance company would pay the first $300,000 and you'd pay the other party the remaining $700,000.

Umbrella policies are relatively inexpensive. It provides a lot of protection for the dollar. Contact your current auto and homeowners insurance agent for more information.

## Keep It Simple

The key to remember in your whole financial scheme of things is that there are both simple and complex ways to protect your assets from creditors, lawsuits, bad business deals, and various other threats against your assets.

Just as you should do regular check-ups of your estate plan, retirement plan, and investment plan, you should also do a periodic risk analysis to see if you have done all you can to avoid having your assets confiscated. Make sure you have enough liability insurance, and make sure you own your assets in the best possible method to make them less of a target.

# What Happens If You Get Sued?

## First Things First

If you are ever served papers initiating a suit against you, the first thing you should immediately do is hire a competent attorney. We wouldn't recommend trying to defend yourself. The legal system is full of details one can easily overlook. There are certain deadlines, evidentiary foundations, subpoenas, and other legal matters that must be addressed in a timely matter.

If you get sued because of an auto accident, immediately contact your insurance carrier. Your insurance company will usually provide an attorney to defend you if your coverage provides for it. If you get sued because of an auto accident and you don't have insurance, don't wait until the day before the court date to find an attorney. Preparation for a trial takes time, and you'll give the other side a huge chance at winning if you don't understand the system. Remember, "ignorance of the law is no excuse."

As you already know, hiring an attorney will cost you some money. No ifs, ands, or buts about it. But if you try to guess at the complex judicial system and do not hire an attorney, there's no question that it will cost you much more in the long run.

Also, make sure that you get an attorney who understands the type of matter you are involved in to make sure you get the best defense. There are different types of lawyers who specialize in different areas. If you're in an auto accident, the real estate attorney who closed on your house may not be the best person to defend you. Your divorce attorney probably can't help you in a wrongful death claim against you, and so on. Find one that studies that particular area of the law as a living.

## Stay Calm

If you get sued, don't panic. Now, that may seem like an unreasonable tip, but you'd be surprised at how many people get scared stiff and start doing crazy things. Some will act guilty, even if they aren't.

What do we mean by that? They get sued, and even though they may be innocent, they start transferring all their assets to their kids, selling the house, and move out of the country. First of all, these hasty decisions are usually an overreaction to being nervous and scared. Second of all, and more importantly, transferring assets after a suit is filed, even small transfers, could be considered a fraudulent transfer that can be quickly reversed by the courts.

If you're being sued for $1 million, and the court says you have to pay up, you shouldn't pat yourself on the back if three days prior you transferred all your assets into your children's names. In fact it is wrong. It won't work. And more importantly, it could get you into more trouble.

Transferring funds after a lawsuit may even be a criminal matter. In other words, it doesn't do you any good to transfer any assets after you get sued. You must act BEFORE any lawsuit, and that takes planning ahead.

# A Word About Criminal Matters

Do you know the difference between civil and criminal charges? If you were in an auto accident and someone is killed, you could face a wrongful death claim, which is a civil claim. Money for damages will be sought, while at the same time there's a possible criminal charge of vehicular manslaughter. And again, money for damages will be sought.

The biggest key is not to go on the advice of your friends or your neighbors or your church group members or your accountant... not even this book. Your best bet is to seek the advice of a good attorney, or several of them.

## How To Start Over

If you happen to get sued, and you lose, there may be some relief. You may be able to file bankruptcy or rely on certain provisions of your state to protect some of your assets. Or, sometimes insurance pays the claim, and the worst thing that happens is your rates go up.

On the other hand, you could lose everything. All that you have worked for in your lifetime could go up in smoke.

To avoid the latter from happening, take a good hard look at your assets. Determine the best methods of protection based on your personal situation, then take the next step and do it.

Good honest people get sued. Good honest people get wiped out because of things they do and don't do with their assets.

One thing is for sure, lawyers are rampant. We live in a treacherous legal environment, and if you don't take some preventative steps now, you may not be able to protect yourself later.

# Emergency Cash Reserve

One of the leading causes for financial ruin and bankruptcy is the lack of emergency savings. You need to plan for the unexpected. Everybody will experience some sort of emergency in their life such as health issues, accidents, job changes, etc.

Setting aside money to meet unexpected expenses provides a financial safety net and allows you to take advantage of financial opportunities as they arise. Most experts recommend an **emergency fund** equal to at least three to six months' living expenses; however, you do not need to set aside the full amount in a low-yielding passbook, certificate of deposit, or money market account.

The amount of your emergency fund depends upon your age, health, job outlook, and personal financial situation (e.g., amount and kind of insurance coverage).

An emergency fund might be adequate with enough to cover three to six months of expenses using a combination of cash and credit if you have a source of low-cost borrowing (e.g., home equity credit-line loan, cash-value life insurance, or retirement plan). If your household has multiple sources of income or dual earners, you can count on those other sources of income in an emergency.

You might want a larger emergency fund if you are in business for yourself, your work is seasonal, or you rely heavily on commissions. If your health is questionable (e.g., you foresee long-term disability or extensive medical expenses), you anticipate a large expenditure for the care of a relative in the near future, or your child is about to enter college, you may also need a larger cash reserve.

Your emergency cash reserve can be subdivided to minimize penalties for early withdrawal of large amounts of funds at one time and to maximize interest earned on accounts should an emergency occur.

Money that would be needed within three months of a financial emergency is best placed in an interest-bearing checking account, passbook savings, money market deposit account, or money market mutual fund.

Funds needed four to six months after an emergency could be placed in short-term certificates of deposit (CDs) as well as three and six-month Treasury bills.

Money that would not be needed for seven months to two years could be placed in 12-month Treasury bills and longer-term CDs (12-, 18-, and 24-month).

Money you can avoid withdrawing for two to five years during a financial emergency could be placed in two or five-year Treasury notes, short-term bond funds, or three to five-year CDs.

# Inflation

One factor that many people fail to consider when it comes to money management is inflation. Inflation is another way of saying: things you have to buy go up in price over a period of time.

Now there are all kinds of technical explanations of why inflation occurs. There are all kinds of scientific theories and economic models that explain how and why prices go up.

We can get this information from all kinds of textbooks, financial journals, published articles by professors, and so on. We're going to skip all that stuff for this book because the reality is that, for you and your family, it doesn't matter why there is inflation. All you need to know is that it is there and understand how to deal with it.

It's kind of like trying to understand why and how the sun works, versus understanding how to live your life while the sun is up, and how to live your life when the sun is down. In other words, how to deal with the fact that there is a sun. That's what we're going to cover in this chapter, how to **deal** with inflation.

There's a very important aspect of inflation that must be discussed. The issue of the government, and how the government relays information about inflation to us as members of the general public.

Now there are all kinds of opinions as to why inflation is created by the government, how the government makes inflation worse than it would have to be otherwise, and all sorts of related topics.

As we said a minute ago, we're not going to get into all of that here in this book. But we do think it's important to understand the difference between what the government *tells you* inflation is all about versus the truth of what inflation *really is* all about.

## The Government's Story

Most of us depend on and turn to the government for our information about things like inflation.

Over the past 80 years the government has created indexes about inflation that they report to us every single month about how fast prices are going up. Back in 1913, the government came out with a new measure of inflation called the Consumer Price Index (CPI). The Consumer Price Index is a government formula to tell the public how high prices have gone up on average in the United States over a month's period of time and is then converted to an annual rate of inflation.

For example, the government might say that this month the CPI went up 0.4%, which translates to an annual rate of inflation of 4.8%. They might also tell us that in May, inflation rose 4/10 of 1% for the month, but because of lower figures in previous months, the average annual rate of inflation for the year is actually running at 3.7%, not 4.8% as you would assume.

Now, what's the problem with the CPI? First of all, since they only use a limited number of items in calculating the CPI, it doesn't necessarily reflect the reality of what you're facing when you buy things on a daily, or regular basis.

For example, housing prices may be down on the nationwide average, which would bring the CPI down, but that may be the only sector of our economy that is going down when other areas of our lives may be increasing substantially in cost. If you're not buying a house, the fact that housing prices went down has no bearing on your life, or on what you pay for everything else.

They pull this trick all the time. In a recent month, for example, they said that inflation was running at 0.4%, which would translate to a 4.8% annual rate of inflation. But, they cautioned, we shouldn't pay too much attention to this, because if you took out the jump in food and energy prices, the index would have only been 0.1%.

How nice of them! They're telling us to ignore the reality that gas and food prices went sky high. They're telling us that if we don't eat or drive, that inflation isn't that bad. It's insulting to all of us to think we're that dumb—that we can't figure out that huge jumps in the cost of eating and driving cannot be ignored.

Another problem with the CPI is that because it is based on a formula that some professors came up with years ago, it doesn't necessarily mean the formula is right, or takes into account all the variables that we face today as consumers.

What is the government's incentive to keep inflation as low as possible? The reason is because the CPI is tied to a minor thing called Social Security benefits. The Social Security benefits are increased based upon the CPI. If the CPI is high, the Social Security benefits will increase a large amount, thus possibly bankrupting the Social Security system. If the government can keep the increases small, it will help keep the Social Security system solvent.

Yet because so many things that we think about in our financial lives revolve around how the government reports inflation to us, this causes a serious problem.

# Betty's Story

Let's take, for example, the story of Betty. Betty was a retiree in 1975. Her husband passed away prior to that, and left her with a relatively modest pension from the teacher's union, a Social Security retirement benefit, an almost-paid-for home, and a few bucks in the bank from some life insurance.

In 1975 when she retired, she was receiving a little over $400 a month. She had about $15,000 in the bank, and a mortgage payment of only $97 a month. Her car payment was only $21 a month and her other fixed expenses such as food, utilities, insurance, health costs, etc. only ran about $200 a month.

By the time she retired, Betty actually had a small surplus cash flow of about $50 a month, money in the bank, and a secure and peaceful retirement in front of her. She thought!

But then things really changed. Betty was in great health, and ten years after her retirement at age 75, she still had basically the same $400 a month coming in, but her expenses had increased to where she was running a negative cash flow-spending more than she took in.

Her savings had decreased a bit because she had gone on a few vacations and helped a few of the grandkids with some education costs, paid for part of a wedding, and so on.

But, she was basically okay. She moved into a retirement home. Her monthly expenses were up to around $700 per month. This negative $300 per month in cash flow didn't seem too bad since she had principal in her bank account to cover the shortfall.

Now we move ahead ten years to 1995. Betty is 85, still in good health, and in financial trouble.

Her bank accounts are zero. She's living in the retirement home, still in decent health but failing, and having to depend on the grandkids to put in money each month to pay her bills and take care of her.

If she needed anything, the family had to buy it for her. The $400 a month she was getting at age 65, which *seemed* OK at the time, *was no where near enough at age 85!*

# The REAL Inflation Story

Now let's talk a little bit more about how Betty's story relates to the government's so-called measure of inflation, and the reality of what Betty faced and what you will be facing as well.

According to the U.S. Department of Labor, Bureau of Labor Statistics, the government figures of what inflation has run on an annual basis since 1975 (the CPI) are an average of 5.3% per year.

For example, let's take a car. A new 2000 model year car would cost you about $25,000. Back in 1975 a similar car would cost you $3,500. If you take the CPI figure of 5.3%, and calculate how much the 1975 cost of $3,500 would grow, it would end up at only $12,728. Significantly less than the $25,000 it actually does cost.

Using these prices, the *REAL* inflation rate on the car, and most other cars, is *ACTUALLY* 8.18%, or 2.88% higher than what the government tells you.

If you want to see another example, let's look at nursing home costs. In 1965, the monthly cost of a top-end, quality nursing home was about $175 a month. In 2000, the average cost, depending on the area, was about $4,000 a month.

Nursing home costs have risen at an annual rate of 9.36% per year. This is almost double what the government says inflation is running. If "true" inflation increases at the same rate, a nursing home stay will cost $9,787 a month only ten years from now.

Let's take college education as another example. In 1975, the cost of a four-year, public, state university in most parts of the country was around $2,000-maybe $3,000 in more expensive schools. Today, that same education would cost around $8,000 per year or about $32,000 for a four-year education.

Same college, same dorm, same books (maybe updated versions), but basically nothing better or different. If you look at the Consumer Price Index and multiply 5.3% out over a 25-year period, the price of a college should only cost $7,275 not $32,000.

Let's take another area, like your home. In 1970, the median home price was around $21,000. Today, the median price of a house is $160,000. Using the CPI factor from Uncle Sam, the median price of a house should only be around $98,871. The real inflation has brought that cost up way more than what the government says. In fact, housing prices have jumped more than 35% higher than the so-called CPI would have you believe.

How about the increased cost of clothing? Or the cost of shoes? Or dinning out? Or sporting tickets? Or auto parts? Or snow skiing? Or stamps? Do you get the idea?

## Two Different Stories

What the government tells us about inflation and what it really is are two different things. In fact, they are so different that our viewpoint is that the CPI is a meaningless piece of information. We don't pay much attention to it and you should be skeptical.

If the government wants to attempt to soften up this problem, that's their choice. But we all know that whatever it costs to buy things is what it costs. We can't go to the department store and tell them they have to charge us less for our clothes because, according to the government, the price should only be about half of what they're charging.

The other aspect that's very important to understand is that different types of items have different amounts of inflation attached to them. Some go up much faster than others.

Medical care and college costs, for example, are significantly more inflated every year than other costs.

Even a general category, like food, may have certain items that explode in price over a period of time because of shortages, increased production costs, etc.

All this can be summarized by saying there is more inflation than we realize. If we don't plan for it and allow our retirement plan to have a built-in inflation factor—if we don't plan our investments to include a generous amount of inflation to our costs—our retirement plan isn't going to work.

Betty didn't realize how bad things were, because she was living her life day-by-day and didn't see the jumps in prices all at once. The cost of living gradually increased everyday. Before she knew it she was in financial trouble.

# Future Costs

The monthly premium on your health insurance that might cost you $500 a month could be $1,080 per month in ten years and $2,330 per month in twenty years.

The average home that now costs $175,000 will cost about $345,000 ten years from now.

The car you bought for $30,000 with monthly payments of $450 might cost you $64,750 with monthly payments of $971 ten years from now.

It's no easier for you to accept paying that much for a monthly car payment than it was for Betty to accept that her $97 monthly mortgage payment would turn into a $4,000 per month fee at the retirement center for her to have a place to live.

It was no easier for Betty to believe that a doctor's visit would cost $125, or that a gallon of milk would be $3. The prices we live with and accept as "normal" would have made Betty think you were crazy if you told her what things would cost.

She wouldn't have been able to understand how anyone could survive with prices like that, and as it happened, she didn't survive financially. She lived in her 1970 mentality.

# How To Deal With Inflation

Now that we understand inflation and how it can destroy your finances, we must now learn how to **PLAN** for it.

First, we must figure out what your monthly budget is today, in today's dollars, and calculate a realistic number of how much after-tax income we need to live on today.

You will need to pick several inflation rates and figure out how much this same monthly budget will cost 2, 5, 10, 15, 20, 25 years from now to have the same life-style based on the inflation rates that you pick.

Then, you have to take a look at your investment portfolio plus your current resources for income such as pension, Social Security, and so on, that you're receiving now. You have to figure out what you're actually getting in interest or return on your investment today, and what your cash flow is today.

Then you will need to figure your future income and investments by adding in inflation. Now chart this year-by-year beginning now and figure in each year. In one column place your monthly budget, next your pension income, then your Social Security, and finally your investment rate of return. The last column will keep track of the running total.

This chart will show you approximately how your finances will fare in years to come in regards to inflation. It will also show what it will cost to live in the future by inflating your budget each year. Even if you don't fill in all the columns, at least you'll know what you will be spending each month.

The advantage of this chart is that you have a realistic plan based on a realistic expectation of inflation and not the phony CPI figures the government would have us use. So we have dealt with inflation realistically instead of the dreamland the government presents to us.

If you look at your completed inflation chart you will see what happens if you don't change the way you invest or spend money. You can see how you may need to alter some of your investments to give you a better, higher rate of return.

A higher rate of return will give you a better chance to outpace inflation and allow you to reach your retirement goals.

## Investing To Beat Inflation

Bulletproofing your portfolio against the threat of inflation might begin with a review of the investments most likely to provide returns that outpace inflation.

Over the long run—10, 20, 30 years or more—stocks may provide the best potential for returns that exceed inflation. While past performance is no guarantee of future results, stocks have historically provided higher returns than other asset classes.

Consider these findings from a study of Standard & Poor's data. An analysis of 20-year holding periods between 1943 and Dec. 31, 1999, found that the average annual return for a portfolio comprised exclusively of stocks in Standard & Poor's Composite Index of 500

Stocks was 11.38%—well above inflation rates for the same period. The average annual return for long-term government bonds, on the other hand, was only 5.13%.

In addition, the study found that the stock portfolio did not suffer a loss in any of the 445 separate 20-year holding periods. In every period, the annual rate of return for the stock portfolio was greater than the inflation rate. The bond portfolio outpaced inflation in only 169 of the 445 20-year holding periods—by a much lower margin.

There are many ways to include stocks in your long-term plan in whatever proportion you decide is appropriate. You and your professional financial planner can create a diversified portfolio of shares from companies you select. Another option is a stock mutual fund, which offers the benefit of professional management. Stock mutual funds have demonstrated the same long-term growth potential as individual stocks. CDA Weisenberger tracked equity mutual funds from 1943 through 1998 and found an average annual return of 13.66%.

## **Summary**

No one wants to end up like Betty. No one wants to end up dead broke and having to depend on their family or other charity to take care of yourself.

Unfortunately, there are lots of Betty's out there, and lots more Betty's who aren't aware of their situation.

We don't want this to be you. Just because you might be okay today doesn't mean you'll be okay somewhere down the road.

People live a lot longer now and this makes inflation problems even worse. All the improvements in health care, and the improvements in the health consciousness of the American public, have created a bigger problem in retirement. The longer time you'll be living, the more you will need your money to grow so you can beat inflation.

Remember that inflation doesn't care whether you have lots of money or a little money; it wipes out your purchasing power at any income level. It is definitely a non-discriminating villain.

Don't be naive and stick your head in the sand and just hope things will turn out okay. These days that type of "planning" won't work. No one has a crystal ball to know exactly what the inflation rate will average over the coming years, but that doesn't mean we can't use the past to help us make some educated guesses in planning for the future.

We think "real" inflation will remain high in years to come. So the "Betty's" out there will need to plan ahead to avoid the inflation dangers.

Make sure you plan in the effects of inflation. Then monitor your plan, update your plan, and make adjustments as necessary so you're always on target and you don't ever end up like Betty.

Inflation is the most overlooked monster lurking out there to bite your financial head off. Don't pretend by ignoring it and hoping it will go away, it won't, no matter what our politicians and economists tell us.

So *YOU* have to take the right actions if you want to be secure and not end up like so many Betty's.

# Chapter 5

---

# Finding Money To Invest

Many Americans are going broke on some of the highest incomes our country has ever seen. Studies estimate that 70% of Americans live from "paycheck to paycheck," courting financial disaster if their income is suddenly reduced or stopped.

Generally, Americans are not saving for a "rainy" day; they are consuming it all today. The individual saving rate in the United States fell from 6% to 4.5% of disposable income between 1980 and 1990. In 1998, Americans saved only 0.5% of their disposable personal income, and in 2000 the average savings rate was a **negative** 1%.

How can you have a negative savings rate? Simple, you just spend more than you make. Many Americans withdraw money from their savings and investments to make purchases.

## Are You Saving Enough Money?

We will help you "find" money to fund your investment plans. We will suggest tools for success, but you have to supply the desire, self-discipline, wise decisions, and good planning to be successful.

Review your financial status by answering these questions:
- Do I have three to six months of expenses in an emergency fund?
- Do I save regularly?
- Do I know how much I need to save to achieve future goals?
- Do I save to purchase big-ticket items instead of buying on credit?

- When I use credit, do I save to make as large a down payment as possible?
- Do I save at least 10% of my personal disposable income?
- Do I know how much I need to save for retirement?

The more times you answer "yes" to these questions, the more likely you are a prudent saver. A "no" can help you identify areas where you could do better. Once you have a sound savings program in place, you are ready to invest surplus funds. Unfortunately, many people feel their savings are not sufficient, and they see no way to meet their immediate needs and have extra funds to invest.

It doesn't take a lot of money to start investing. There are investments that require as little as $25 for a U.S. savings bond or $250, $500, or $1,000 to open a mutual fund account, depending on account requirements.

# Strategies For Saving Money To Invest

## Establish A Regular Savings Program

The first strategy is to set up a regular savings program if you do not already have one. Saving means putting money aside from present earnings to provide for a known or unexpected need in the future. It is an integral part of family and personal financial planning. Having a specific goal provides motivation to save. You probably will not get very far saving for the sake of saving.

### Needs Versus Wants

Individuals and families save to satisfy their needs and wants. **Needs** are items that are necessary for survival such as food, shelter, clothing, and medical care. **Wants** are all the other things we think we need, but could do without. If we spend our money to satisfy wants before we meet our needs, we will probably experience financial difficulties. The pressure to acquire present wants is often greater than the willingness to provide for future needs or even future wants.

Generally speaking, four major financial needs require planning for the near and distant future:

**Emergencies** from the normal course of living such as car repairs, illness, or replacing a major appliance.

**Loss of income** as a result of death, divorce, disability, or unemployment.

**Other family goals** such as education for your children or a special vacation.

**Retirement** with financial freedom to do various activities.

Once goals have been set, a major thought in most people's minds is "How am I going to reach this goal? There is no way I can save that much money!" However, most people find that—if they really put their minds to it and they have set realistic goals—they can save the necessary money.

As we noted earlier, a regular savings program is critical to a family's immediate well-being as well as their long-term security. To adequately fund a savings program and begin an investment program, you must identify a specific amount to save from each paycheck and honor that commitment. Regular savings in small amounts is generally more effective than setting aside larger sums at sporadic intervals. As your salary increases, increase the amount you commit to savings.

## Pay Yourself First

Another important concept for your savings program is to "pay yourself first." Make your "savings bill" a part of your spending plan, just like rent or mortgage, utility bills, clothing, car payment and upkeep, childcare, or any other bill that you normally incur.

When you pay your other bills, pay your savings bill by depositing the money into a savings account or other financial instrument. One painless way to accomplish this is payroll deduction, if it is available. Your employer deposits your savings directly from your paycheck into a credit union, bank account, or a money market fund for a higher interest rate.

If you never see the money, you won't miss it or be tempted to use it for something else before it reaches your savings account. Note how quickly small amounts of money can grow with time (Refer to Table 1).

**Table 1    How $10.00 a Month Will Grow**

| Year | 3% | 4% | 5% | 6% | 7% | 8% | 9% | 10% | 11% | 12% |
|---|---|---|---|---|---|---|---|---|---|---|
| 1 | $122 | $122 | $123 | $124 | $125 | $125 | $126 | $127 | $127 | $128 |
| 2 | 247 | 249 | 253 | 256 | 258 | 261 | 264 | 267 | 270 | 272 |
| 3 | 376 | 382 | 389 | 359 | 402 | 408 | 415 | 421 | 428 | 435 |
| 4 | 509 | 520 | 532 | 544 | 555 | 567 | 580 | 592 | 605 | 618 |
| 5 | 646 | 812 | 683 | 701 | 720 | 740 | 760 | 781 | 802 | 825 |
| 6 | 788 | 812 | 841 | 868 | 897 | 926 | 957 | 989 | 1,023 | 1,058 |
| 7 | 933 | 968 | 1,008 | 1,046 | 1,086 | 1,129 | 1,173 | 1,220 | 1,268 | 1,320 |
| 8 | 1,083 | 1,129 | 1,182 | 1,234 | 1,289 | 1,348 | 1,409 | 1,474 | 1,543 | 1,615 |
| 9 | 1,238 | 1,297 | 1,366 | 1,435 | 1,507 | 1,585 | 1,667 | 1,755 | 1,849 | 1,948 |
| 10 | 1,397 | 1,472 | 1,559 | 1,647 | 1,741 | 1,842 | 1,850 | 2,066 | 2,190 | 2,323 |
| 15 | 2,270 | 2,461 | 2,684 | 2,923 | 3,188 | 3,483 | 3,812 | 4,279 | 4,589 | 5,046 |
| 20 | 3,283 | 3,668 | 4,128 | 4,644 | 5,240 | 5,929 | 6,729 | 7,657 | 8,736 | 9,991 |
| 25 | 4,460 | 5,141 | 5,980 | 6,965 | 8,148 | 9,574 | 11,295 | 13,379 | 15,906 | 18,976 |
| 30 | 5,827 | 6,940 | 8,357 | 10,095 | 12,271 | 15,003 | 18,445 | 22,793 | 28,302 | 35,299 |

The table can be used to find out how long it will take to reach your financial goals. It shows the growth of monthly $10 deposits invested at various interest rates. Put aside $10 a month for five years at 10%, for example, and you'll have $781—the figure at the intersection of the year five and 10% interest columns. If you can invest $50 each month, you will have five times $781, or $3,905.

## Strategies to Stretch Your Money

Whether you save pennies to make dollars, break habits and bank the savings, or find that you are the beneficiary of a long-lost life insurance policy, *you* are the one who has to manage your funds to best meet your individual and/or family goals.

Remember that saving money does not make one a tightwad. On the contrary, saving money often allows you to have more of what is important to you and your family. As you continue on your path to saving money, you may find that the following ideas will serve you well as road marks on your journey.

## Adopt The Two-Week Rule

If you think you really want something, wait two weeks to get it. The purpose of this habit is to make you an impulse saver, not an impulse spender. The two-week rule does not mean losing out on a once-in-a-lifetime opportunity.

How many items, such as expensive clothing, a new piece of furniture, a boat or recreational vehicle, or a new car, would not be there in two weeks? If you wait two weeks to buy big-ticket items, two good things can happen. You may find the same item at a lower price somewhere else, or you may discover that you really did not want the item once the initial excitement wore off.

## Avoid Unnecessary Waste

Another principle to practice is keeping items that are still good. You can avoid waste, which translates into savings or more money for other activities. You don't have to keep using items that need to be replaced, but do continue using those that still have value. The money that you would use for premature replacements can fund your savings and investment programs or purchase other goods and services for you and your family.

In a similar vein, don't waste goods and services. Don't leave the television on when nobody is watching it or operate the air conditioner when nobody is going to be in the house for hours. Don't throw away a tube of toothpaste that is good for a few more brushes.

These actions are related to the conservation of resources, not money; but in the end you save money, too.

Another related principle is to develop a positive philosophy regarding care and maintenance of goods. By taking proper care of products, using them in the intended manner, and maintaining them according to manufacturer's instructions, you can greatly extend the useful life of an item. Instead of buying a new item, use the well-cared-for item and invest the money you would have spent. Let it be earning interest for you and contributing to your long-term financial security.

## Become A Coupon Clipper

Would you think it was crazy to take a few dollar bills out of your wallet each week and throw them into the garbage can? That is exactly what you are doing by not using coupons for items that you normally buy or taking advantage of dozens of money-saving opportunities each day.

If you spent 5 minutes a week cutting out coupons for your grocery shopping and saved at least $6.00 a week, that is the same as getting paid $72.00 an hour after taxes. In a year, you would save a minimum of $300.00. You would need to deposit $5,000.00 and get a 6% yield tax-free to make that much money. Remember, pennies do make dollars.

And finally, practice treating yourself. Having saved money by not buying things you don't need allows you to spend money for the things you want and that make your life enjoyable. Learn to truly enjoy the fruits of your labor.

## Save Bonus Money

Saving "bonus" money is also an easy strategy. Bonus money is money earned or received that was not expected, such as tax refunds, gift money, overtime pay, rebates, and refunds. Saving this money over time will boost your saving dollars and provide a larger balance on which to earn interest for the future.

Note: if you consistently receive a large tax refund, you may want to adjust your withholding. A tax refund means that the government has had your money during the year; you were losing the use of the money to fund your financial goals.

## Save Coupon Money

Another strategy to boost your savings is to save coupon money. Many people use coupons to reduce their grocery and personal care bills, but few think of actually saving the money they saved. To make this strategy a reality, put aside the amount you "saved" by using coupons at the grocery store or drugstore. The amount saved is probably printed on each receipt.

Put the "savings" (the money you did not spend) in a special "coupon saving jar." Every month or so add this cash to your savings account. Saving just $2 a week for 52 weeks gives you a savings total of $104, which could be your "seed" money to open an investment account. However, remember that you aren't saving if you buy something that you don't need or that costs more than a comparable product even with the coupon.

## Continue Installment Loan Repayments

Most of us have one or more installment loans that we are repaying. Once you pay off an installment loan (assuming other loans are not overdue), continue to make "payments" to your savings account. For example, when you pay off your car loan, continue writing a check for the same amount, but make the check payable to your savings account.

You were able to get along without this money for the duration of the car loan, so continue to live at the same level and save the "car payment." This is a good way to save for the down payment on your next car when the old car needs to be replaced. It also adds a substantial amount of money to your savings account on a regular basis. This same strategy can be used when other household expenses end (e.g. childcare).

## Collect Loose Change

Another painless strategy is to collect loose change. At the end of each day, empty out your pockets and wallet and put the change in a special container. Every other week or once a month, deposit the change in your savings account.

Don't cheat on yourself by "stealing" change that has been collected. Take it all to the bank. Some people even go so far as to keep *all* their change. They only pay for cash purchases with bills and save all their coins. Develop a plan that works for you and stick to it.

## Save Lunch Money

Saving lunch money is another way you and your family can save money. Get up 10 minutes earlier each morning and make your own lunch. Save the money you would have spent on lunch. If all family members do this, the family can realize a nice sum which they can add to their savings. Working together to reach a family goal, such as a new TV or a summer vacation, can be an excellent family activity.

## Shop For Sale Prices

Another strategy that can work for all family members on a wide variety of purchases is to save the money you "save" when you buy items on sale. When you buy an item on sale, save the difference between the sale price you paid and the "full" price you would have paid if the item had not been on sale.

Put this money in a safe place and on a regular basis deposit it into your savings or investment account. Using this strategy can add large amounts to your savings program. The key is that you actually keep this difference and apply it to your savings or investment program.

## Plan A "Nothing Week"

Once in a while, have a "Nothing Week," an entire week when you and your family agree not to spend any more money than is absolutely necessary. You would not go to the movies, out to eat, bowling, etc. Plan to do special activities, but save the money instead of spending it. Add this money to your savings program.

Another similar strategy is to use a crash budget approach. A crash budget works like a crash diet—you try to cut out all unnecessary spending and save as much as possible in a given period of time, say two weeks or a month. Add all the savings to your savings or investment program.

If the "Crash Budget" sounds unbearable, consider a "Cut-Back Week." During this week, do what the family would normally do, but think of ways to make it less expensive and save the difference. For example, rent a movie instead of going to the theater, make long-distance phone calls on the weekend when the rates are lower, write a letter or send an e-mail instead of calling, drink mix-your-own lemonade instead of soft drinks, etc.

## Avoid Paying Credit Charges

A critical savings strategy to consider is avoiding the use of credit. Unless credit purchases are paid off in full each month, interest consumes dollars that could be spent funding your saving and investing goals.

Suppose that you have a balance of $1,000 on a credit card that carries a 19.8% interest rate and a full grace period. If you make no more charges against the account and only pay the minimum payment of 3% per month, you will pay approximately $165 in interest over one year. If you continue making only minimum monthly payments for the rest of the $1,000 with no additional charges, you will take eight years and three months to pay it off, and you will have paid $843 in interest.

Carefully evaluate all spending decisions, especially those being paid with credit. Make every spending decision on the basis of how it will satisfy your goals. Eliminate spending for items that have little or no value relative to your goals. Also be aware of your needs and wants as you make purchases.

## Breaking Habits Can Yield Dollars To Invest

Some of the items we buy are needs, items that are necessary for survival. Other purchases are wants, all the things we think we need, but could do without. Buying items to satisfy our wants can become a habit; before we know it, we are spending lots of money on these items.

Find money to improve your financial situation by identifying some of your money habits. Then break those habits or at least reduce the number of times you enjoy the habit each day, week, or month. Review Table 2 for specific examples.

### Table 2  Looking For Money

| Cable TV | | $40/month = | $480/year |
|---|---|---|---|
| Video rentals | 3 @ $9/weekend = | $36/month = | $432/year |
| Movie tickets | 2 @ $7/visit = | $14/month = | $168/year |
| Treat at movie | 2 @ $5/visit = | $10/month = | $120/year |
| Dry cleaning | 3 garments $4 ea /month = | $12/month = | $144/year |
| Car wash | $5/week = | $20/month = | $240/year |

Going further, if your family drinks iced tea instead of a 2-liter soda for the evening meal, you can probably save at least $5 a week or $260 ($5x52=$260) a year. By drinking tap water instead of other beverages, you can save $7 a week or $364 ($7x52=$364) a year.

Let's look at those who feed the soda machines at work. By bringing soda from home ($.30 each) instead of feeding the machine ($.75 each), a person who drinks two sodas per day could save $234 over the course of a year ($.75-$.30 = $.45x2/day = $.90x5 days/week = $4.50x52 weeks = $234).

Changing or adjusting a few habits can result in big savings for you and your family. To see how easy this can be, use the following steps to help you identify and change habits.

# Steps To Breaking Money Habits

**Step 1.** Identify the habit, determine frequency, and calculate total cost

**Step 2.** Make a decision to change

**Step 3.** Act immediately

**Step 4.** Share your plan

**Step 5.** Stick with your plan to change

**Step 6.** Celebrate your success.

By following these six easy steps, you can gain better control of your financial resources and increase the money available for investing. Put this six-step plan to work for you and your family.

## Step 1. Identify The Habit, Determine Frequency, And Calculate Total Cost

Using Worksheet 1, "So Where's The Money?", think of some habits you might be able to adjust. Select from the products or services listed or add your own choices to the list. Then determine how often you purchase the product or service. Next, calculate the total cost of enjoying the product or service for one year. Armed with this information, you are ready to advance to Step 2 in your quest to break habits and collect funds for investing.

Calculate your total monthly and yearly costs. Are you happy with where your money is going? If you aren't, now is the time to learn about ways to break habits and begin a savings program for you and your family.

# Worksheet 1.  So Where's the Money?

| FREQUENCY | | COST | |
|---|---|---|---|
| **Product or Service** | **How Often Used** | **Monthly Cost x 12** | **=Yearly Cost** |
| Hair Care (example) | 4 Times/Month | $100.00 x 12 = | $1,200.00 |
| Nail Care | | | |
| Dry Cleaning | | | |
| Eating Out | | | |
| Cell Phones/Pagers | | | |
| Pop/Snacks | | | |
| Music CDs/Tapes | | | |
| Cigarettes/Alcohol | | | |
| Brand Name Clothes | | | |
| Video Rentals | | | |
| Cable Television | | | |
| Movie Tickets/Snacks | | | |
| Pay-Per-View TV | | | |
| Poker/Lottery | | | |
| Video Purchases | | | |

## Step 2.  Make A Decision To Change

The second step to breaking habits involves looking for alternatives and choosing a different way of spending your money. This action step demands that you take control of the situation.

One way to do this is to review your money habits and where you spend money, then identify how you can make changes. For example, have you ever stopped to consider how much you and other family members are spending for hair and nail care? If you spend $15.00 per week for hair care, that's $60.00 per month or $720.00 per year. Add a nail care bill of $15.00 per month or $180.00 per year. That is a lot of money.

What can you do? It is important for you and other family members to look good and feel good about yourselves. You can take control and make changes that will help you capture some of the money going to these expenditures and redirect its use toward other family goals and still be well-groomed. "How can I do that?" you ask. Learn how to do these tasks yourself, or barter with a friend or neighbor who has these skills. You do something for them that they can't do, and they do your hair and nails.

Every once in awhile, you might treat yourself or other family members to a special makeover. Otherwise, save the money you would be spending on hair and nail care, and put this money toward your family goals.

Once you get into the swing of breaking habits, you and your family can come up with ideas on how to change and adjust spending.

**Ask yourself:**

- Am I getting the best buys?

- Am I spending more than I need to?

- How could I change my spending?

Be specific and honest as you review expenditures. Come up with creative ways to save money, and share these ideas with others. Here is an example from the clothing area to get you started.

- First, do inventories of each person's clothing: evaluate items— which are still useable, need replacing, or need to be added?

- Once you know what needs to be purchased, check out sales at different stores and look for the best buys.

- Avoid buying designer clothing, as it is usually very expensive. Ask yourself and family members if it is worth the extra cost. Consider what else you could buy if you bought items that cost less and had money leftover.

- Check out second-hand outlets, flea markets, thrift stores, and manufacturers' outlet stores.

- Be a knowledgeable shopper; don't think that the outlet stores are always cheaper than other stores.

- Know the prices of what you plan to buy and comparison shop for the best deal.

- Make simple repairs.

- Swap clothing with family and friends.

- Develop a positive attitude about recycled clothing and share that attitude with your children. Well-maintained clothing from relatives and friends can greatly enhance a wardrobe.

When shopping for clothes, read all care labels very carefully. Only buy washable items. Dry cleaning can become quite expensive over the life of a garment.

By adopting these strategies, you will see your clothing budget shrink. Add the money you no longer spend on clothing to your investment plan. With these budget reduction ideas for clothing in mind, brainstorm ways to save money in other budget categories with family, friends, neighbors, and co-workers.

Develop money saving lists for:
- Using utilities
- Buying home furnishings
- Purchasing health and beauty aids
- Shopping in the grocery store
- Buying a car (new and/or used)
- Selecting telephone and cable television features
- Buying toys and other gift items
- Selecting insurance coverage
- Financing large ticket items and other purchases.

Some habits are very hard to break even when they are dangerous to our health and physical well-being, as well as financial well-being. Examples that quickly come to mind are smoking, overeating, drinking alcohol, and gambling. These activities can be life threatening and/or result in financial ruin. If you smoke a pack of cigarettes a day, what is the cost for a year?

A pack-a-day habit adds up fast:
$2.50/pack/day = $17.50/week = $70.00/month = $840.00/year.

Remember, if you believe in yourself, you can kick any habit. Once you get into the swing of breaking habits, you and your family can come up with numerous ideas on how to change and adjust spending.

Perhaps together the family could turn the task of saving into a friendly competition for the "Saver of the Year Award." The winner would be the person who saved the most dollars or the largest percentage of their income in a given period of time. By making the decision to change, you are ready to advance to Step 3 in breaking habits and finding money to invest.

## Step 3. Act Immediately

Now that you have all these great ideas to keep more of your money, how will you keep yourself motivated? Writing down your new desired behavior is one strategy. By recording the change, you are committing yourself to a new behavior. It is necessary to start your new behavior immediately.

For best results, begin within 24 hours after making the decision to change or adjust spending. The sooner you begin a new behavior, the sooner the new behavior will become a habit. Step 4 will further assist you in adopting new behaviors.

## Step 4. Share Your Plan

To further establish a new behavior, share your plan with others. Tell family, friends, and co-workers about your plan. By giving others the opportunity to support you, you boost your determination to succeed. If your behavior change involves the entire family, all family members must work together in order for the family to succeed.

Refer back to the worksheet, "So Where's The Money?". Go over the chart with the entire family. Together, decide ways the family can break habits and develop a savings plan. Now is also a good time to make a family "piggy bank." The "bank" can be an empty jar or a small box. Once the family decides on a family financial goal, they can put a picture identifying the goal on the "bank."

Examples of goals include paying off a bill, buying something for the house, visiting family in another state, or accumulating money for a car. The "bank" needs to be kept where all can see it and all can help by adding money. After accumulating a sum of money, the family might want to open a savings account at a local bank or mutual fund money market. Once this account has grown to cover emergencies, additional savings may then be invested so the family will realize a larger return on their money.

Even with the best of intentions, sometimes staying focused on your savings plan is hard. The next step of the action plan will help you move forward.

## Step 5. Stick With Your Plan To Change

This is a critical step toward breaking habits and increasing family savings. You and your family members must always look for new ways to reduce spending and increase savings. It is important to reinforce the fact that you can change your attitudes and break habits. Stay focused on your goal. It takes about 30 days for a new behavior to become a habit.

Here are some specific activities for you and your family that will help you gain control of your finances, but still have fun as a family. By engaging in activities such as these, we are changing our attitudes and choosing activities that are more "money friendly." Changing attitudes and lifelong habits will serve you well immediately, and over a lifetime, and set an example for your children by instilling the value of saving.

Yes, you can do it—you can change your attitude. You can break habits and save for things that are really important to you and your family. You just have to stick with your plan. If you are diligent, you will reach Step 6 of our action plan.

## Step 6. Celebrate Your Success

The last step to breaking habits is to celebrate your success. Once you have reached your initial goals, let others know of your success. Enjoy the fruits of your savings. Then continue with your new behaviors that are now habits.

You have the tools necessary to be successful. Remember to trim all unnecessary expenses and keep your needs and wants in perspective. Watch the pennies you save grow into dollars that can be used to fund your saving and investment programs.

# Be A Comparison Shopper

Comparison shopping is the customer's best, but least used, technique when spending regardless of the type of expenditure. Comparing prices and products can save as much as 50% off a price you might have paid without making the comparison. Comparison shopping makes good sense.

It is important to remember that an over-spender isn't just someone who spends more than he earns. An over-spender is also anyone who pays too much for things, especially when items or services purchased are conveniently available for less.

The benefits of comparison shopping are more than the money saved. Comparison shopping puts you in control of your finances. It helps you learn more about the products and services you are interested in buying.

As a more informed consumer, you are able to make better spending decisions. Additionally, each success will reinforce your resolve to comparison shop again. By making wise consumer decisions and getting a good value for less, shoppers are able to save and/or invest the money saved.

# Missing Money

Do you know that sometimes you can collect dollars instead of pennies by becoming a more knowledgeable consumer? By using the strategies that follow, you may be able to add large sums of money to your family's saving and investment program.

Throughout the country, billions of dollars remain in accounts that have been abandoned or forgotten. These accounts include checking and savings accounts, pension benefits, and insurance benefits.

How could anyone possibly forget about something of value? Well, maybe you neglected to retrieve a security deposit after moving out of an apartment. Perhaps dividends on a stock or mutual fund have been going to the wrong address. Maybe you switched banks and failed to close out your old accounts. Or you changed jobs frequently and previous employers don't know where to send pension benefits. Perhaps you are entitled to benefits of a life insurance policy or cash left by a relative who has died.

In any event, you might be entitled to unclaimed property held by your state or the Pension Benefit Guaranty Corporation. Or you might be the beneficiary of a long-lost insurance policy. Fortunately, receiving your just rewards is not extremely difficult if you know how to proceed.

To locate missing bank accounts and other unclaimed cash, contact your state's unclaimed property office. In most states, owners can recover their cash whenever they learn about it, no matter how long it has been in the state fund.

About half of the states pay interest on money left in interest-bearing accounts. Instead of waiting for a state to find you, which is unlikely, you can contact the state's unclaimed property office. If you have access to the Internet, the CapitaLink site on the World Wide Web (www.ifast.com) allows you to search $50 million in unclaimed mutual fund, insurance, and financial accounts at no charge. It also lists all of the states' unclaimed property offices.

When you write or call about abandoned property, give your name (maiden or former names, if necessary), Social Security number, current address, and all previous addresses while you lived in the state. If you are applying for property that was held in someone else's name, provide his or her Social Security number and former addresses. States normally take 2 to 3 weeks to write back saying whether there is property waiting for you. If you are due a windfall, they will send you an abandoned-property claim form to complete.

Return the completed form with proof that the cash belongs to you. If it's in your name, you will need to supply only a current ID, such as a copy of your driver's license, and any document that links you to the money (e.g., a pay stub, savings passbook, or utility bill). For property that belonged to you when you lived at an earlier address, you must provide proof that you lived there. A copy of a tax return will do. Expect to get your check in about two months.

From time to time, you may see advertisements of asset finders, people who offer to find lost property for you. Beware of such ads. If you decide to hire such a firm, pay no more than 10% of the assets recovered and check out the firm with the Better Business Bureau.

According to one state property fund director, "If you ever get a card or letter from a company offering to find your money, take that as a tip that the firm knows you have money waiting. So call or write to the state fund yourself. Then you'll get all the money you're due."

According to the Pension Benefit Guaranty Corporation (PBGC), more than 12,000 people in the United States are owed uncollected pension benefits. The PBGC, a federal agency, has launched a nationwide search on the Internet to find workers who are owed benefits and who could not be located when pension plans closed.

To check if your name is on the list of hard-to-find beneficiaries, log onto the Pension Search Directory at http://search.pbgc.gov. The directory identifies about 1,000 companies mainly in the transportation, machinery, retail trade, apparel, and financial services industries. If you do not have a computer, check for availability at a public library or libraries at high schools, community colleges, or universities. If you are not able to access a computer and you feel you are owed benefits, write to the Pension Benefit Guaranty Corporation, Missing Participant Program, 1200 K Street, NW, Suite 930, Washington, DC 20005. Include the participant's or beneficiary's name, address, daytime telephone number, Social Security number, date of birth, and the name and location of the employer.

Another place to look for lost cash is the Internal Revenue Service. Yes, the IRS has more than $68 million in unclaimed tax-refund checks that were returned because of an incorrect address or other delivery problems. The average check amount is $690.

The last place where you might look for ready cash is lost insurance policies—yours or those of relatives where you might be the beneficiary. If you think there is a lost policy in your family, send a stamped, self-addressed business envelope to the Missing Policy Service, American Council of Life Insurance, 1001 Pennsylvania Avenue, NW, Washington, DC 20004-2599. The Council will send you a tracer form to complete and return. Then they will circulate copies to about 100 large life insurance companies. The service is free and takes from 3 to 6 months.

## Summary

If you are able to provide the desire and self-discipline, you will be able to "find" the money necessary to fund your saving and investment programs. Improving your financial health through increased savings is not a matter of luck, rather it reflects planning, defined goals, wise decisions, and a desire for personal success. The various savings strategies included in this chapter offer you the groundwork needed to initiate a saving and investment program for you and your family.

# 21 Ways To Keep More Cash

1.  Pay yourself first. Have automatic contributions from your paycheck or checking account go to a savings or investment plan. Money that you do not see is often easier to save.

2.  Find money to save by refinancing your mortgage. Cutting your rate by a percentage point will probably pay off if you plan to be in your home for an additional 18 months.

3.  Switch to a credit card that charges a lower interest rate, but be aware of low rates that increase after six to twelve months. Be ready to switch cards again.

4.  If you are offered a no-fee, no-points home equity loan, sign up. Use this line of credit to pay off higher-cost debt. Do not use it to increase your debt load.

5.  Pay ahead on your mortgage. An extra $25 to $50 a month can make a big difference in the amount of interest you pay as well as the number of years you pay. Or pay your monthly payment in two installments (if allowed)—one payment 2 weeks before the due date and the other on the due date. You will reduce the total cost of the mortgage and the length of the loan.

6.  If you are incurring late fees or extra finance charges because bills come due before you get paid, ask to have the due date changed to after payday.

7.  If you have a computer, cut your telephone costs by e-mailing children in college and far-off friends. Other money savings tips include buying your own phone and blocking "900" numbers if you have youngsters.

8.  To cut your utility bill, unplug the extra refrigerator or freezer that is used infrequently. Also lower the thermostat on your water heater to 120 degrees, install high-efficiency showerheads and faucets, switch to compact fluorescent bulbs in fixtures that are on at least 4 hours a day, replace an inefficient heating and cooling system if you are likely to stay in your current house for a decade or more, and check with your utility to see if they have programs that will pay you to insulate your home.

9. Sign up for overdraft protection on your checking account; dodge unnecessary bank fees; avoid keeping large balances in your checking or savings accounts earning low interest rates—invest them in higher-yielding investments; and compare costs of checks from your bank and other sources for the best buy. Join a credit union for potential savings on your banking and credit transactions.

10. Shop for the best price on all your insurance needs. Reduce costs by having home and auto insurance with one insurer, installing safety devices in your home, canceling private mortgage insurance when you have sufficient equity in your home, purchasing life insurance only on breadwinner(s) or primary caregivers, and avoiding single-disease health insurance policies.

11. If available, use your employer's plan that lets you set aside part of your salary to pay medical bills with pretax dollars. Carefully evaluate health care plans available to you and select the one that best meets your needs.

12. Comparison shop for the best prices on prescription drugs. When available use generic drugs for both prescription and over-the-counter drugs, and utilize mail-order pharmacies for drugs taken regularly.

13. If you smoke, stop. It is bad for your health and costs about $800 a year for a pack-a-day smoker. A year after you quit, check with your life insurance agent for reduced premiums.

14. Save big by buying a nearly new rather than a brand-new car. Other savings related to your car include pumping your own gas, buying the octane fuel recommended for your car, raising your collision and comprehensive deductibles to $500, and avoiding four-wheel drive vehicles unless needed (they cost more up front and you pay more for gas, tires, and insurance). If you buy a new car, order from the factory, selecting only the options you want unless the dealer is willing to discount the price of unwanted options.

15. Buy in bulk at discount and warehouse stores. Always shop with a list to avoid impulse buys and use coupons when appropriate. Try store brands for considerable savings.

16. Instead of beginning your landscaping projects the first warm day of spring when plants and related materials are most expensive, wait until the items go on sale.

17. Encourage your college-bound students to apply for scholarships and offer to pay them a lump sum to graduate on time (or early) to avoid having to pay for a fifth year of college. If your child attends college at least 150 miles away, check with your agent regarding lowering your auto insurance premium (it could drop as much as one-third). Even if the student takes the car to school, costs may be lower due to the location of the school.

18. Maximize contributions to your tax-deferred retirement plan and contribute to an IRA. Even though you may not be able to deduct IRA contributions from your taxes, the money in your account grows tax-deferred until it is taken out.

19. To save dollars on your entertainment and education budget categories, use the local library. They have the latest books, magazines, journals, and newspapers as well as music compact discs, Internet access, investment research, and a host of other services.

20. Other quick ways to add cash back into your budget include canceling subscriptions to magazines you do not read or could access at the library, dropping club memberships you do not use, canceling credit cards you no longer use, disconnecting cable television or at least dropping some of the options you probably have, and trimming back the options you carry on the telephone.

21. Catch your coins and bank your surprises. At the end of each day, put all your loose change into a savings container and once a month deposit the collection into your savings account. Whenever you receive a raise or unexpected money such as a gift or contest winnings, put all or part of the money into your savings account.

# Chapter 6

---

# Discovering Investment Vehicles

In the investment world, there are many different types of investment vehicles in which to place your money. Which vehicle you choose depends on your goals. It depends on your time range, your objective, your risk tolerance, and the rate of return you are attempting to achieve.

This chapter will explain many investment vehicles that you may have in your investment portfolio.

## Checking Accounts

Checking accounts are best used as your everyday type of account. You can deposit payroll checks and other income and then pay your expenditures. This account is like a revolving door with money coming in and going out rapidly. It has a quick cash flow. It is generally best to keep approximately two months' of expenses in this account so it can handle the cash flow and emergencies.

Be sure to shop around at banks, savings and loans, and credit unions for the best service and lowest rates. Focus on avoiding the monthly service charge as this can add up quickly over several years. Shop for other fees such as low balance charges, ATM fees, check charges, and other fees.

Don't buy your checks from your bank; instead buy them from one of the many mail order check-printing companies available in newspapers and magazines.

Look for an account that offers interest with checking. If the fees are low enough, it can add a small amount to your account.

## Savings Accounts

Savings accounts are found at banks, savings and loans, and credit unions. You receive interest for placing your money in an account there. The interest rate however is usually quite small, under 5% per year.

Bank savings accounts are backed by the Federal Deposit Insurance Corporation (FDIC) insurance. Many people, usually older ones, clamor after savings accounts because of the insurance, remembering back to the days of bank failures. They generally have no risk tolerance and don't realize or care that they are receiving a much lower interest rate for the insurance.

The 1980s highlighted how poorly much of the savings and loan industry was run and showed that banks are not perfectly safe, either. The FDIC insurance system is just an insurance system. If there were ever such an economic disaster in the U.S. that money in savings accounts declined in value, the whole U.S. banking system could be in jeopardy and the FDIC insurance system could collapse.

## Bank CDs

This investment vehicle is an extended type of savings accounts. A bank CD (certificate of deposit) is an interest-bearing bank investment that locks you in for a specific period of time. Generally the bank offers certificates from 6 months to 5 years. This locked-in time range allows the bank to pay you a higher interest rate than a standard savings account. If you need to withdraw funds from the CD prior to maturity, the bank will charge you a penalty for early withdrawal. Like savings accounts, bank CDs are also backed by FDIC.

There are two primary considerations in planning for your investment in a CD:

1) *Term:* The most popular type of CD is the 6-month certificate, but CDs are available with maturities ranging from 7 days to 15 years. During the term of your CD, the money you've invested is relatively costly to liquidate. If an emergency arises which requires you to withdraw your money before maturity, you'll be penalized for it. This penalty is known as early withdrawal penalty and will vary from bank to

bank. Thus you'll want to consider carefully when you're likely to need the money before you invest in a CD.

2) *Rate of Return:* The interest paid on a CD will vary not only according to the term of the certificate but, from time to time, as interest rates fluctuate, as well as from bank to bank. Don't buy your CD at the first bank you visit. Check the Internet for rates, contact your investment advisor for the highest rates available. Ask about how the bank credits the interest earned to your account. The more frequently interest is credited, the better for you, since each time your account grows through an interest payment, the amount of money you have working for you grows as well.

## Who Should Purchase CDs?
Generally, certificates of deposits should not be in an investment portfolio because there are so many alternatives. Millions of people own them because of their safety, convenience, and confidence in their bank, yet investors lose because they deny the chance for higher yields, which come with accepting more risk. However, there are certain times when CDs do make sense.

1) *Emergency savings:* We recommend an emergency fund equal to at least three months of expenses. A short-term CD (three months or less) can be a good choice for emergency savings since the funds are relatively liquid.

2) *Short-term goals:* Savings for a car, house or any other item in the next one to two years can make a good justification for CDs.

3) *The parking lot theory:* An inheritance, lottery, or any windfall may give you a large sum of money. However, you may need a little time to decide where to invest. CDs make a fine short-term parking lot for those funds.

# Treasuries

The U.S. Treasury Department provides for the enormous financial needs of the federal government. Much of the money the Treasury raises comes from the sale of securities to the general public. These securities are known as Treasury obligations and consist of Treasury bills, notes, and bonds.

Conservative investors often invest in Treasuries because they are safe and secure and are a good alternative to bank CDs. In comparison with similar obligations issued by corporations, Treasury obligations usually pay a yield, which is one or two percentage points lower. However, many people are willing to accept the slightly lower yield in exchange for absolute safety.

## Treasury Bills

Treasury Bills (T-Bills) are short-term federal debt, sold in denominations of $10,000, with $5,000 increments thereafter. T-Bills are issued in original maturities of 13, 26, and 52 weeks. The first two are auctioned weekly, while the 52-week bill is auctioned every 28 days. They can be purchased through brokers or directly from the Federal Reserve. They are issued on a discount basis under competitive bidding, with the face amount payable at maturity. The investment return on bills is the difference between the cost and the face amount. Bills may be sold prior to maturity at a competitive market rate, which can result in a yield greater or less than the original acquisition rate. T-Bills are an extremely safe type of investment vehicle.

## Treasury Notes

Treasury Notes are similar to T-Bills except they mature in one to ten years and are sold in denominations of $1,000 to $100,000. Treasury notes, like T-bills, pay interest rates determined by auction. However, they are not sold at a discount. Instead, they pay interest every 6 months at a rate fixed at the time of purchase. In this respect, they resemble corporate bonds. Treasury notes can be bought and sold on the secondary market.

## Treasury Bonds

Treasury Bonds are similar to T-Bills and Notes except they mature in five years or more and sell in denominations of $1,000 to $1,000,000.

## U.S. Savings Bonds

These bonds are issued by the U.S. Treasury and are designed for the conservative investor. Presently, they pay a flexible interest rate based upon 85 percent of yields on five-year government treasury securities. The rates change each May and November.

If you hold the bond for five years, you will receive the average of all the rates in effect while you owned the bonds, but they pay a fixed rate if cashed before five years. You can buy a $50 bond for $25 or a $10,000 bond for $5,000. The maximum amount of bonds a person can purchase during one year is $15,000 ($30,000 face value).

The most common U.S. savings bond is the Series EE, which the United States Treasury began issuing on January 2, 1980, to replace the series E bond. Series EE bonds also have a guaranteed minimum yield if the bonds are held for five years. Call your local bank for current minimum yield. Presently, U.S. savings bonds are exempt from state and local taxes, and federal tax is deferred until the year cashed. As of January 2, 1990, Series EE bonds that are used for higher education are exempt from federal tax. Note: They must be bought in the parent's name, not the child's.

U.S. savings bonds Series HH are sold at face value, with $500 being the minimum investment. The bonds mature in ten years. The interest is paid every year; therefore, when the bond matures you have already received your interest. Interest is taxed each year.

## Money Markets

A money market account is offered by mutual fund companies and brokerages. They are like a mutual fund that invests in short-term issues such as Treasury Bills, bankers notes, and corporate commercial paper, which is issued by the largest and most credit-worthy companies and U.S. government securities.

There are hundreds of money market funds that invest billions of dollars. Money market funds are closely regulated by the U.S. Securities and Exchange Commission. Money market funds' investments can exist only in the most credit-worthy securities and must have an average maturity of less than 120 days. Money market funds maintain a constant $1-per-share price.

Even though this vehicle is NOT insured by FDIC, it is considered to be a safe investment, and to date no major money market fund has lost investors' principal investments. If the lack of insurance on money market funds still spooks you, consider a fund that invests exclusively in U.S. government securities. These money markets are virtually risk-free because they are backed by the full strength and credit of the federal government. These types of accounts typically pay a lower interest rate, usually ¼ percent less (even though the interest is state tax free).

# Municipal Bonds

When a city, state, or county needs funds to build schools, roads, or water and sewer facilities, they offer bonds. Because municipal (muni) bonds are tax-free, the interest rates offered are lower than regular bonds of similar type. Tax-exempt municipal bonds yield about 85 percent of compatible taxable instruments; the investor in the 28 to 39.6 percent tax bracket has a chance to lock in excellent returns.

Municipal bonds that offer higher interest rates than what is presently being offered are most likely to be called in, because the issuer will want to redeem them with new ones paying lower yields. When a bond is callable, it may be redeemed by the issuing agency prior to the maturity date, usually within 10 years after issue, and usually at a premium. Of course, this places a lid on potential profits, which may be a significant loss to you if interest rates decline greatly after the bond is issued.

As with any investment, risk is a factor to consider in purchasing municipal bonds. Like corporate bonds, municipal bonds are rated by two major independent rating services: Moody's and Standard & Poors. The AAA rating is the highest; the C rating is the lowest. In general, the lower the rating, the higher the yield. However, we don't recommend that you purchase bonds with a rating lower than A, since the slightly higher interest rate you may be offered on the lower-rated bond isn't worth the sacrifice in safety. Also, when financial times are uncertain, investors will look for high-quality bonds even though they do produce a lower yield.

A technique when investing in municipal bonds is known as laddering. What is done is that you purchase bonds maturing in different years. Therefore, if rates have risen when a bond matures, you will be able to reinvest the proceeds into an instrument paying the new high yield. Conversely, if interest rates should fall, a portion of your holdings will still earn interest at the higher rates.

When a municipality issues muni bonds, the city's or state's credit is on the line. If bonds are somewhat lower-rated, the municipality must pay higher-than-normal interest on the issued bonds. To save money, it may purchase insurance that guarantees that all payments of principal and interest will be made on time. Thus it may appear that the insurance is free to the investor, but that is not true. Since the insurance raises the quality of the municipality's credit, the yield on the bond issued will be lower. Because the cost/yield difference between an insured and an uninsured bond is narrow, the insurance has become a "good buy."

## Municipal Bond Funds

A municipal bond fund is similar to a money market fund: its shares are highly liquid. Each fund sells or redeems shares at its net asset value (NAV) at any time. The managers of a municipal bond fund are constantly trading. Thus the fund as a whole never matures but goes on indefinitely buying and selling bonds to take advantage of changes in the marketplace.

One advantage that municipal bond funds have is that buyers can invest a much smaller amount of money than they would need to buy a municipal bond on their own. Most municipal bond funds require an initial investment of at least $1,000. Any time thereafter you can buy additional shares in the fund. You have the option of receiving a check for your monthly earnings or having them automatically reinvested to purchase additional shares in the fund. Whenever you wish, you can sell your shares back to the fund. However, since the value of the bonds in the fund's portfolio fluctuates over time, you may or may not get back your original investment when you sell your shares.

# Bonds

Bonds are a type of loaner-ship. This is where you invest (loan) some money and that organization pays you back interest for using the money. In a way you are a bank. The types of organizations that may sell bonds are corporations, local, state, and federal government, foreign governments, and other entities.

When investing in bonds, you should be aware of some of the terms. *Principal* is what you originally invest. The *maturity* date is the date on which the loan must be paid in full; it can range from one day to thirty years. If it is less than one year, it is called short-term debt, if it matures within a few years then it is called intermediate bonds, and if longer than ten years, it is called long-term debt. *Interest* is the money you receive in return for loaning your money.

There are three types of risk involved in bonds: (1) the interest will not be paid; (2) the principal will not be returned; (3) the market value of the bond might decline due to rising interest rates, making your investment worthless. For example, if you're holding a bond issued at eight percent, and rates increase to ten percent, your bond decreases in value. Because why would anyone want to buy your bond at the price you paid if it yields just eight percent and they can get ten percent elsewhere?

Unless the Federal Government defaults, there is "no risk" when you loan money to the government. So government securities are the safest of all debt instruments available. However, government securities, like other bonds, can lose market value if interest rates rise.

Corporate bonds can be purchased the same way as stocks—through a brokerage firm. Government bonds can be purchased from commercial banks or a Federal Reserve branch bank. Corporate bonds have more risk than government bonds due to the fact that corporations are less stable than the U. S. Government.

High-yield bonds, also known as Junk Bonds, are speculative bonds that have a poor rating. These bonds pay a higher interest rate but are a higher risk. Generally bonds with a B or lower rating are classified as high-yield bonds.

## Mortgage-Backed Securities

Mortgage-backed securities are investments in a portfolio of home mortgages and are sometimes referred to as "pass-through" securities because homeowners' mortgage principal and interest payments are "passed through" to investors.

The most well-known mortgage-backed security is the Ginnie Mae, which is issued by the Government National Mortgage Association (GNMA). Ginnie Maes carry the "full faith and credit" guarantee of the Federal Government and generally pay a slightly higher rate than Treasury bonds. Ginnie Maes require a $25,000 minimum purchase, with $5,000 increments, from brokers, but can also be purchased indirectly for $1,000 through units in a Ginnie Mae unit investment trust. They can also be purchased through mutual funds that invest in U.S. government agency securities (minimum amounts vary per fund).

Two other mortgage-backed securities that are not backed by the federal government are Freddie Macs, issued by the Federal Home Loan Mortgage Corporation (FHLMC) and Fannie Maes, issued by the Federal National Mortgage Association (FNMA). They also require $25,000 and typically pay a higher rate than Ginnie Maes to compensate investors for the extra risk of not being government-insured.

The biggest disadvantages of all three mortgage-backed securities are an uncertain maturity and irregular monthly payments. Although the mortgages in their portfolios are issued for 30 years, the average life of a mortgage-backed security is only 10 to 12 years because homeowners frequently move or refinance. Also, if investors spend the part of their monthly check that is a return of principal, instead of reinvesting it, they will have nothing left when the last mortgage in their Ginnie Mae portfolio is repaid.

## Collateralized Mortgage Obligations

Collateralized mortgage obligations (CMOs) are another type of mortgage-backed security. CMOs were developed to address investors' concern about receiving income from other mortgage-backed securities in unpredictable increments.

With CMOs, the portfolio of mortgages is divided into various classes, called tranches, thus offering investors a choice of estimated maturity dates to match financial goals. Investors in a particular tranche typically receive semi-annual interest payments that differ from period to period and from other tranches. Tranches with a longer maturity generally pay a higher return to compensate investors for incurring greater interest rate risk. The principal portion of mortgage payments corresponding to all tranches goes to investors in a single tranche until that tranche is retired. Each tranche gets its principal back when all the tranches before it have been repaid. CMOs are available in $1,000 increments through brokerage firms and pay a higher yield than comparable mortgage-backed securities.

The two disadvantages of CMOs are their complexity and the fact that principal prepayment can still come sooner (or later) than expected. Just as with other mortgage-backed securities, investors must realize that principal is being repaid throughout the life of a CMO, not at maturity like bonds. Investors who mistakenly think that CMO payments are just interest may inadvertently spend their principal.

## Zero-Coupon Bonds

Zero coupon bonds (zeros) are issued at a deep discount but don't pay interest until they mature. Zeros are usually sold in denominations of $1,000 per bond, at prices far below par value. During the term of the bond you receive no interest—hence the term *zero coupon*—since coupon means interest in bond terminology.

When the bond matures, you are paid face value, including the interest that's accumulated over the term of the bond. For example, you may purchase a $20,000 zero-coupon bond with a six-year term for $13,500. At the end of the six years, you will receive $20,000.

One advantage of zeros is that you can invest relatively small amounts up front and choose maturity dates to coincide with times you know you'll need the money—for example, college tuition.

One drawback to zeros, however, is that taxes are due annually on the interest that accrues, even though you don't receive the actual payment until the bond matures. Another drawback is that zero-coupon bonds are very volatile in the secondary market, so if you have to sell them before maturity, you might have to sell at a loss.

## Convertible Bonds

As their name suggests, convertible bonds are a type of corporate bond that allows investors to "have their cake and eat it too," almost. They provide the upside potential of stocks (the opportunity to participate in company earnings) with the downside protection of bonds (a fixed return and repayment of principal at maturity).

Convertible bonds can be exchanged for a specified number of shares of common stock of the issuing company. As the price of the company stock increases, the convertible bond price also increases because the option to convert becomes more valuable. This correlation is true whether an investor chooses to convert or not. The trade-off is that convertible bonds generally convert to fewer shares of stock than you could buy for the cost of a bond. Almost all convertible bonds are callable.

Even though they are a "hybrid" investment, convertibles, like all bonds, are sensitive to interest rate fluctuations. They can be purchased as individual securities in $1,000 increments or through convertible bond mutual funds.

## Preferred Stock

Although technically a form of stock, preferred stock is often listed as a fixed-income investment because it behaves more like a bond, but has no fixed maturity date. The word "preferred" refers to the fact that shareholders receive preferential treatment. They are paid dividends before common stock shareholders and, in the event of a corporate liquidation, can claim corporate assets after bondholders but before common stock shareholders.

Preferred stock typically pays a fixed dividend rate similar to the coupon rate on a bond. Share prices fluctuate inversely with changes in interest rates. Par value on preferred stock is usually about $25 per share so a round lot (100 shares) would cost $2,500. Dividends paid are a fixed percentage of par value. Preferred stock shares are available through brokerage firms.

## Common Stock

All corporations have common stock. If you organized a corporation for the purpose of manufacturing widgets, and sold one share of common stock to each of nine people at $100 per share and one share to yourself At $100, the corporation would be capitalized at $1,000 and would have ten stockholders. In buying one of these shares, you became a shareholder or part owner of the corporation. You took an equity position and will participate in the future gains, or lack of gains, of the corporation for as long as you hold your share.

Stocks are the most common investment traded on securities markets. Companies that issue stock are from every industry and sector including: airlines, computer manufacturers, department stores, oil drillers, restaurants, and many others. You can buy stock in more than 9,000 publicly-traded companies, though chances are your portfolio will only have a tiny fraction of what's available.

Since shareholders are part owners of the corporation, if the company does well, you may receive part of its profits as dividends and see the price of your stock increase. But if the company fares badly, the value of your investment can drop, sometimes substantially.

A stock has no absolute value. At any given time, its value depends on whether the shareholders want to hold it or sell it and on what other investors are willing to pay for it. If the stock is hot and lots of people want lots of shares, the value will go up. If a company is losing money, the stock value will probably drop. Some stocks are undervalued, which means they sell for less than analysts think they're worth, while others are overvalued.

Investors' attitudes are determined by several factors: whether or not they expect to make money with the stock, by current stock market conditions and the overall state of the economy.

The caution that past performance is no guarantee of future profits is absolutely valid, especially for stocks. Investing isn't about balancing risk with reasonable expectations of reward.

## Dividends

If a corporation makes a profit (earnings), the board of directors has the option to reinvest the profit back into the corporation and/or pay it out to the shareholders. The money paid to shareholders is called a dividend.

Generally, larger and older corporations pay more dividends than younger and smaller ones. Often newer and smaller companies need the profits to help grow the business.

If you are dependent on dividends for your groceries and if the price of food continues to rise, you must increase your income or reduce your intake. Most of us would probably be a lot healthier if we did the latter, but we have a tendency to reject this alternative. Therefore, you will want to select stocks that pay good dividends consistently.

We prefer stocks that have raised their dividends in at least eight of the past ten years and whose dividends today are 100 percent higher than they were ten years ago. We also prefer those that have held their dividend payout to less than 60 percent of earnings and have kept their debt under 25 percent. A record of strong and consistent dividends points to companies that are committed to similar performance in the future.

Holding payouts under 60 percent of earnings helps eliminate companies that don't retain enough earnings to sustain growth. Keeping long-term debt low protects future earnings. But don't reach too far for yield and jeopardize your capital. Usually the reason for the high yield is the poor evaluation that the market has given to the future prospects of the company, or it may be paying out an inordinately large percentage of its earnings, which could adversely affect future earnings.

So in selecting stocks for dependable income, it is obvious that you will want to choose quality issues with long established dividend records rather than younger, less tested companies that have not been in business long enough to establish extended dividend payment records.

During times of market corrections, we often have calls from less sophisticated holders of income stocks who are worried that their dividend will be cut because the market price is down. If all is well with the company, we try to calm them with the explanation that short-term market prices often have no relationship to earnings. In the long term, however, they usually do.

## Blue Chips

The stocks we have just described would generally be called blue chips. What is a "blue chip" stock? First, the name can be traced to the game of poker, in which there are three colors of chips: blue for the highest value, red for the next in rank, and white for the lowest value.

Occasionally someone will come into my office and say "I only invest in blue chip stocks and throw them in a drawer and forget about them." We consider this approach to be very risky. I would prefer to see them monitor their holdings on an ongoing basis. In today's investment world, a particular stock can drop over 50% in one day if they happen to report poor earnings or bad publicity is reported on the company.

In summary, if your desire is for income from stocks, you should:

- Look for companies that have a long, unbroken dividend record.

- Don't reach too far for yield and jeopardize principal.

- Remember that too high a yield can be dangerous and misleading.

- Favor companies producing consumer goods and services.

- Select sound companies that continue to increase their dividends.

Make sure you do your homework carefully before buying any income stocks. Read the research reports and look for any potential problems the company may be having or expected to have in the future. If you do not need income now, consider companies with slightly lower yields. Often these companies are plowing back a larger portion of their earnings into expanded facilities that should in time yield higher earnings that would allow them to pay out higher dividends.

# Yield

The yield on stock is the relationship of the dividend it pays to its market price. Every shareholder is entitled to the same dividend per share. However, the price you have paid for your stock may differ from the price paid by another shareholder. If you paid $50 for a share of stock and the dividend is $2, the yield on your original investment is 4 percent ($2 divided by $50). If you paid $35, the $2 represents a return, or yield, on your original investment of slightly more than 5.7 percent. You should, however, continue to calculate your yield on current market price, because you have the option of repositioning your assets.

## Growth Stocks

A growth company is usually one that is increasing its sales and earnings at a faster rate than the growth rate of the national economy. The growth investor is not as focused on earnings and dividends as the income investor.

To be a successful investor in growth stocks, you must be aware of current events: supply and demand, general market trends, psychology, and money markets. In fact you must be truly current in all respects. One of the most stimulating characteristics of my profession is that every day is a new day in the market. Nothing remains static. There is no way you can be a truly top-notch investor by buying blue chips and throwing them in a drawer and forgetting about them. This only increases your risk and lowers your opportunity for gain.

There are two irreversible structural changes occurring in the United States that are permanently transforming our economic base. First, our transformation from a smokestack to a microchip economy. Second, the United States is no longer an economic fortress unto itself, but rather now a part of a global economy. And its potential for growth is boundless because its new thrust comes from our richest and most renewable resource—the human mind.

# Exchange Traded Funds

At the most basic level, exchange traded funds (ETFs) are just what their name implies: baskets of securities that are traded, like individual stocks, on an exchange. They currently trade on the American Stock Exchange.

An ETF is an investment in a particular stock index. For example, there are ETFs that invest in the stocks that comprise the Dow Jones Industrial

Average, Standard & Poor's 500, and Nasdaq 100. You can also invest in ETFs that invest in certain industry sectors, such as technology, health, energy, or transportation.

Unlike regular open-end mutual funds, ETFs can be bought and sold throughout the trading day. They trade like stocks instead of mutual funds that trade at the end of the day. They can also be sold short and bought on margin—in brief, anything you might do with a stock, you can do with ETFs. Most also charge lower annual expenses than even the least costly mutual funds.

All currently available ETFs are passively managed, tracking a wide variety of sector-specific, country-specific, and broad-market indexes. Their passive nature is a necessity: The funds rely on an arbitrage mechanism to keep the prices they trade at roughly in line with the net asset values of their underlying portfolios. For the mechanism to work, potential arbitragers need to have full, timely knowledge of a fund's holdings. Active managers, however, are loath to disclose such information more frequently than the Securities Exchange Commission requires them to.

Another advantage is that, because you buy and sell ETFs at your discretion, you only incur a tax liability when you decide to sell your ETFs. Investors in no-load mutual funds are beholden to the fund manager when it comes to possible tax liabilities.

Since you buy ETFs like stocks, you will incur a brokerage commission when you buy and sell ETFs. This differs from no-load mutual funds, which don't charge a commission for transactions. Thus, when buying or selling ETFs, it is important to control your transaction costs.

One last point about ETFs is worth mentioning. These vehicles can be extremely effective ways to diversify a stock portfolio with relatively small amounts of money. Indeed, a portfolio holding a few ETFs, especially ETFs that mimic a broad index (such as the S&P 500), plus a few individual stocks can be surprisingly diversified. Thus, ETFs allow an investor to hold fewer stocks. This simplifies portfolio record keeping and monitoring while still being prudent from a portfolio diversification standpoint.

## Are ETFs Right for You?

ETFs have several clear advantages over traditional mutual funds, but they aren't suitable for everyone.

91

## Trading Flexibility

ETFs trade throughout the day, so you can buy and sell them when you want. However, the arbitrage mechanism isn't failsafe. Heavily traded issues such as SPDRs (which track the S&P 500) and QQQs (which track the Nasdaq 100) should trade right around the value of their underlying securities, but premiums and discounts can arise, especially for thinly traded funds. Moreover, it is not yet known how ETFs might behave in the face of a full-fledged market correction. It's conceivable that investors wishing to sell in the midst of such an event could have to part with their shares at prices below their net asset values.

## Costs

In terms of the annual expenses charged to investors, ETFs are considerably less expensive than most mutual funds. SPDRs, for example, set their annual expense ratio to just .12%.

Still, investors need to put these numbers in perspective. On a $10,000 investment, you'd save just $9 a year by choosing an ETF S&P 500 Index fund over a mutual fund S&P 500 Index fund.

The expense advantage of ETFs may also prove to be more mirage than fact for most investors. That's because you must pay commissions to buy and sell ETFs, just as you would for stock transactions. If you plan on making a single, lump sum investment, then it may pay to choose an ETF. However, if you plan to buy or sell shares more than once a year, ETFs' cost advantage could be obliterated quickly. That may be ETFs' greatest weakness. The fund companies behind them tout ETFs' expense advantages and trading flexibility as their key benefits, but the fact remains that if you trade very much, you actually end up costing yourself far more than you would with almost any mutual fund.

## Taxes

With a regular mutual fund, investor selling can force managers to sell stocks in order to meet redemptions, which can result in taxable capital gains distributions being paid to shareholders. In contrast, most trading in ETFs takes place between shareholders, shielding the fund from any need to sell stocks to meet redemptions. Furthermore, redemptions made by large investors are paid in-kind, again protecting shareholders from taxable events.

Keep in mind, however, that ETFs can and do make capital gains distributions, as they must still buy and sell stocks to adjust for changes to their underlying benchmarks.

## Performance

Because they are shielded from investor trading, ETFs shouldn't suffer from having to keep cash on hand to meet redemptions, or from being forced to sell stocks into a declining market for the same purpose.

An ETF is fully invested where a mutual fund must leave some money in cash to allow for withdrawals. For example, if a mutual fund has 5% in cash for withdrawals, only 95% of the fund is growing and paying dividends as opposed to 100% of an ETF.

## Summary

ETFs have a lot to offer. They're flexible and low-cost, and their underlying portfolios are protected from the impact of investor trading. There are also ETFs that address specific subsectors that regular mutual funds do not. Nevertheless, look carefully before you leap.

ETFs' cost advantage isn't always as large as it might seem, and trading costs can quickly add up, if you are dollar-cost-averaging. Particularly if you're in the market for a fund that tracks a broad index such as the S&P 500, it can make a case yet for choosing an ETF over one of the mutual-fund options.

# Equity Unit Investment Trusts

Unit investment trusts (UITs) are an unmanaged portfolio of professionally selected securities that are held for a specified period of time. They were first issued in the 1960s as a way to "package" and sell portfolios of professionally selected bonds, especially tax-exempt municipal bonds. The cost of a unit is generally $1,000. During the 1990s, the UIT concept was extended to stocks.

Unlike mutual funds—which are professionally managed—equity UITs are a "buy-and-hold" investment. Securities in the portfolio are held for a pre-determined time to generate dividends and capital gains for investors. At maturity, investors can take their cash and invest elsewhere or can "roll over" their balance into a new UIT.

Like their bond counterparts, equity UITs are an unmanaged portfolio of stocks that usually remains unchanged throughout the life of the trust. Some equity UITs follow a specific investment strategy such as investing in the five or ten highest yielding stocks among the 30 stocks included in the Dow Jones Industrial Average or only in stocks listed on foreign stock exchanges.

Like mutual funds, an increasing number of equity UITs also select stocks from a particular industry sector (e.g., technology) or companies located in a particular state or region of the country. Like individual stocks, UIT dividends and capital gains are taxable, whether earnings are distributed in cash or reinvested in additional UIT units. If the value of a UIT portfolio increases, that capital gain is taxed. Most equity UITs have maturities of six years or less. Shares can be sold prior to the trust's maturity at a price determined by market conditions.

Two advantages of equity UITs are not having to worry about changes in portfolio holdings or management and tax efficiency (low taxes because stocks in a UIT portfolio are rarely traded). A major disadvantage is their up-front cost. Equity UITs typically charge a front-end load (commission) of about 3% of the amount invested.

## **Mutual Funds**

A mutual fund is a corporation that pools large sums of money ranging from one million to several billions of dollars, pooled from millions of individual investors, just like you, who wish to save or make money. Mutual funds are run by an individual or a team of professional money managers who invest the pool of money into stocks, bonds, or other securities. The combined holdings of a mutual fund are known as the fund's portfolio.

An individual who owns shares in a mutual fund may invest as little as $25 to $50, or as much as $2,500 or more. By investing money into a mutual fund, your money is spread out and diversified among hundreds of stocks, bonds, or other securities, minimizing risk.

You do not need to buy bonds and stocks directly. You are not limited to the volatile performance of merely one or two stocks. In addition to this, you pay minimal fees, often less than 1% of your investment (per annum), while earning money with the expertise of the mutual fund managers. But, most of all, you will certainly be making more money than leaving it in a bank account where you may actually lose spending power.

The goal of a mutual fund is to provide an efficient way for an individual to make money. There are several thousand mutual funds with different investment strategies and goals to choose from. Choosing one can be overwhelming, even though it need not be. Different mutual funds have different risks, which differ because of the fund's goals, fund manager, and investment styles.

Money from a mutual fund is made when the stocks, bonds, or other securities increase in value (a capital gain), issue dividends, or make interest payments. When investing in a mutual fund, the income you make is the result of income received from dividend-paying stocks, and interest from bonds. If the fund sells a holding whose value has increased, you make money. Even if the fund does not sell that specific holding, the fund itself will still increase in value, and in that way you may also make money. Therefore the value of the shares you hold in the mutual fund will increase in value when the holdings increase in value. Capital gains and income or dividend payments are best reinvested for younger investors.

Retirees often seek the income from dividend distributions to augment their income. With reinvestment of dividends and capital gains distributions, your money increases at an even greater rate. When you redeem your shares, what you receive is the value of the shares.

## What Is A Mutual Fund?

Although their popularity has mushroomed in recent years, mutual funds have been around a long time. The oldest mutual funds in existence today are more than 70 years old, having survived the Great Depression, World War II, and other turbulent economic and political events. In all, investors have entrusted more than $5.5 trillion to more than 12,000 mutual funds in the United States. (Source: Investment Company Institute, December 2001.)

Before making any investment, you should try to learn as much as you reasonably can about the asset you plan to purchase and how it works. Many different types of mutual funds are offered to individual investors, and the characteristics of each type will determine whether it is appropriate for your investment goal—whether it be funding your retirement, paying college tuition, or some other purpose.

The idea behind the mutual fund is simple: Many people put their money in a fund, which invests in various types of securities to pursue a specific financial goal. Then, each investor shares proportionately in the income or investment gains and losses that the fund's investments produce.

Because investors may sell their shares or buy new shares each business day, mutual funds are called "open-end investment companies."

Each mutual fund has a manager, or investment advisor, who directs the investing of the fund's assets according to the fund's objectives. Some common objectives of mutual funds are long-term growth, high current income, stability of principal (the amount of your own money that you put into an investment), or some combination of the three. Depending on its objective, a fund may invest in common stocks, bonds, cash investments, or a combination of these three types of financial assets.

## Major Fund Categories:

| Money Markets | Short term T-Bills, CDs, commercial paper. |
|---|---|
| Bond Funds | Seek income from the interest rates of government and/or corporate bonds. |
| Income Funds | Seek income through the dividends and income provided by stocks and bonds at regular intervals. Income may be reinvested automatically to increase capital appreciation. |
| Balanced Funds | Capital gains and income earned from a mix of investments from bonds and stocks. Bonds add stability during down and volatile periods, while stocks provide growth. |
| Stock Funds | Includes a wide variety of funds seeking capital gains from small portfolios of 50 stocks to large portfolios of hundreds of stocks. There are various categories, including sector funds (such as tech & health care funds), region specific, and international stock funds. |

## Fund Objectives/Goals:

| Aggressive Growth | Great for longer-term investors who do not need their money within the next five years. Small-Cap funds invest in the stock of small and new businesses, which have greater potential for growth, yet have higher risk of short-term volatility. Short-term losses of 20-30% may occur in a high volatility dip, but in the long term these funds, as a rule, have had great potential for high returns despite volatility. |
|---|---|
| Growth | Seek high returns, yet have less volatility than aggressive growth. Investment portfolios consist of large, medium and small sized companies. Managers tend to utilize more conservative strategies than their aggressive fund counterparts. |
| Index | This category seeks to replicate the market trends by investing in the same stocks measured by indexes such as the S&P 500 and NASDAQ. Returns match the market. Management fees are usually extremely low. |

| Growth, Income | Funds that tend to invest in both stocks and bonds. Bonds provide a safety cushion during volatile periods; dividends and income provide extra capital appreciation, in addition to appreciation made from stock appreciation. |
|---|---|
| Income | Funds that invest in bonds. Money is made from bond income, and also from bonds, which increase in value. |
| Capital Preservation | Money market mutual funds preserve initial investment. Interest rates vary, but are usually much higher than in a savings or money market account. |

## Types Of Mutual Funds

| Your Objective | Type of Mutual Fund | What These Funds Hold | Capital Growth Potential | Current Income Potential | Stability of Principal |
|---|---|---|---|---|---|
| Current income, stability of principal | Money market | Cash investments | None | Moderate | Very High |
| Tax-free income, stability of principal | Tax-exempt money market | Municipal cash investments | None | Moderate | Very High |
| Current income | Taxable bond | Wide range of government and/or corporate bonds | None | Moderate to High | Low to Moderate |
| Tax-free income | Tax-exempt bond | Wide range of municipal bonds | None | Moderate to High | Low to Moderate |
| Current income, capital growth | Balanced | Stocks and bonds | Moderate | Moderate to High | Low to Moderate |
| | Equity income stock | High-yielding stocks, convertible securities | Moderate to High | Moderate | Low to Moderate |
| | Growth & income stock | Dividend - paying stocks | Moderate to High | Low to Moderate | Low to Moderate |
| Capital growth | Domestic growth stock | U.S. stocks with high potential for growth | High | Very Low | Low |
| | International growth stock | Stocks of companies outside U.S. | High | Very Low to Low | Very Low |
| Aggressive growth of capital | Aggressive growth stock | Stocks with very high potential for growth | Very High | Very Low | Very Low |
| | Small-capitalization stock | Stocks of small companies | Very High | Very Low | Very Low |
| | Specialized stock | Stocks of industry sectors | High to Very High | Very Low to Moderate | Very Low to Low |

# Making Money With Mutual Funds

Of course, when you invest any money there is always some degree of risk, but the bottom line is this: in the long run, stocks bonds and other securities increase in value and make money. In the short term, stocks are volatile. The amount of volatility, if any, depends on the nature of the stock. Stock issued by large and established companies are less volatile, steady growers. Stocks of new and smaller companies tend to have more volatility but greater growth potential over the short run.

The volatility and aggressiveness of a mutual fund also lies with the manager's investment strategies. These will be described in the individual mutual fund's prospectus—an informational booklet that describes a fund's returns, risks, portfolio, and investment strategy.

One way investors insure their failure and doom is to become nervous and sell out as soon as the value of the investment drops. In the short term, fluctuations in the value are normal and are to be expected. Do not sell on down fluctuations, because down fluctuations will almost certainly go back up, in the near to immediate future.

You probably have heard of market crashes. But, if you had kept your investments in the stock market of the Great Crash of 1929, instead of pulling out at a loss, you would have eventually recovered your loss and much more! Remember this, mutual funds are never as volatile as stocks themselves, because of the fact that a mutual fund consists of a portfolio of several stocks it is practically impossible for all to go down, even in a market crash.

When the investors all pulled out their money, instead of holding out, they contributed to the declining prices of the stock, which contributed to the severity of the crash and the Great Depression. Investor panic and the "herd mentality phenomenon" essentially resulted in the Great Depression, which could have been avoided.

Once you are invested into a mutual fund, when to sell becomes another important issue. A bad mutual fund is a fund that does consistently poorly, losing money, even in a good market when other mutual funds are making money. These funds can easily be avoided in the first place, by comparing their five-year return averages with other mutual funds.

A simple rule to follow is this: if the three to four year return is negative, do not buy the fund in the first place. If you check your mutual fund's performance every day, either through the phone, newspaper, or computer on-line service, and see short-term volatility, don't pull out, this is normal.

If you are seeking a specific goal, and have attained the amount desired, then pull out that amount of money. Partial redemptions can easily be made, usually over the phone if you desire.

Money invested in mutual funds for the purposes of retirement—in IRAs (individual retirement accounts) or 401k plans (company retirement plans)—can be withdrawn at age 59½ without any taxes. Withdrawing early will incur a heavier tax penalty.

## The Advantages Of Mutual Funds

There are four key attributes that help make mutual funds America's most popular medium for investing.

### Diversification

A single mutual fund may hold securities from hundreds of different issuers, a level of diversification that few investors could achieve on their own. By pooling their money, mutual fund shareholders are able to spread their assets among many different securities, sharply reducing the risk of loss from problems with any one company or institution.

### Professional Management

A professional investment manager—who has access to extensive research, market information, and skilled securities traders—decides which securities to buy and sell for a mutual fund. Professional management can be a valuable service, because few investors have the time or expertise to manage their personal investments on a daily basis or investigate the thousands of securities available in the financial markets.

### Liquidity

Shares in a mutual fund may be sold whenever you want. At your request, a fund is required to redeem shares any business day, based on that day's closing price—at the net asset value. Net asset value is the share price, or market value, of a fund's total assets, less its liabilities, divided by the number of shares outstanding.

## Convenience

Mutual funds offer a variety of services that can make investing easier. Fund shares may be purchased or sold by mail, telephone, or by the Internet, and your money can easily be moved from one fund to another as your investing needs change. You may arrange to have automatic investments made into a fund to steadily build an investment portfolio, or to redeem some of your shares automatically to meet monthly living expenses. You can have distributions of fund income paid directly to you or automatically reinvested in more shares of your fund. Extensive record keeping services are provided to help you track your transactions, assist you in completing your tax returns, and follow your fund's performance. You can monitor the price of your fund shares daily in newspapers, by telephone, or via a variety of online services.

## The Disadvantages Of Mutual Funds

There are some disadvantages associated with investing in mutual funds that you should consider before investing.

## No "Guarantees"

Unlike bank deposits, mutual funds are neither insured or guaranteed by the Federal Deposit Insurance Corporation (FDIC) or any other agency of the U.S. Government. The market value of a mutual fund may fluctuate, even if the fund invests in government securities. Mutual funds are regulated by the U.S. Securities and Exchange Commission (SEC) and by state securities officials, who require funds to provide full disclosure of information an investor needs to make an informed decision. But this regulation does not eliminate the risk of an investment falling in value.

## The Diversification "Penalty"

Because a mutual fund typically holds a large number of securities, fund shareholders give up the chance to earn the higher returns that are sometimes achieved by holding a single security or a handful of individual securities. In other words, just as diversification eliminates the risk of catastrophic loss from holding a single security, it limits the potential for a "big score" from holding a single stock or bond whose value shoots up. It also is important to understand that diversification does not protect an investor from the risk of loss from an overall decline in financial markets.

## Potentially High Costs

Mutual funds can be a lower-cost way to buy securities when compared with buying individual securities through a broker. However, a combination of sales commissions and high operating expenses at some funds may offset the efficiencies that can be gained through mutual fund ownership. It's important for you to compare the costs of mutual funds that you are considering, because high costs can significantly erode the returns you receive as a shareholder.

# The Nuts And Bolts Of Mutual Funds

People invest in mutual funds because they have specific goals they want to reach, such as building a nest egg for retirement, putting a child through college, or saving for a major purchase. Understanding how funds work and how they can help investors reach their goals will help you choose the investment most appropriate for your situation.

There are two basic ways a mutual fund investor may make money from fund shares: current income and capital gains.

## Income

A mutual fund may produce current income for its shareholders from the fund's investments in interest-bearing securities—such as bonds or cash investments—or from dividends paid on common stocks owned by the fund. Such income, whether earned as interest or dividends, must be paid out each year to fund shareholders in the form of income dividends. Depending on the fund, income dividends may be paid monthly (for money market funds and bond funds), quarterly (for many balanced funds and stock funds), semiannually, or annually. Fund shareholders can choose to receive income dividends in cash or to have the dividends reinvested in more shares of the fund. A shareholder designates the method of payment when an account is opened, but may change the selection at any time.

The annual income produced by the fund, expressed as a percentage of the fund's current market value, is known as its yield. For example, a fund with a share price, or net asset value, of $20 that pays out $1 per year in income has a yield of 5% ($1 ÷ $20 = .05).

Not all mutual funds seek to produce investment income. For example, many stock funds—especially growth and aggressive-growth funds—

primarily seek price appreciation from the securities they hold and may produce little or no income from interest or dividends.

## Capital Gains

When the securities that a fund has purchased rise in value, or appreciate, the fund has an unrealized capital gain. Such unrealized gains remain in the fund, raising the market value of its shares. This gain, or appreciation, is "on paper" until an investor sells the shares.

If the fund itself sells securities at a profit, a capital gain is realized. These realized capital gains are periodically paid out to shareholders in a capital gains distribution. When a fund pays out its realized capital gains, the fund's share price is reduced by the amount of the distribution since the shareholders, not the fund, now have the proceeds. As with income dividends, the proceeds of capital gains distributions may be received by a shareholder in cash or reinvested in more shares of the fund.

Of course, stocks and bonds fall in value as well as rise, and funds from time to time may incur capital losses, which reduce the market value of fund shares. Likewise, an individual investor may suffer a loss by selling shares for a price lower than the investor paid for them.

## Measuring Mutual Fund Performance

**Figure 1**

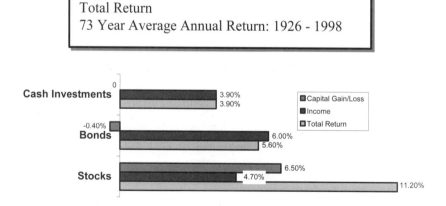

A mutual fund's investment performance is best measured by its total return. A fund's total return is the change in the value of an investment in the fund, taking into account any change in the fund's share price during the period and assuming the reinvestment of income dividends and capital gains distributions. **Figure 1** shows the average annual total return for cash investments, bonds, and common stocks from 1926–1998, how much of that return came from income, and how much from capital gains (or capital losses, in the case of long-term bonds).

Total return may be negative if a fund's share price has declined during the period being measured. **Figure 2** provides an example of how to calculate a fund's total return.

**Figure 2**

## Total Return Calculation

Purchase price (per share)................ ...........................$50
Income distribution.................... ......................$2
Capital gains distribution............ .....................$1
Share appreciation (shares now worth $52)..........$2

### Total Return

Income + Capital Gains + Appreciation
Original Purchase Price

$$\frac{\$2 + \$1 + \$2}{\$50} \quad = \quad \frac{\$5}{\$50} \quad = \quad 10\%$$

This example assumes that only one investment was made over a single period.

Total return is commonly presented in two ways. One way is called the fund's cumulative total return, or the total rise in the value of a fund's shares over time, assuming that dividend and capital gains distributions were reinvested.

The other way is called average annual total return, which is the compounded total return it would take each year to produce the fund's cumulative total return. Seemingly modest annual returns can be

103

converted, through the power of compounding, into impressive cumulative returns. For example, an average annual total return of 7% would, after ten years, amount to a cumulative total return of 97%.

## The Power Of Compounding

Compounding is when you earn interest, dividends, or capital gains on both your original investment and on the reinvested earnings of your investment. As Benjamin Franklin put it many years ago: "The money that money makes, makes money."

The steady but powerful effects of compounding are why it is so important to begin investing as early as possible in pursuit of your goal, whether that goal is retirement, financing college, or saving for a down payment on a house.

**Figure 3**

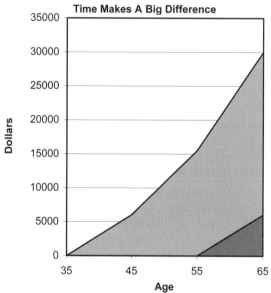

Consider, for example, a single investment of $3,000 in a mutual fund that earns an average annual total return of 8%, after taxes. As **Figure 3** shows, if someone invested $3,000 at age 55 and all earnings were reinvested, it would grow to $6,480 in ten years when the investor reaches age 65 and retires. If the investor had instead invested $3,000 at age 35 and reinvested all earnings, the amount would have grown to $30,190 at retirement, a difference of $23,710, or nearly eight times the original investment.

It is never too late to start an investment program, but it is clear that the earlier you start, the more benefit you will derive from compounding.

## Evaluating Fund Performance

The best way to check the performance of your mutual fund is to compare its total return with the returns of similar funds or with the return of an appropriate market index or benchmark over the same time periods.

A stock fund should be compared with other similar stock funds—ones that invest in the same types of companies.

A bond fund should be compared with bond funds that invest in bonds of similar maturities and credit quality.

You would want to compare a long-term U.S. Treasury bond fund with other funds holding long-term Treasury bonds, not with funds that hold short-term bonds or mortgage-backed securities. You can usually find the name of the appropriate market index in a fund's prospectus or annual report.

When comparing funds, it is best to focus on long-term performance because financial markets—and the economy, for that matter—tend to go through cycles that can last for several years. For example, small-company stocks (and funds investing in such stocks) will at times outperform large-company stocks (and large-company funds).

At other times, the large-company stocks will be the star performers. A common mistake investors make is to constantly "chase" the best-performing funds from the recent past. Unfortunately, last year's "hot" sector of the financial markets is likely to be replaced this year by a different sector. Sadly, some mutual fund companies encourage this practice with advertisements that trumpet performance from the recent past, while simultaneously conceding (usually in small print) that past performance is no indication of future results.

## Fund Expenses

Risk and return are not an investor's only considerations. Another critical factor is cost. Expenses have an important impact on your investment results. All mutual funds have expenses, but some funds are much more costly to own than others. Once you understand fund expenses, you'll find it easier to select the most cost-effective funds.

Fund costs fall into two categories: sales charges, or "loads," and operating expenses. Not all mutual funds impose loads, but all funds have ongoing operating expenses that are deducted from the income each fund earns before that income passes through to fund shareholders.

Sales loads may be charged up front as a percentage of the sum you invest. These front-end loads range from 4% to 6%. Funds that charge sales fees ranging from 1% to 3% are called "low-load" funds. Another form of sales charge is the back-end load, which is applied when an investor sells fund shares. Back-end loads, also called contingent deferred sales charges, may be as high as 6% for a redemption that takes place within a year of the original investment. The charge typically declines over time, disappearing by the seventh year after the original purchase of fund shares.

All funds incur expenses from basic operations—including investment advisory fees, legal and accounting services, postage, printing, telephone service, and other costs of running the fund. These expenses are paid from income earned by the fund. The total of these costs is known as the expense ratio, which is expressed as a percentage of the fund's average net assets during the year. This annual expense ratio typically ranges from a low of about 0.20% (or $2 per $1,000 in assets) to 2% ($20 per $1,000 in assets).

Some funds add to their operating expenses a 12b-1 fee, which goes to pay marketing and distribution costs of the fund. This 12b-1 fee, which is sometimes used instead of a sales load to compensate salespersons, can be as much as 1% of assets, or $10 each year for each $1,000 invested. Funds that are sold without 12b-1 fees or sales loads are called pure no-load funds.

## How Costs Affect Returns

All mutual funds have expenses, but some are much more costly to own than others. And there is no evidence that higher costs lead to better performance. You should pay careful attention to all the fees and expenses charged by a fund because they directly reduce your investment return.

Paying a load or higher operating expenses might make sense if the end result were higher returns to the investor. But paying more to purchase shares or to operate a fund does not necessarily mean that you receive better investment management. According to William Sharpe, recipient of the Nobel Prize in Economic Sciences: "There is virtually no evidence to suggest that funds with higher expense ratios do better, before expenses. Which therefore suggests they will do worse, after expenses."

## How To Compare Fund Costs

It is easy to research the costs of a mutual fund. The SEC requires that information about sales charges and operating expenses be disclosed in a document called the prospectus, which must be given to all investors at or before the time of purchase. The information about sales charges and expenses is spelled out in a fee table near the front of the prospectus. This table makes it easy to compare the costs of one fund with those of another.

## Constructing Your Investment Portfolio

How you divide your investments among stock, bond, and money market funds will largely determine your long-term investment returns and the volatility (short-term variability) of those returns. For instance, stock funds can be expected to provide much higher long-term returns than money market funds, but they also fluctuate quite a bit in value. Having a mix of the different types of investments can help to offset the volatility of the financial markets because one type of asset might be rising when another is falling. This cushioning effect makes it easier for investors to continue with a long-term investment plan even during a sharp downturn in the stock market.

Choosing an appropriate mix of investments for a specific financial goal is known as **asset allocation**. Because investors usually have several goals, they often think of their investments as a collection of separate portfolios, each designed for a different goal.

When selecting an asset allocation, consider four factors:

## Your Goal

This is simply a purchase or series of expenditures you want to make at some time in the future. For instance, one goal might be to make a down payment on a house, while another might be to ensure financial security in retirement.

## Your Time Horizon

This is the number of years you have to invest before reaching your goal, including the period during which you are spending your investment.

The time horizon for making a down payment on a house might be two or three years, while the time horizon for retirement might be 40 years, including your years in retirement.

## Your Risk Tolerance

This is the ability to endure the inevitable fluctuations that come with investing. Knowing that you have many years to reach a goal may make you more comfortable with investments, such as stocks, that are likely to provide higher long-term returns but also have higher risks. Keep in mind that you can't avoid all investment risks, and, if you select only very stable investments, you run the risk of losing purchasing power to inflation.

## Your Financial Condition

This is the stability of your job and the state of your personal finances. A person with a steady job and well-established investment programs can afford to take on more investment risk than someone with an unstable job and few assets.

## Rebalance Your Portfolio

Because stock, bond, and money market investments will each provide different returns, you may need to "rebalance" your portfolio over time—moving assets from one fund to another to maintain the desired asset allocation.

If you do not rebalance, you could end up with a portfolio that carries more risk than you want or that is not likely to fulfill your financial goals. Keep in mind that if you rebalance by selling one type of asset and buying another, you may incur an income tax liability and you may have to pay fees and commissions.

You may want to review your asset allocation each year to make sure it is still appropriate. As your time horizon decreases, consider gradually changing your investments to a more conservative mix.

## Build Your Portfolio With One Or More Funds

In selecting mutual funds that best match your asset allocation plan, you could select stock and bond funds to create a portfolio of funds, or you could choose a balanced fund, which is a single mutual fund that invests in stocks, bonds, and (sometimes) cash investments. In many cases this is a good strategy for someone just starting out with a small amount to invest. Many balanced funds maintain a fairly stable mix of such assets.

## Fund Style

Two important considerations when choosing funds are deciding whether to use:

- An "actively" managed fund **or** an index fund.

- A taxable fund **or** a tax-advantaged fund.

Your portfolio can be built using either actively managed funds or index funds, but you should understand the difference before selecting one. Actively managed funds seek to produce investment returns that exceed a target market average, such as the Standard & Poor's 500 Index (the S&P 500) by researching and selecting specific securities. The alternative approach—an index fund—holds securities in the same proportion as that of a market index (or average) in order to closely match the index's performance.

Some investors favor an actively managed fund in hopes that it will provide above-average returns. Others prefer an index fund because few professional managers can beat the market consistently. Over the last ten years, the overall U.S. stock market (as represented by the Wilshire 5000 Equity Index) has outperformed 82% of all actively managed stock funds, according to fund researcher Lipper, Inc.

Some investors are unsure which investment approach is best, so they hedge their bets by owning both actively managed and index funds. It's a good idea to diversify with both styles of funds.

## Taxable Versus Tax-Advantaged Funds

Most mutual funds are not managed with an eye on the impact of taxes, but some funds are tax-friendly by nature. For example, a stock fund that buys and holds securities rather than actively trading them is less likely to realize taxable capital gains that must be passed along to fund shareholders.

Stock index funds—by pursuing a buy-and-hold strategy—can reduce an investor's exposure to taxes. Some other funds, called tax-managed funds, take indexing a step further to minimize taxable gains and income

109

through strategies that include low turnover, careful selection of shares to sell at a loss to offset capital gains, and redemption fees to discourage short-term investing and market-timing that can hurt the other investors in the fund.

You can receive tax-free income by investing in municipal money market and bond funds, which invest in securities issued by state and local government entities. The interest earned through these funds is generally exempt from federal income taxes and, in some cases, from state and local taxes. These funds are also known as tax-exempt funds. Keep in mind that, while interest income is tax-exempt, you may still incur taxable capital gains through an investment in a municipal bond fund.

Tax-exempt funds are typically appropriate only for investors in a high tax bracket because they pay lower yields than taxable funds—and that lower yield could easily offset any tax advantage. To determine if a tax-exempt fund is a good choice, you should compare its yield (not total return) with the after-tax yield you would receive from a comparable taxable fund. Tax-exempt funds should never be used in a tax-deferred account such as an individual retirement account (IRA), Roth IRA, or 401k. The reason for this is that retirement accounts already grow tax-deferred.

## Taxable Versus Tax-Exempt Bond Funds

To decide if you should invest in a taxable fund or a tax-exempt fund, use this formula to determine the "taxable-equivalent yield" of the tax-exempt fund.

Tax-exempt yield ÷(1 - your federal tax rate*)= Taxable-equivalent yield

*In decimal form. For example, 0.31 if in the 31% bracket.

If the taxable-equivalent yield is higher than the yield on a taxable fund with a similar maturity, then you may wish to invest in the tax-exempt fund. Bond fund investors should check their marginal tax rates each year to determine if a tax-exempt fund or a taxable fund is appropriate.

**Note:** Income received from a tax-exempt fund may be subject to state and local income taxes or to the federal alternative minimum tax. If you invest only in municipal bonds from your state, the interest income may also be exempt from state and local income taxes. In that case, add your marginal state and local tax rate to the federal rate in the formula above.

## How To Read A Mutual Fund Prospectus

A recent survey of retirement investors revealed some significant misperceptions about mutual funds:

Nearly 90% of investors surveyed didn't know that money market mutual funds contain only short-term securities.

About 75% of respondents didn't know it's possible to lose money in a government bond fund.

Almost half of respondents didn't know that they could lose money in a bond fund.

Fortunately, there's a tool designed to thwart such misinformation—the mutual fund prospectus. Wading through this sometimes complex document, however, may take perseverance and a strong cup of coffee.

Think of the prospectus as your travel guide to the world of mutual funds—it provides all the details you need to map out a successful investment plan. At first glance, of course, a prospectus may not look as reader-friendly as you would hope. It is, after all, a legal document that must adhere to rigorous standards set forth by the Securities and Exchange Commission (SEC), the federal agency that oversees the mutual fund industry.

With a little basic knowledge of the information contained in a prospectus, you can make effective use of this valuable investment-planning tool.

## Questions To Ask Before Investing

- What does this fund invest in?

- What is the long-term rate of return?

- How much has return fluctuated in the past?

- How does the fund's performance compare with that of the underlying market?

- Is the fund seeking income or capital growth?

- What time frame is appropriate for an investor in this fund?

- What are the costs involved with this fund?

## How Can A Prospectus Help You?

Consider these examples of hypothetical situations in which the information found in a prospectus could have been very useful:

An investor sells his mutual fund shares and is surprised to learn that a portion of the sale price is paid to the fund company in the form of a back end load.

An investor exchanges her investment in one fund for another fund in the same fund family. She did not know that fees were charged for the exchange.

A retiree in search of income invests in a high-yield bond fund but doesn't know it is also high-risk and is disturbed by its fluctuating value.

Attempting to make a mortgage payment with money from a money market account, an investor discovers that the fund places a minimum amount on its check writing privilege.

All of the necessary information to prevent these occurrences is contained in every mutual fund's prospectus.

Take a look at these key elements:

**Date Of Issue** — First, verify that you have received an up-to-date edition of the prospectus. A prospectus must be updated at least annually.

**Minimum Investments** — Mutual funds differ both in the minimum initial investment required, and the minimum for subsequent investments.

**Investment Objectives** — The goal of each fund should be clearly defined—from income with preservation of principal to long-term capital appreciation. Be sure the fund's objective matches your objective.

**Investment Policies** — A prospectus will outline the general strategies the fund managers will implement. You'll learn what types of investments will be included, such as government bonds or common stock. The prospectus may also include information on minimum bond ratings and types of companies considered appropriate for a fund. Be sure to consider whether the fund offers adequate diversification.

**Risk Factors** — Every investment involves some level of risk. In a prospectus you'll find descriptions of the risks associated with investments in the fund. Refer to your own objectives and decide if the risk associated with the fund's investments matches your own risk tolerance.

**Performance Data** — You'll find selected per-share data including net asset value and total return for different time periods since the fund's inception. Performance data listed in a prospectus are based on standard formulas established by the SEC and enable you to make comparisons with other funds. Remember that past results do not guarantee future performance. When evaluating performance, look at the track record of a fund over a time period that matches your own investment goals.

**Fees And Expenses** — Sales and management fees associated with a mutual fund must be clearly listed. The prospectus will also display the impact these fees and expenses would have on a hypothetical investment over time.

**Tax Information** — A prospectus will include information on the tax status and implications of a fund's distributions—whether they will be treated as dividend income or capital gains.

**Investor Services** — Shareholders may have access to certain services, such as automatic investment of dividends and systematic withdrawal plans. This section of the prospectus, usually near the back of the publication, will describe these services and how you can take advantage of them.

## The Summary Prospectus

The Securities and Exchange Commission recently approved use of a simplified summary prospectus to help investors better understand key characteristics of a mutual fund investment.

Ask your mutual fund company for a summary prospectus in addition to the regular prospectus.

To simplify the process of reviewing mutual fund prospectuses, certain information is required to appear in the same place. For example, the fee table and performance table must appear at the beginning of the prospectus.

While the rest of the material can appear in any order, you'll generally have no trouble finding the information you need. Prospectuses generally range from 10-20 pages and include a table of contents. And after reviewing a few prospectuses, you'll become accustomed to the language and be able to reduce the time it takes to find the information you need to make a sound investment decision.

You can receive prospectuses free from mutual fund companies, a broker, or a registered representative. Be sure to read the prospectus and ask questions about items that you are not sure about before investing. Your financial planner or broker should be able to answer any questions.

## Real Estate

Real estate is one of the best investments you can make, but you must know what you are doing. Just because a home is a good investment does not mean it's a "sure thing."

When you buy a home, you are probably making one of the largest investments you will ever make, so you need to totally understand the basics of making such a purchase. If a home is bought in the right location and at the right price, it can be very worthwhile. But, if you make a mistake in either of these areas you can suffer financially.

When you buy real estate for use as rental property, you can benefit by the purchase in at least three ways: it provides current income; it provides tax benefits through business expense deductions and depreciation; and, if you like, it can provide a place to live when you retire.

Let's consider first the tax benefits that result from offering property you own for rental purposes. First, any expenses you incur in operating the rental property are deductible from your income as business expenses. These might include repair and maintenance of the house or other property, interest payments on a mortgage, or an occasional trip to inspect the property if it is outside the area where you live.

Second, depreciation can be deducted from your income as well. This is the annual decline in value of any property, which results from its increasing age and is determined according to a fixed schedule depending on the nature of the property. This is a noncash deduction, since you are not actually expending any money; yet you reap the tax benefits just as if you were.

Real estate values usually increase each year rather than decrease, despite what happens in "soft" markets such as from the mid 1980s to the early 1990s. Therefore, you could say that you benefit twice: the actual resale value of your property will generally grow, while you get a tax deduction because of the theoretical decrease in the value of your property over time.

Real estate offers decided advantages to the canny investor. But like any other investment, it carries risks as well. The greatest is the risk of buying a property whose rental or resale value is minimal. My real estate agent associates tell me that the three most important rules of real estate investment are location, location, location, and that is pretty sound advice.

Another important aspect of real estate investments is the selling of your home and its tax ramifications. When you sell your home and you realize a profit, you will receive two favorable tax treatments:

**1)** You will be able to postpone the tax on the profit indefinitely if you purchase another primary residence within 2 years.

**2)** Before May 1997, a one-time tax exclusion of $125,000 was available to those over the age of 55 while other homeowners could be taxed on any profit from the sale of their home as capital gains. Under the Taxpayers Relief Act of 1997 that exclusion, regardless of age, has been raised to $500,000 for gains on the sale of the home for married couples and $250,000 for single filers as long as the property was held as a primary residence for two of the past five years. However, homeowners can no longer plow gains in excess of the exclusion into a new house.

## <u>REIT</u>

If you're interested in real estate but somewhat hesitant to get involved directly, consider a real estate investment trust (REIT). It is the simplest and most direct way to invest in real estate. Like a mutual fund, a REIT pools money from many investors who buy shares in the trust's portfolio.

However, rather than investing in stocks or bonds, a REIT invests in real estate.

Purchasing a REIT could be looked at as investing your money in real estate by the share instead of by the brick. When you receive shares in a trust, you are buying a stock that trades on a stock exchange just as any other stock does. Income from the rent or interest on the mortgages is paid as dividends. When the property is sold, capital gains will be given to the stockholders as a special dividend; or the sale may increase the earnings per share, thus raising the value of the stock.

A REIT may invest in various properties such as: office buildings, apartments, shopping malls, hotels, and resorts. Some REITs are regional, meaning they invest only in a city or state.

REITs have several advantages for investors. They allow small investors to participate in real estate investments that would otherwise be unavailable. Shares in a REIT are liquid and can normally be sold near their full value. They are a liquid method of owning what is traditionally an illiquid asset and are easier to buy and sell than physical property.

As long as a REIT meets certain requirements, it pays no corporate tax. Thus, while other investments, such as mutual funds, pay after-tax dividends, the REIT can distribute pretax dollars.

REIT investments may be very conservative or highly speculative depending upon the policy set by the management of the trust. You'll want to make sure that the objectives of the trust match your own investment plans before you get involved.

## **Precious Metals**

Gold and silver has been used as money since biblical times. It has several characteristics that make it desirable as a medium of exchange. Gold is scarce and it is durable. More than 95 percent of all the gold ever mined during the past 5,000 years is still in circulation. And it is inherently valuable because of its beauty and its usefulness in industrial and decorative applications.

One advantage of precious metals as a currency is that they can't be debased by the government. With a paper-based currency, such as U.S. dollars, the government can print more to pay off debts. This process can lead to the devaluation of a currency and inflation.

One hundred years ago one ounce of gold would buy about one average men's suit. Today at about $300 per ounce, one ounce of gold will buy— you guessed it—one average men's suit. With all the fluctuations in price, the real value of gold hasn't changed in a hundred years.

## Why Is Gold Considered An Investment?

Scared investors often invest in precious metals as a hedge against economic collapse or hyperinflation. They read some of the many doom-and-gloom books available and think back to the Great Depression and then insist on buying gold to protect them.

Gold has long been referred to as the "doomsday metal" because of its traditional role as a safeguard against economic, social, and political upheaval and the resulting loss of confidence in other investments, even those guaranteed by national governments. Yet this may not be true, as was seen during the stock market crash of 1987 when the price of gold was expected to soar. As you may be aware, nothing occurred to its price even though the volume of sales increased 300 percent. Gold prices also remained relatively stable after the terrorist attack on September11, 2001.

# Commodities

At the very top of the investment risk pyramid are commodities. These include bulk goods and raw materials such as pork, grain, coffee, sugar, cocoa, metals, etc. The term also describes financial products, such as currency or stock and bond indexes, that are the raw materials of trade.

Commodities are bought and sold on the cash market, and they are traded on the futures exchanges in the form of futures contracts. Commodity prices are driven by supply and demand: when a commodity is plentiful—corn in August, for example—prices are comparably low. When a commodity is scarce because of a bad crop or because it is out of season, the price will generally be higher.

Financial expert Andrew Tobias says that since 90% of the people who speculate in commodities lose (and 98% may be a more accurate figure), the key is how to be among the 10% or (2%) who win. He simply compares investing in commodities to gambling. At the top of the investment risk pyramid, you have high potential for return, but also high risk. To invest there, you need to be able to afford to lose your entire investment.

Costs include brokerage fees. You also need considerable knowledge of the commodity in question and the markets in which it is created and sold as well as the changing situations of the buyers.

# Annuities

An annuity is a contract between you (the annuity owner) and a life insurance company. In return for your payment, the insurance company agrees to provide either a regular stream of income or a lump sum payout at some future time (generally, once you retire or pass age 59½ ).

Your premiums are invested in one or more security portfolios and fixed interest accounts, where they earn interest and/or capital appreciation. No taxes are due until these earnings are paid out. If you make a withdrawal before age 59½, you could incur a 10% tax penalty.

All annuities have several things in common:

1. Inside the annuity, the money compounds tax-deferred. Beyond this, each annuity has its own cost structure, characteristics, and rate of return. Taxes are paid on the earnings when money is withdrawn at retirement either in a lump sum or as a series of periodic payments.

2. There is no tax deduction for the money used to purchase the annuity (exception: IRAs, retirement accounts, and tax-sheltered annuities in 403b plans).

3. If the annuity holder (investor) dies during the accumulation phase, that is, before receiving any payments from the annuity, the beneficiary is guaranteed to receive the amount of the original investment.

Annuities are sold by commissioned sales persons such as: bankers, stockbrokers, financial planners, insurance agents, or through mutual funds, but regardless of who makes the sale, an insurance company always backs the annuity.

## Definition Of Annuitize

Choosing to receive payments at regular intervals over time is "annuitizing." Most companies offer several annuity options, based primarily on how long you want the income to last.

How is the amount of the payment/withdrawal determined if it's annuitized? First, the insurance company converts the accumulation units to "annuity units," which allow payouts that are partly a tax-free return of principal and partly taxable earnings. Meanwhile, the undistributed portion of the investment continues to compound, tax-deferred. The amount of each payment will depend on the annuity option selected, annuitant's age, the number of annuity units, and the performance of the securities in the portfolio(s) selected.

An annuity may be either an immediate annuity or a deferred annuity.

## Immediate Annuities

An immediate annuity pays a lifetime income starting now. In return for a lump sum of money, the purchase of an annuity guarantees a fixed income for life.

## Deferred Annuities

A deferred annuity allows the annuitant to initially purchase accumulation units prior to the payout period.

Deferred annuities may be purchased in one of two ways. Single premium annuities are purchased with a lump sum and flexible payment annuities may be purchased by installment payments over a period of years.

Deferred annuities accumulate money for the future and come in two types. A fixed annuity pays a specified interest rate for a period of time. A variable annuity puts your money in stocks, bonds, or money market mutual funds, and returns are dependent on the financial market volatility and performance.

## Fixed Annuities

A fixed tax-deferred annuity is a contract between you and an insurance company for a guaranteed interest bearing policy with guaranteed income options. The insurance company credits interest, and you don't pay taxes on the earnings until you make a withdrawal or begin receiving an annuity income. Your annuity contract earns a low rate of return that is safe.

Fixed annuities are like certificates of deposit (CDs) offered by insurance companies. The early withdrawal fee or penalty from a fixed annuity will be even greater than on CDs. On the positive side, tax planning can be accomplished by using an annuity to push income from this year into next year, lowering income for tax purposes.

But, once you own them for more than a year, your flexibility drops significantly. Too many people allow the unpaid tax or expense penalty to handcuff them into holding the annuity, missing wonderful investment opportunities. In the years I've been managing money, I've seen this happen much too frequently.

## Variable Annuities

A variable annuity is an insurance wrapper around equity mutual fund investments. Variable refers to the fact that the market value and/or income generated by the underlying securities is not fixed; your return may vary due to prevailing interest rates and other market factors.

It allows the client investment choices in separate accounts. The separate account investments are similar to mutual funds. Choices range from very conservative options such as money market and government bonds to more aggressive choices such as medium and small company stock funds.

You pay an extra 1% to 1.5% (or more) annually for your equity fund never to be worth less than your original investment should you die prior to withdrawing the money. This is called mortality and expense charges.

The performance of your investment does not depend on the insurance company's portfolio. Only the performance of the variable portfolios you have chosen will affect your results.

You allocate your money to purchase accumulation units in different portfolios, depending upon how aggressive or conservative you wish to be.

You choose the portfolios in which you will invest from among those offered. The insurance company backing the annuity develops a relationship with a professional money manager, whose experts decide which specific stocks and bonds will be a part of each portfolio.

In some newer variable annuities, you can take advantage of the wisdom of more than one expert money manager, allowing you even more flexibility in structuring your investment.

120

If you'll need the money in such a short time as to not let the stock market go through its normal cycles, equities are not the place to invest. If you have long-term investment capital, which qualifies to take the risk of the stock market, you don't need to insure it.

Even if you invest in a single separate account, your risk is spread among many securities, reducing the possibility of losing a substantial amount due to any one security.

Another feature a variable annuity has is switching privileges. Most variable annuities permit you to reallocate your money among the portfolios, usually without charge as long as you don't move the money too often.

A variable annuity has two stages: the accumulation period and the payout period. The accumulation period begins as soon as you invest. You invest with one large payment if you select a single premium annuity. Or you may make one or more payments of various amounts to a flexible premium annuity. Once you make a payment, your money begins to accumulate tax-deferred earnings. Later, your principal and interest can be paid out to you in the form of a regular income or as a lump sum.

Your premium usually purchases "accumulation units" in the insurance company's separate account, which is maintained separately from the company's regular portfolio of investments. This separate account in turn purchases shares in professionally managed securities portfolios. Each unit's value or "price" is determined by the value of the portfolio, divided by the number of units outstanding.

Each unit represents a share of the total worth of the portfolio. For example, assume a $10 million portfolio has one million accumulation units: each unit has a current value of $10. If the portfolio appreciates to $12 million, the unit value rises to $12 each. Divide your premium by the unit value at the time you invest to approximate the number of units you'll purchase.

## Payout Options

The payout from annuities may be taken in several ways. Ordinary taxes (not capital gains tax) are owed when the money comes out, and there is 10% penalty on earnings withdrawn before age 59½. You can take monthly payments for the rest of your life, or you can make periodic withdrawals.

If you make regular withdrawals, part of each withdrawal is treated as taxable income, and the rest is a nontaxable return of your own capital. If you make occasional withdrawals, the entire withdrawal is treated as taxable income. Taxes are levied until you have taken all of the earnings on the original capital invested. Other payment options include taking the money in a lump sum or rolling your savings into another annuity tax-free.

Because annuities are purchased with after tax-dollars, it is usually recommended that pre-tax investment plans (e.g., IRAs, 401ks) be used to the maximum first.

## Surrender Fees

Like Certificates of Deposits, annuities have a penalty for early surrender, however most annuity contracts have a minimal "free withdrawal" provision.

Annuities are notorious for their lack of liquidity. When you buy an annuity, you are making a long-term commitment (15 to 20 years). Moving the money to another annuity may be difficult, and quitting is expensive. You usually have to pay a surrender fee to the insurance company for selling an annuity too soon (e.g., withdrawing money from an annuity after the third year). A common fee is 7% the first year, which is reduced to 0% by the seventh year.

For our purposes, "liquidity" refers to the ability of an investor to have *unrestricted* access to his/her money. For example, an investment would be characterized as "liquid" if it were available without penalty or additional fees at any time. On the other hand, an investment would be deemed "illiquid" if there were impediments to the investor accessing the money. A variable annuity falls into this "illiquid" category for two reasons.

First, the insurance company makes withdrawals costly by imposing a surrender charge of between 6 and 8 percent of the withdrawn amount. While this surrender charge phases out over time, and while most variable annuity contracts allow the owner a 10% penalty-free withdrawal annually, investors who value unrestricted access will be frustrated.

The second factor affecting a variable annuity's liquidity comes courtesy of the Internal Revenue Code (IRC). The IRC requires that if you withdraw money (in excess of the 10% annual allowance) from an annuity before age 59½, an additional 10% penalty applies. Of course, like the insurance company's surrender charge, the IRC tempers its restriction with a limited escape clause. That escape clause says that if you irrevocably elect to annuitize the account (give up all access to principal and begin periodic distributions), the penalty is waived.

## Tax Advantages

You pay no taxes while your money is compounding inside an annuity. You can also pay a lower tax on random withdrawals because you control the tax year in which the withdrawals are made, and only pay taxes on the interest withdrawn. Tax deferral gives you control over an important expense—your taxes. Any time you control an expense, you can minimize it.

The longer you can postpone this particular expense, the greater your gain when compared to the gain you would make with a fully taxable account.

## Tax-Deferred

Tax-deferred means postponing your taxes on interest earnings until a future point in time. In the meantime, you earn interest on the money which you're not using to pay taxes. You can accumulate more money over a shorter period of time, which ultimately will provide you with a greater income.

To illustrate the increased earnings capacity of tax-deferred interest, compare it to fully taxable earnings. $25,000 at 6.0% will earn $1,500 of interest in a year. A 28% tax bracket means that approximately $420 of those earnings will be lost in taxes, leaving only $1,080 to compound during the next year. If these same earnings were tax-deferred, the full $1,500 would be available to earn even more interest. The longer you can postpone taxes, the greater the gain.

## The Difference Of Taxable And Tax-Deferred Investments

When you invest in a taxable investment such as mutual funds, stocks, or some bonds, any dividends or interest you earn during the year are considered taxable income. Also, if you sell the investment or the mutual fund money manager sells an investment and gives you a distribution, you'll owe capital gains taxes.

When you invest in the underlying securities of a variable annuity, growth is credited to your account but is not taxed in that year. You pay taxes only on money withdrawn.

When you make a withdrawal, you'll owe income taxes at your current rate on any portion of the withdrawal that is considered growth. For tax purposes, withdrawals are always considered interest first, so unless you begin to exhaust principal, you'll owe taxes on the full amount of your withdrawal. In addition, because the IRS set up tax deferral rules in order to encourage Americans to save for retirement, if you make a withdrawal before age 59½, you're likely to owe a 10% federal tax penalty on the amount withdrawn. (Only under certain IRS-defined situations, such as disability, will you be exempt from this penalty.)

If you purchase your annuity in a qualified plan such as an individual retirement account or Keogh account, different tax rules apply. The full amount of any withdrawal, even an amount attributed to principal, is taxable. This is because in a qualified plan, the contributions to the annuity are made on a pretax basis—since you didn't pay tax on that money in the year it was earned and invested you owe tax when you receive it out of the annuity.

## No Withholding Tax

There is no withholding tax while your annuity is compounding; it is completely tax-deferred. If you request a distribution (random withdrawals or annuity income), taxes will be withheld – unless you elect differently. Your election not to withdraw can be made at the time you make your request. Because the interest is tax-deferred, it is not necessary to issue a Form 1099 while your money is compounding. Only when your interest is distributed (withdrawal or annuity income) will a Form 1099 be sent, reflecting the amount of interest actually received.

## Tax Disadvantages

Many commissioned annuity sales people fail to tell the truth about the taxation of annuities. They only tell the positives.

The main part that they fail to tell you is that when money is withdrawn it is taxed as ordinary income tax. That is if you are in the 31% tax bracket you pay 31% on any money withdrawn. However, if you owned a mutual fund or stock and owned it for more than one year when you

124

sell it you are taxed at the capital gains rate of only 20%. This is an 11% savings!

Another aspect annuity sales people fail to tell you is that if your investment drops in value, you don't get to write off the losses against the gains. For example, you invested $10,000 in a stock and the stock price drops to $8,000 after you purchase it you could sell it and offset gains with the $2,000 tax loss.

If you would lose money in a variable annuity you don't get the advantage of offsetting gains as you would in a standard account.

Step up in cost basis is another advantage a standard account has over the annuity. For example: you purchased a stock for $10 per share and over several years that stock grew to $40 per share. If you died while still holding that stock, your heirs would receive it at the price at the date of death (in this example $40 per share). Your heirs would avoid any capital gains taxes incurred over the years. In an annuity the heirs would have to pay ordinary taxes on *any* gains.

Charitable giving is another disadvantage of annuities. For example: you purchased a stock at $10 per share and over several years that stock grew to $40 per share. You would be able to gift that appreciated stock to a registered charity and get the full tax deduction *and* avoid any capital gains tax.

## Safety

The fixed tax-deferred annuity is a safe investment. A qualified legal reserve life insurance company is required to meet its contractual obligations to the annuitant.

Legal reserve refers to the strict financial requirements that must be met by an insurance company to protect the money paid in by all policyholders. These reserves must be, at all times, equal to the withdrawal value (principal plus interest less early withdrawal fees, if any) of every annuity policy. State insurance laws also require that a life insurance company must maintain certain minimum levels of capital and surplus, which provide additional policyholder protection.

## When Does The Money Mature?

An annuity policy does not "mature" like a bond or certificate of deposit. Both the principal and interest will automatically continue to earn interest until withdrawn or you reach age 100. You can let your money continue to grow, make withdrawals, or begin receiving an annuity income at any time.

## Spendthrift Protection

If you are someone that is a mindless spendthrift who would have spent the money frivolously if you had it as a lump sum, an immediate annuity serves the situation well since you would get payments over a period of time but no access to the principal. Better you only get monies in drips and drabs and not allow the principal to be squandered.

Additionally, annuitization could be used for many people who are not spendthrifts per se but are so lacking in basic budget planning they tend to spend the assets well before their actuarial lifetime. But that is just being foolish.

## Avoid Probate

If a premature death should occur, the accumulating funds within your annuity may be transferred to your named beneficiaries, avoiding the expense, delay, frustration, and publicity of the probate process. Like most assets, the annuity is part of your taxable estate. Your heirs can choose to receive a lump sum payment or a guaranteed monthly income.

The beneficiaries that do receive the money will need to pay ordinary tax on the funds. Annuity beneficiaries do not get the step-up in cost basis, as stocks would offer.

## What Guarantees Do I Have?

The guarantee that annuity owners receive is the "guaranteed death benefit." The insurance company generally guarantees that in the event of death before annuitization, your beneficiary will receive the greater of a) the entire amount of your premiums, less withdrawals, charges, and fees; or b) the current contract value. Some annuities provide more generous options.

Another guarantee that annuity owners receive is the "fixed interest option." Most annuities also let you allocate funds to one or more "fixed account" options in which the insurance company guarantees your interest rate.

# Can I Have Access To My Money Before I'm 59½ ?

Most annuities provide for withdrawal of a specified amount free of charge, excluding taxes. Withdrawals in excess of the amount specified are possible but, in the early years of the contract, may trigger surrender charges. Most annuities require the annuitant to hold the funds there for at least eight to ten years.

As discussed previously, if you are younger than age 59½, the IRS may impose a 10% penalty tax.

You may also encounter a "market value adjustment" (MVA) if you withdraw money from fixed interest options before the end of the interest rate guarantee period. An MVA ensures that you receive the market value of assets withdrawn before their maturity date and may increase or decrease the value of your account.

Also, be aware that some annuities allow you to make systematic withdrawals from your account on a regularly scheduled basis, which can help in providing you with a steady income. Systematic withdrawals are subject to the same tax rules as other withdrawals.

# Are Taxes Different On Payouts Than On Withdrawals?

Once you have annuitized, each payment is structured as a partial return of principal and part interest. Only the interest portion of the payment is taxable. In addition, you can annuitize over your lifetime before age 59½ and your regular payments will not be subject to a tax penalty. You should consult your financial advisor before deciding to annuitize.

# What Happens If The Money Is Paid Out To My Beneficiary?

An annuity provides a death benefit that avoids probate and is paid directly to your beneficiary, thereby avoiding costs and delays. The guaranteed minimum death benefit is generally the greater of either the total amount of your premiums, less withdrawals, or the current value of your investments.

Some companies are more generous in their contracts, allowing for a guaranteed increase in the premium amount or a step-up in the guaranteed death benefit value at certain contract years. Read the literature and contract language for the annuity you choose to find out exactly what type of death benefit the company offers.

Again, remember that annuities are taxed differently than non-annuities, as discussed previously.

## How Do Variable Annuities Compare To IRAs?

Annuities and IRAs both provide tax-deferred growth, but there are differences. A qualified IRA owner also receives a tax deduction on the money invested into an IRA each year.

Anyone can invest in an annuity, in an unlimited amount. With an IRA, only those with earned income can invest, and contributions are limited. Also, an annuity can guarantee you an income for life; most IRAs cannot. In addition, the IRS says you must begin taking distributions from your IRA at age 70½; most annuities do not require you to begin taking regular payments before age 85. For information on the tax deductibility aspects of IRAs, consult your tax advisor as tax laws constantly change.

## What Should I Consider When Selecting A Variable Annuity?

The historical performance of the underlying portfolios, while not a guarantee of future results, should tell how well the annuity's investment manager has done in both positive and adverse markets. This is more important to the growth potential of your investment than any short-term figures.

Fees and charges should be carefully reviewed. Some annuities have a surrender charge that declines over a number of years. Others maintain a high charge for a stated period of time. No-load variable annuities are an excellent option if you feel you need to buy an annuity. Be sure to look at annual administration fees and asset charges, and find out if the insurance company charges for transfers among the portfolios. It's important that you understand the fees before you purchase your annuity.

The soundness of the insurance company is important. Find out whether the company is rated "Excellent" (A) or higher by independent industry analyst A.M. Best Company.

## How Do I Get Out Of The Annuity That I'm In?

You don't get in them to begin with, truthfully. Because an annuity is a contract and in essence qualifies as insurance even though there's no insurance around while your money is in the annuity, it's called an annuity.

Many investors want to come out of the annuities because there are a few things that are happening. For those of you who are in annuities, you are stuck, because if you take your money out in one lump sum you're going to pay ordinary income taxes on it (and penalties if you're under age 59½) and you might look to taking 10% what you can withdraw at once. Slowly but surely get it out of there. But be very careful before you get into one because they're not all that they are made up to be.

## Business

Ownership of a business is another investment option. There are many different kinds of businesses and many ways to be involved. You may own and operate a business yourself or hire someone to operate it. You can start your own business or purchase a franchise of a larger business.

While businesses certainly offer opportunity for income, they also have many risks. Careful attention must be given to the financing, cash flow needs, and reserves.

For small businesses it is important to separate business expenses from the family budget. A separate checking account for the business is crucial. In many cases a more sophisticated software such as QuickBooks © may be more helpful.

Another advantage to keeping your business separate from your personal life is protecting your home and belongings during difficult financial times.

If you are considering starting a business, there are many resources to help you. For instance, in many states a cooperative extension office offers education on micro and home-based businesses. The Small Business Administration also offers assistance. Other organizations in communities and in state government have valuable resources as well.

If you are considering such an investment, search widely for information. Do your homework! The failure rate of small businesses is very high. Planning, especially development of a business plan, is critical.

Remember, running a business can be the riskiest investment you have ever made. However, if done correctly it can be the best and most rewarding venture. The truly successful people on earth are business owners.

# Collectibles

People collect just about anything—stamps, coins, dolls, art, cars, and autographs. To be financially successful with collectibles as an investment, however, a high level of knowledge is required. Some people collect as a hobby and enjoy spending their time this way.

To make money with this type of investment, you need a collection of items in top condition. You probably cannot regularly use or touch the collectible and will need to safely store them in a protective environment.

Keep documented evidence of the value of your collection, (e.g. an appraisal of antiques). Regular maintenance and insurance may be necessary, too and there could be storage costs. The specific needs and the type of collectible will determine costs.

Generally, collectibles do not provide a regular or periodic income. When you sell an item, you see the gain in value. When you want to sell, it may take a while to find the buyer willing to pay what you think your collectible is worth. A professional appraiser or auction house may also be required to sell items to other investors.

As you make investment decisions about collectibles, it is important to be sure that you are truly focusing on the value of the investment and that you are not unduly influenced by the psychological pleasure you receive from owning it.

# Chapter 7

---

# Investing Wisely

Learning the basic fundamentals to investing will give you an advantage over other investors. This chapter will help explain many basic investing techniques that are effective to maximizing performance and minimizing risk.

## <u>Dollar Cost Averaging</u>

Dollar-cost averaging is a systematic method of investing, by putting away a predetermined amount of money on a regular basis. This is a proven way to pursue the accumulation of wealth over time. It helps to smooth out the ups and downs when investing.

By automatically investing the same amount of money every month or quarter over a long period, dollar-cost averaging accomplishes several goals:

**Encourages discipline.** Once you have begun, it serves as a strong reminder to invest at the appointed time. An automatic bank draft into the investment is useful for consistency.

**Eliminates the need to decide when to invest.** When it's time to invest, you do so, regardless of what is going on in the market.

**Avoids the temptation to time the market**. Some investors cannot resist the urge to try to invest at a market low and take their profits at a market high. They usually fail because the task is virtually impossible, even for the experts.

## How Dollar-Cost Averaging Works

The object is to invest a set amount of money at regular intervals so the average cost of shares tends to even out the market's peaks and troughs. Your dollars purchase fewer shares when the market is up, but they buy more when it's down.

While you may not achieve the positive results of buying at the market's low point and selling at its high point, neither will you suffer the consequences of doing the opposite. On average, in a generally rising market, you have the opportunity to accumulate wealth over time in a systematic, organized way.

In the long run, it doesn't matter when you start, just that you start. Over a long enough period, it makes little difference whether the market was up or down when you began.

Making monthly additions to your account allows you three times as many opportunities to benefit from favorable market swings as investing on a quarterly basis. On the other hand, of course, it provides three times as many chances for your account to be adversely affected by market swings. The more frequently you invest and the longer you keep investing, the smoother the average-share-cost line becomes.

A market decline can mean bargain prices. Unless you are selling shares, a fund's price quote in the daily paper is not relevant for anyone who is not planning to sell, so don't panic if it is down. In fact, a downturn provides the opportunity to buy more shares at attractive prices—shares that have the potential to grow in value when the market finally turns upward.

Be prepared to weather a sustained market decline. Keep in mind that in order for dollar-cost averaging to work, you must be prepared to commit the financial resources and have the resolve to make the contributions on each appointed date.

Regular investing does not ensure a profit and does not protect against loss in declining markets. Investors should consider their ability to invest continuously during periods of fluctuating price levels.

# Example

In the figure below, we explain how effective dollar cost averaging works. For example, there are two investors, investor A and investor B. They both buy a mutual fund initially priced at $5 per share. They each invest $100 per month into their respective fund regardless of what happens to the fund price. The mutual fund that investor A buys generally grows over the year and ends at $10 per share. The mutual fund that investor B buys, however, drops and stays low for the entire year and finally ends up at $5 per share.

**Table 1**

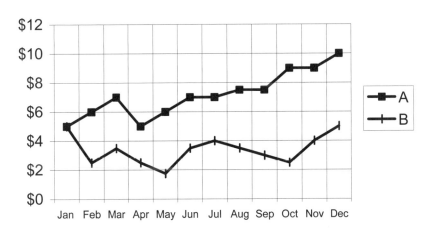

Which investment will provide the better return?

Before we answer the question, let's look at the numbers. If we add up all the shares investor A bought through the year we end up with 173 shares. To get the ending value of investor A, we multiply the number of shares (173) by the ending price ($10 per share) to get an ending value of $1730. To get the ending value of investor B we multiply the number of shares (410) by the ending price ($5 per share) to get an ending value of $2050. So investor B ended up better.

Initially looking at the graph, you would assume that investor A had a better investment than investor B, but you would be wrong! Why did investor B do better? Because when you are dollar cost averaging you are buying the same dollar amount each month, but you buy more SHARES when the stock price drops. Look at the month of May for investor B; he bought 66 shares compared to only 17 shares for investor A.

Investor B ended up with more than twice the number of shares than investor A because the fund price stayed low throughout the year, thus purchasing more shares each month.

On another point, if the investors purchased a "lump sum" at the beginning of the year, then investor A would have doubled his investment in the end while investor B would have finished back where he started.

The advantage of dollar cost averaging is you don't know what the markets will do in the future so you protect your assets by buying into the market gradually.

## Investing Versus Timing

Many investors make the mistake of believing that they can time the market. Those who have been most successful find the buy and hold strategy works the best. In fact, billionaire investor Warren Buffett goes one step further. He recommends that one buys good companies and holds them "forever."

In a quote from the Owner's Manual for Berkshire Hathaway stock, Chairman and CEO Warren E. Buffett writes: "As owners of, say, Coca-Cola or Gillette shares, we think of Berkshire as being a non-managing partner in two extraordinary businesses, in which we measure our success by the long-term progress of the companies rather than by the month-to-month movements of their stocks. In fact, we would not care in the least if several years went by in which there was no trading, or quotation of prices, in the stocks of those companies. If we have good long-term expectations, short-term price changes are meaningless for us except to the extent they offer us an opportunity to increase our ownership at an attractive price."

Not everyone is as perfect at picking stocks as Warren Buffett. So the idea that you hold a company forever may not work. Knowing when to sell your stocks or mutual funds requires regular monitoring of the quarterly reports you receive either from an individual company or from a mutual fund company, depending on the type of investment you select.

Market timers believe that they can buy low and sell high. The problem is that few can accurately time the market.

## Example:

If you stayed fully invested in stocks as measured by the S&P 500 Index from January 1, 1989, to December 31, 1998, you would have earned an annual return of 16%. If you had tried to time the ups and downs of the market, however, you would have risked missing the days when the market registered some of its biggest gains. And as the chart below illustrates, missing only a few of the best days would have had a dramatic impact on your total return.

**Buy And Hold verses Timing**
**S&P 500 Index: 1989 – 1998 Annualized Returns**

# Why Timing Doesn't Work

With daily market fluctuations now commonplace, accurate market timing has become a near impossible task. Accordingly, today's investor should commit to a long-term investment strategy that addresses their individual goals.

## Missing The Market

Jumping in and out of investments, or "market timing," does not work for most investors. Selling when the market moves down could mean missing periods when stocks recover. Clearly, investors could pay heavy penalties for not being in the market for the best performing days.

If market timing really works then every great mutual fund manager and institutional manager would be practicing timing. The only way market timing can really work is if you knew the future, and no one really does.

There are many investors who tried market timing but now are broke and understand the importance to staying with the basics, such as dollar-cost-averaging, asset allocation, and diversification.

## Bear Markets

A bear market is usually defined as a stock price decline of at least 20% over an extended period of time and remains a true test for the long-term investor. Because it is nearly impossible to anticipate changes in the market over time, an investment portfolio should be properly positioned for constantly changing environments. Good investment strategies are designed to respond to market fluctuations.

Market timers, however ignore the investment basics and abandon the investment policy they originally began with. During bear markets, market timers try to anticipate when the markets will move up. Market timers lose a vast amount of money when the bear market lasts two or more years.

## Buying On The Dips

During a down market, it is sometimes hard for investors to avoid selling everything. But, for long-term investors, market declines should actually be viewed as buying opportunities.

The enduring bull market of the 1990s caused several stocks to reach record highs. The market correction in 2000 and 2001 provided opportunities to buy these high-quality stocks at a reduced price. Although it's virtually impossible to buy at the lowest price every time, patient investors usually reap the benefits of a recovery by buying on the dips and holding on despite the possibility of further market decline.

## Conclusion

Given the convincing evidence, a "buy and hold" strategy appears to be the most profitable for the long-term investor. Despite the rational appeal of this approach, however, not all investors leave their money in a volatile market.

This disciplined strategy neglects to address the high level of emotion that often drives investment decisions. Even the most experienced investors may find it difficult to hold on during corrections as the value of their assets rapidly declines.

The important thing to remember is the long-term investor usually wins in the end. Although periods of decline in the market are inevitable, no one is capable of determining exactly when those periods will occur or when declining stocks will recover.

Keys to successful long-term investing include setting strategic long-term goals and avoiding the temptation to sell simply because the market is down. Experienced investors are prepared for market fluctuations and will use periods of volatility to add to their long-term investment strategy.

# The Rule Of 72

Einstein's "RULE of 72" gives us an easy formula to figure how long it takes to...*double our money!* The Rule of 72 is a rule of thumb that can help you compute when your money will double at a given interest rate. It's called the rule of 72 because at 10%, money will double every 7.2 years.

The investment can be a stock, a bond, a CD, and other ways of getting a return on your money. You don't need a calculator and you can use this method to quickly calculate in your head how long it takes to double your money. You can use it for many purposes such as buying a car, figuring college cost, comparing interest rates, etc. All you need to do is divide 72 by the annual rate of return. The result would be approximately the number of years required for your investment to double in size.

## EXAMPLE:

If you have $10,000 in a savings account at a bank, earning you 2.5%, divide 2.5% into 72 = 28.8 *years to double your money.*

This shows why Einstein said, "If people really understood the Rule of 72 they would never put their money in banks!"

If you have $10,000 invested in an investment that returns 12% divide 12% into 72 = 6 years to double your money. A much better return!

Knowing this, why would you put money in a bank? It's probably the worst place to put it. They seldom pay over 4 to 5%, even in CDs. There are MUCH better places to invest your money.

How many doubles do you have left?

Doubling your money is a VERY important part of wealth accumulation.

If you are 35 years old, with money earning a measly 3% in a bank and doubling only every 24 years, you only have ONE DOUBLE by age 60. If you figure that inflation averages 3% you're just breaking even, if you don't figure the income taxes you paid on the 3% growth.

If you're 35 and your money is growing at 12%, you have SIX DOUBLES by age 60!

If you're 50 and your money is growing at 12%, you have 1.6 DOUBLES LEFT by age 60!

What is this really saying? Start investing as soon as you can! Today!

# Time Value Of Money

Let's turn to an element that is at the heart and soul of building wealth and financial security...**TIME**.

The longer you invest, the more money you will accumulate. The more money you invest, the more it will accumulate because of the magic of compound interest.

Compounding works like this . . .

The interest earned on your investments is reinvested or left on deposit. At the next calculation, interest is earned on the original principal PLUS the reinvested interest. Earning interest on accumulated interest over time generates more and more money. Compounding also applies to dividends and capital gains on investments when they are reinvested.

## How Time Affects The Value Of Money

Too many investors have perfected the art of procrastination. They come up with numerous excuses to delay saving for their goals. I have heard excuses ranging from "we just got married, we have lots of time to invest later" or "raising children is too expensive, we will start when we can afford it."

The key point to remember is that every day you delay beginning investing, the more you need to invest later.

The example below illustrates the importance of starting early.

Investor A invests $2,000 a year beginning at age 22 for eight years, and then stops. Investor B waits eight years, then invests $2,000 a year for 36 years. Compare the total contributions and the total value at retirement of the two investments. This example assumes a 10% fixed rate of return, compounded monthly. All interest is left in the account to allow interest to be earned on interest.

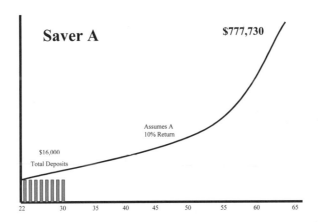

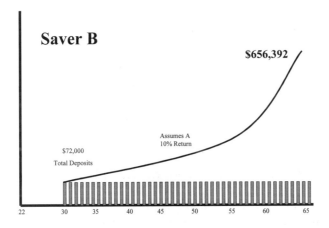

Note that Investor A, who invested much less than Investor B, has a much higher nest egg at retirement age, because of an eight-year head start. As you can see from this example, compound interest is especially magical when money is steadily invested and left to grow over a long period.

The key to this example is to start investing as early as possible. Every year you delay, the more money you need to invest to catch up to your goals.

# Diversification

Diversification means spreading your risk. The old adage of not putting all your eggs in one basket has considerable merit in designing a good investment portfolio.

Don't put all your faith in one company or in one industry, because it may disappoint you. If you buy a diversified group of fundamentally sound stocks with good earnings and growth, the chances are that in a good market you will catch at least some of the winners, since most big money in a diversified portfolio comes from one or two big winners.

**NON-DIVERSIFIED**
**Investing in a Single Source**

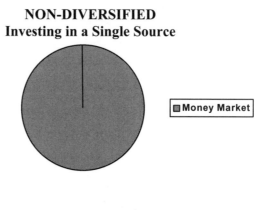

**DIVERSIFIED**
**Spreading Out Your Investments**

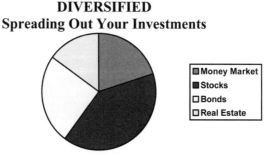

There are two benefits to diversification. First, it reduces the volatility in the value of your portfolio. When one of your holdings is down, odds are that others are up. This stabilizes your portfolio performance. Secondly, diversification allows you to obtain a higher rate of return for a given level of risk.

Don't be deceived into thinking that eight airline stocks or eight computer stocks represents diversification. They do not. You should strive for a portfolio covering a wider range of industries. For example, you may have some stocks in the health care industry, the retail area, automotive, beverage, telecommunications, electronics, and others.

Now don't over diversify, because you may find that you are unable to manage a large number of companies. If you limit your holdings to ten stocks and a stock comes to your attention that you feel you should buy, what will this force you to do? Probably eliminate one.

In order to move to strength, it would now be prudent to go through your list and sell the one that is doing the poorest job. The way to upgrade a portfolio is to sell your losers and keep your winners, as this allows you the possibility of continuously moving to a position of strength.

When managing your portfolio, you may find it extremely helpful to utilize mutual funds. A mutual fund generally has anywhere from 20 holdings to as many as 500, usually from a wide spectrum of industry groups.

By purchasing a mutual fund, you will find that it will help your portfolio become more diversified. Diversification such as this can permit you to own your slice of the U.S. economy by becoming a part owner of the major companies whose products and services you use regularly.

When researching mutual funds, remember to look at the industry sector weightings. Many popular mutual funds may have a high percentage in a certain industry, for instance technology. If you design a portfolio with several mutual funds, be careful that your overall portfolio is not weighted too heavily in one industry.

One final point: make sure the mutual funds in your portfolio have a low over-lap ratio (correlation). A portfolio with many mutual funds and a high overlap is not diversified. For example at one time in 1999 Janus Funds had four mutual funds with very high correlations. So if an investor owned two or more of them it did not help diversify their portfolio.

# Asset Allocation

Asset allocation is a disciplined, systematic approach to investing that seeks to enhance your portfolio's returns at a level of risk that you feel comfortable undertaking. It is a basic financial building block that uses diversification as a means to help you achieve your ultimate financial goals.

Asset allocation is based on the notion that diversification among different types of investments and markets is an essential component of a balanced portfolio. Because markets rarely move in lockstep, proper diversification among different classes—typically stocks, bonds, and cash, may help offset losses in one with the stability or gains from another. If stocks are plummeting, gold is going through the roof, or bonds are declining, you will probably be more relaxed knowing that your asset allocation program was specifically designed to help compensate for this type of volatility.

Asset allocation allows you to be objective and helps you resist the temptation to try to time the market—a practice that, as history has shown, rarely, if ever, benefits even the most savvy investor. You might be more at ease knowing that your portfolio is well equipped to try to handle the market—no matter the direction it is headed or the current asset class being favored.

Asset allocation seeks to provide a degree of steadiness, order, and balance to an investment world of ups and downs. The following questions are considerations that you should take into account when developing your asset allocation strategy.

## What's Your Investment Objective?

You and your financial advisor should establish the investment goal you are trying to achieve. Younger investors generally concentrate on saving for long-term goals such as a new home or a college education for their children. Therefore, they need to invest for growth. Older investors, on the other hand, are usually more concerned with maintaining a high standard of living during their retirement years and are looking for investments that provide income. Different goals, whether short or long term, aggressive or conservative, will call for different investment approaches.

## What's Your Time Horizon?

Knowing how much time you have to invest will determine the amount of risk that you can afford to incur while reaching for your desired goal. Long-term investing is one way to reduce the impact of short-term risk. So, in general, the more time you have to work toward your investment objective, the more risk you can afford to take on. And, conversely, as you get closer to meeting your objectives, the more conservative your portfolio should become. Your portfolio should be adjusted regularly, according to where you are in your investment time horizon.

## How Much Risk Are You Willing To Incur?

While your portfolio is focused on working toward your predetermined goals, it should do so at a level of risk that you feel comfortable with. Your risk profile can range from conservative to aggressive, depending on how much short-term uncertainty you are willing to undertake and how much growth potential you require.

Are you a more conservative or more aggressive investor? Will you panic if the market dips? Or do you think such downturns are cause for little concern? Is your investment motto "slow and steady"? Or do you prefer a faster, bumpier ride? These questions are key because an investment that keeps you awake at night or one that is working too slowly may not be appropriate for you.

## What's Your Current Financial Situation?

Your asset allocation plan should take into consideration your current financial situation. The more money you have set aside for emergencies, the more risk you may be able to take on. The less savings you have to draw on in a financial emergency, the more conservative you should be with your portfolio.

## Examples Of Investment Portfolios

Below are three generic asset allocation models—aggressive, moderate, and conservative. Your investment mix may differ, and you should consult with your financial advisor to help you determine the best strategy and investment mix for your goals and investment style. Please note that these models assume that you have set aside adequate reserves for short-term needs and that your income needs are focused on current income and potential growth of future income.

## Investor Profile: Aggressive
## Goal: Growth

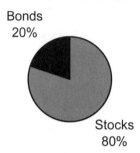

Bonds
20%

Stocks
80%

## Investor Profile: Moderate
## Goal: Growth and Income

Bonds
40%

Stocks
60%

## Investor Profile: Conservative
## Goal: Income

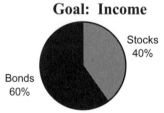

Stocks
40%

Bonds
60%

# Risk

Risk is an inherent part of investing. Generally, investors must take greater risks to achieve greater returns. Those who do not tolerate risk very well have a relatively smaller chance of making high earnings than do those with a higher tolerance for risk.

It's crucial to understand that there is an inescapable trade-off between investment performance and risk: Higher returns are associated with higher risks of price fluctuations. Stocks historically have provided the highest long-term returns of the three major asset classes and have been subject to the biggest losses over shorter periods. At the other extreme, short-term cash investments are among the safest of investments when it comes to price stability, but they have provided the lowest long-term returns.

Over short periods—even periods lasting a few years—lower-risk investments may provide better returns than higher-risk investments. But historically over long periods, riskier assets have provided higher returns.

There are various types of risk. We will discuss a few here:

## Personal Risks

This category of risk deals with the personal level of investing. The investor is likely to have more control over this type of risk compared to others.

**Timing risk** is the risk of buying the right security at the wrong time. It also refers to selling the right security at the wrong time. For example, there is the chance that a few days after you sell a stock it will go up several dollars in value. There is no surefire way to time the market.

**Tenure risk** is the risk of losing money while holding onto a security. During the period of holding, markets may go down, inflation may worsen, or a company may go bankrupt. There is always the possibility of loss on the company-wide level, too.

## Company Risks

There are two common risks on the company-wide level. The first, **financial risk**, is the danger that a corporation will not be able to repay its debts. This has a great affect on its bonds, which finance the company's assets. The more assets financed by debts (i.e., bonds and money market instruments), the greater the risk. Studying financial risk involves looking at a company's management, its leadership style, and its credit history.

**Management risk** is the risk that a company's management may run the company so poorly that it is unable to grow in value or pay dividends to its shareholders. This greatly affects the value of its stock and the attractiveness of all the securities it issues to investors.

## Market Risks

Fluctuation in the market as a whole may be caused by the following risks:

**Market risk** is the chance that the entire market will decline, thus affecting the prices and values of securities. Market risk, in turn, is influenced by outside factors such as embargoes and interest rate changes. See Political risk below.

**Liquidity risk** is the risk that an investment, when converted to cash, will experience loss in its value.

**Interest rate risk** is the risk that interest rates will rise, resulting in a current investment's loss of value. A bondholder, for example, may hold a bond earning 6% interest and then see rates on that type of bond climb to 7%.

**Inflation risk** is the danger that the dollars one invests will buy less in the future because prices of consumer goods rise. When the rate of inflation rises, investments have less purchasing power. This is especially true with investments that earn fixed rates of return. As long as they are held at constant rates, they are threatened by inflation. Inflation risk is tied to interest rate risk, because interest rates often rise to compensate for inflation.

**Exchange rate risk** is the chance that a nation's currency will lose value when exchanged for foreign currencies.

**Reinvestment risk** is the danger that reinvested money will fetch returns lower than those earned before reinvestment. Individuals with dividend-reinvestment plans are a group subject to this risk. Bondholders are another.

# National And International Risks

National and world events can profoundly affect investment markets.

**Economic risk** is the danger that the economy as a whole will perform poorly. When the whole economy experiences a downturn, it affects stock prices, the job market, and the prices of consumer products.

**Industry risk** is the chance that a specific industry will perform poorly. When problems plague one industry, they affect the individual businesses involved as well as the securities issued by those businesses. They may also cross over into other industries. For example, after a national downturn in auto sales, the steel industry may suffer financially.

**Tax risk** is the danger that rising taxes will make investing less attractive. In general, nations with relatively low tax rates, such as the United States, are popular places for entrepreneurial activities. Businesses that are taxed heavily have less money available for research, expansion, and even dividend payments. Taxes are also levied on capital gains, dividends and interest. Investors continually seek investments that provide the greatest net after-tax returns.

**Political risk** is the danger that government legislation will have an adverse affect on investment. This can be in the form of high taxes, prohibitive licensing, or the appointment of individuals whose policies interfere with investment growth. Political risks include wars, changes in government leadership, and politically motivated embargoes.

# Chapter 8

---

# Planning for Retirement

Retirement planning is an essential element of any financial plan. It is a comprehensive process for determining how much money you will need when you retire. Retirement planning also helps you identify the best ways to save for retirement given your financial situation.

If you are like most people, you probably think retirement planning is only important when you retire. However, proper planning requires a much longer period of time—from the day you start working until well beyond your actual retirement date. In fact, it's never too early to start planning for your retirement.

Even so, many people put off retirement planning because they're too busy trying to meet their immediate financial needs to think about what will happen in 20 or 30 years. It's easy to understand why meeting your monthly bills seems more important, especially if your retirement is still far off. Procrastination is too prevalent in today's society.

Here's something to think about: As you move through your life, you will experience many life events that will affect your future financial security—such as getting married, starting a family, purchasing a home, and sending your children to college. Each of these events will affect your ability to plan for your future financial security. If you develop a flexible long-term plan, you can overcome these obstacles and ensure financial independence in your retirement years.

In this chapter we will help you understand the importance of retirement planning and provide you with a process for planning so you can get started now. We will then examine different sources of retirement income and how these sources can be measured and maximized. You'll also learn how to compute your retirement income shortfall and plan for a variety of issues that can affect your retirement at various times during your employment.

One additional note to bring up: the principles of retirement planning discussed in this chapter are merely tools or aids. A successful retirement plan requires your active involvement and long-term commitment.

# Retirement Goals

When defining your retirement goals, your description should be specific and measurable. For example, a goal to "retire at age 60 with resources to sustain current living expenses of $25,000 per year" is a goal, which is both specific and measurable. Other examples of workable goals are "to have sufficient insurance coverage to fund long-term nursing home care" or "to build a retirement home costing $80,000."

If you have several goals, you should prioritize them so your resources will be allocated to the most important goal first. By assigning a priority to each goal, you also ensure that secondary goals won't take precedence over primary goals.

## Gather Data

In this process, it is important to understand your needs for retirement. Many planners estimate retirement income needs by using a benchmark of between 70 and 100% of your current spending levels. To determine the appropriate percentage for your retirement, you need to determine if any of your current expenses will change when you retire. Will your travel and leisure expenditures increase? Will your job-related expenses for commuting and clothing change? Will you have to pay more for medical costs?

It's generally accepted that many of your routine annual expenses will change during your retirement years. The trick is determining whether those expenses will increase or decrease, and by how much.

For instance, some retirees may spend less on gasoline, credit cards, and dining out while others may spend more on health care, insurance, and hobbies.

Another consideration in retirement planning is inflation. Because people are retiring earlier and living longer, the impact of inflation can be substantial. For example, a couple spending $25,000 per year for living expenses when they first retire can expect to spend more than $56,000 for the same living expenses 20 years later, due solely to annual inflation of 4%.

## Impact Of Inflation

| Based on 4% Inflation | | | | Based on 8% Inflation | | | |
|---|---|---|---|---|---|---|---|
| Cost of Living | | | | Cost of Living | | | |
| $25,000 | $37,000 | $45,000 | $56,900 | $25,000 | $54,000 | $79,250 | $116,500 |
| $30,000 | $44,400 | $54,000 | $67,700 | $30,000 | $64,800 | $95,100 | $139,800 |
| $50,000 | $74,000 | $90,000 | $109,600 | $50,000 | $108,000 | $158,500 | $233,000 |

Both living expenses and inflation are important in understanding your retirement needs because you are planning for a period of time, not a point in time.

Once you develop your estimated living expenses over your retirement, you need to inventory the sources of your retirement income. Your retirement funds will probably come from a variety of sources. While you may have little control over amounts that will be paid from some sources, amounts from other sources are completely dependent upon your decisions. For example, your company's pension plan provides benefits commensurate with your salary level and years of service. The same is true for your Social Security benefit. These benefits are based upon formulas incorporating your age, income, and years of employment.

On the other hand, you can have significant influence over your contributions to company-sponsored savings plans, known as 401k plans. Although your employer must sponsor the plan, and may even provide matching contributions, it's up to you to use the plan. To make the most of this savings opportunity, you must be disciplined and establish regular contributions based on a percentage of your income. You're also responsible for learning about the available investment options. Your contributions are generally portable—which means that if you change employers, the funds can be transferred to your new employer's plan or rolled into an Individual Retirement Account (IRA).

Finally, you have absolute control over your personal savings programs. You can select your own bank savings accounts or Certificates of Deposit (CD), manage investment mixes in your mutual funds, or select maturities of bonds purchased by your broker. Federal tax laws can also influence your retirement resources. Pension plans can be distributed in lump sums or paid to you over your life or the joint lives of you and your spouse. Your distributions are taxed as you receive the benefit payments. Social Security benefits are taxed at a different tax rate for some individuals and the benefits can be reduced if you earn too much from part-time employment during retirement.

Perhaps the greatest impact of federal tax laws on retirement planning is the fact that taxes on contributions to funds and investment earnings in company qualified savings plans, IRA's, and other tax-deferred vehicles such as annuities are not paid until the funds are withdrawn from the account.

In analyzing your retirement resources, it's important to note that all assets must be converted into a common form that will reveal your expected income stream during retirement.

## Evaluate Goals And Identify Obstacles

Using the data gathered, you can now compare your retirement income needs to the projected income stream generated by your retirement resources. If your retirement resources exceed your needs, the excess can be used to fund other goals. If there is a shortfall (or retirement gap) you are now able to quantify the amount needed to fill the gap.

Before you retire you must know if your resources exceed your expenses or vice-versa. If you don't know this before you retire, you may be in for a rude awakening.

## Develop Strategies

The first step of the retirement process is to calculate the difference between your estimated needs and your projected resources. If there is an excess, you can develop and prioritize new goals for using the additional funds. These goals may include more retirement travel, earlier retirement, or providing for your grandchildren's college education.

## Design Action Steps

After you develop and document the strategies or alternatives that can be utilized to achieve your goal, you should create an action plan that reflects the alternative or alternatives you select to meet your goal. This plan should list:

**Example Action Plan**

* The action - increase retirement resources.
* The person who is responsible for completing the action – ie Mary.
* The completion date - to do on payday each month.
* The expected cost - cost is $100 per month.

## Review The Progress

Once you develop your plan, the process is dynamic. As you revise and prioritize your projected goals, you may see changes in your estimated income needs, projected resources, and other assumptions. It's a good idea to review your action plan regularly and, if necessary, make changes to be sure it still meets your needs.

# The Beginning

## Take Control Of Your Money

Whether you are getting started in your career, accumulating cash, or positioning yourself for retirement, now is the time to take control of your money. This is the only way most people can accomplish their short-term and long-term goals.

People who fail to take control of their money do not attain their goals or are forced to attain them in another manner—by winning the lottery, inheriting a fortune, or general "good luck."

Understanding your options and making informed decisions now can add thousands of dollars to your retirement nest egg. Your financial future will be much smoother if you take an active role in managing and planning your finances now. In fact, your decisions—or lack of decisions can make you or break you.

## Understand Your Employer's Benefits

When you begin your career, your employer will provide you with a summary of the benefits that are available to you. These benefits may include qualified and non-qualified retirement benefits, medical and dental benefits, life insurance, disability insurance, flexible spending accounts, and savings plans.

Some benefits require you to make important choices that can affect you and your family (e.g., how much life insurance do I want?). Other benefits are provided as part of your employment, such as your employer-provided pension.

Some benefit choices give you the option to reduce your current income to make "pre-tax" contributions to a retirement plan, for childcare expenses, or for uninsured medical and dental expenses.

Generally, you will have some benefit choices that can be changed, usually on an annual basis. Other choices may be irrevocable as long as you remain with that particular employer or as long as the terms of the particular employee benefit plan stay the same.

These benefits can have an impact on the amount of money you have to spend, the amount of money you need to have available in an emergency fund to cover unanticipated expenses such as medical insurance deductibles, and the amount of money you need to save for retirement.

## Seek Qualified Financial Advisors

Depending on your background and how much time you have (or want to allocate) to educate yourself on the available financial options, you may want to seek qualified financial advisors. For example, if you have various investment alternatives in your retirement plan and you don't know the basics about the trade-off between risk, reward and your time horizon, there is a good chance you will make an investment decision that could have a negative impact on your financial future.

Before seeking any advice, be sure that you know how much the advice will cost. Be sure to find out whether your advisor charges a straight fee or whether he or she is paid through commissions on your investments, or some combination of fee and commission.

## Understand Investments

The investments that you will deal with at this stage are stocks, bonds, and cash or cash equivalents (such as certificates of deposit). As a general rule, stocks have historically outperformed bonds and cash equivalents over the longer holding periods (10, 15, and 20 years). However, as with anything in life, you have to accept additional investment risk if you are looking for a higher reward. The stock market can be very volatile—especially if your time horizon is less than seven or eight years.

After stocks, bonds generally outperform cash and cash equivalents over longer time periods. However, the bond market can also be very volatile as interest rates rise and fall. Although you will generally receive the funds you invested when the bond matures, this may not necessarily be true if you have to sell the bond before maturity.

If you expect to need the funds within a year or two, you may want to stick with cash and cash equivalents. Although you give up some investment return, you don't have to worry about losing any of the funds you have invested.

## Understand The Impact Of Income Taxes

Although income tax laws are constantly changing, you should be able to project your annual federal and state income taxes. As a general rule, as your taxable income increases, so does the percentage of income tax that you will be paying.

Most people understand how income taxes affect them because taxes decrease their spendable income. What many people do not realize is how important it is to maximize pre-tax contributions to retirement plans and flexible spending plans for health and child care expenses.

In general, most retirees will enjoy a lower tax bill during retirement. However, some will have a higher tax bill because their 401k or IRA accounts are so large their tax bracket will be bumped up when they are forced to withdraw funds at 70½.

# The Accumulation Years

## Develop A Budget

Developing a budget and sticking to it may be one of the most difficult challenges for most people. Many people think that preparing a budget is so complicated that it requires assistance from an accountant or a background in accounting. Plus, sticking to a budget requires a lot of self-discipline—especially if you're not used to watching your finances. After reading this, we hope that you will be able to overcome both of these obstacles.

First, let's see how easy it can be to develop a budget. A budget is simply a listing of your income and expenses that ensures that you have enough income to cover your expected expenses as well as sufficient savings to cover any large purchases or emergency expenses. Borrowing the funds may be an acceptable alternative—as long as you remember to budget the additional interest expense associated with borrowing. Remember, you need to take control of your money. Don't resort to unplanned borrowing unless you have no other alternative.

If your expenses exceed your income, you may already be in trouble. This means that you already have to borrow money just to meet your ordinary living expenses. If your income exceeds your ordinary living expenses, you should be able to invest this amount in your savings program.

Once you have established whether you can invest in a savings program, you should make a list of your short-term and long-term goals. For example, your short-term goal may be to purchase a new automobile within the next two or three years, or to establish an emergency or contingency fund to cover unexpected expenses. As a rule of thumb, your emergency fund should equal three to six months of your ordinary living expenses. Your long-term goal might be to retire at age 65 with the same standard of living you enjoy today.

After setting your short-term and long-term goals, you will have to adjust your goals (either the timing or the amount), or adjust your budget. Your goals and budget will be continually changing. But as you can see, developing a budget doesn't have to be difficult. Since we assume that you really want to attain your goals, we believe that you will find the necessary discipline to stick to your budget.

## Understand Income Sources

Let's assume you want to retire at age 65. What are you going to live on after you retire? Hopefully, you will have some savings—but will you have enough?

Before you can quantify how much you need to have in savings at retirement, you need to understand the sources and projected amounts of your retirement income.

**Possible sources of retirement income include:**
- Employer-provided pension plans
- Employer-provided savings plans
- Non-qualified retirement plans
- Social Security
- Savings and investments.

## Employer-Provided Pension Plans

If you have a pension plan, you are generally entitled to an annual pension or income when you retire. These benefits are typically based on a formula that includes your length of service with the employer, your age at retirement, your annual Social Security income, your pre-retirement earnings, and whether you elect to take a pension based on your life expectancy or for your and your spouse's life expectancy. In some cases, you may be able to take a lump sum at retirement instead of taking an annual amount.

## Employer-Provided Savings Plans

Many employer-provided savings plans permit the employee to elect to contribute a certain percentage or a certain amount of pre-tax income to a retirement savings account. In some cases, these plans also allow post-tax contributions. Many employers (but not all) make "matching" contributions in cash or employer stock to subsidize these accounts. Under the terms of many of these plans, you may have significant, if not total, responsibility for investing your contributions.

Understanding the importance of electing the maximum contribution amount to these savings plans cannot be overstated. Anytime you have the ability to contribute pre-tax (or post-tax) income to an account that will grow at a tax-deferred rate, you should do so unless you clearly can't afford to do so. (Presumably you would have a very important reason for not participating). To the extent your employer matches any portion of your contribution, it becomes even more important to contribute. Receiving an employer match is the same as receiving an annual increase in pay.

## Non-Qualified Retirement Plans

Almost any plan designed to increase an employee's retirement income or savings available for retirement can be considered a non-qualified retirement plan. These plans can be provided by an employer, or established by an employee. Because these plans are non-qualified, employers who provide these plans do not receive any income tax deduction until the funds are actually paid to, and subject to tax by, employees. Until the funds are paid to employees, there is some risk that the funds will not be available to the employee at retirement. If you participate in this type of plan, you may want to consider this risk when determining your projected retirement income.

There may be less risk with employee-funded non-qualified retirement plans, but there is still generally some risk. For example, if you purchase a deferred annuity or a cash value life insurance contract for tax-deferred growth, there is still some investment risk, as well as the risk that the company selling the products will not perform as well as expected.

## Social Security

There is a lot of skepticism as to whether younger workers will ever receive any Social Security income. In fact, many financial planners do not even consider Social Security in their sources of retirement income. That is why we call it "Social Insecurity!" As a general rule, if you are in your thirties or forties, you may not want to assume that you will receive any Social Security income. If you do, it's a bonus.

If you develop a budget without including any Social Security, you are only being conservative. If the laws do change, you will be ahead of the game. If Social Security is still around as you get closer to retirement, you may have the opportunity to change your investment strategy, budget, or goals (maybe even retire earlier).

The formula for determining your Social Security benefit is similar to the formula used to determine employer-provided pension benefits. The primary differences are that Social Security income is never available in a lump sum, and as a general rule, the maximum annual amount payable is generally much smaller than the amount provided under an employer-provided pension.

## Savings And Investments

If there is any income source that you have control over, it's your savings and investments. Since there are no limitations, you have the choice whether to increase or decrease your payments. You also have many investment choices to choose from to use in your accounts.

Once you assume how much you will be saving each year and how much your savings should increase each year, you can project the amount of savings you will have at retirement.

# How To Compute Your Retirement Income

Before you can determine whether you have a retirement gap, you will need to convert all sources of your retirement income to an annual income stream (adjusted for inflation). This is easy for those sources that are already expressed in annual amounts, such as your employer-provided pension and Social Security benefits. However, your other sources of retirement income need to be converted from a projected lump sum at retirement to an annual amount (inflation-adjusted) that will be available until the death of you and your spouse.

**COMPUTATION OF RETIREMENT GAP**

| Projected Retirement Needs of $88,000 | |
|---|---|
| Social Security | $18,000 |
| Company Pension Plan | $30,000 |
| Company Savings Plan | $32,000 |
| Personal Savings | $5,000 |
| **Total Sources** | **$85,000** |
| Retirement Gap | ($3,000) |

# Develop An Investment Strategy

At this point, you have established some short-term and long-term goals. You have also developed a budget which will assist you in attaining those goals. You are saving any excess income in an emergency fund or another savings account so you will have the cash when you need it. You have established a goal to retire at age 65 and you know your projected retirement income. But how much do you need to save and how much does this amount have to grow if you want retire at age 65? These questions reflect the importance of a sound investment strategy.

## Starting Out

Initially, your investment strategy will be relatively simple. For example, until you have a sufficient amount in your emergency fund to cover three to six months of expenses, you will want to invest most of your excess income in investments that are liquid and risk-free. Because these funds need to be available for unexpected expenses, you will generally invest them in cash and cash equivalents. Examples of cash and cash equivalents would be savings accounts, money market accounts, certificates of deposit, and U.S. Treasury Bills.

## Accumulation

At the other end of the spectrum is the investment strategy that you should develop for the funds in your employer-provided retirement accounts. At this point in your career, you probably don't intend to use any of these funds for at least ten to twenty years. Because you have a long time horizon, you can accept some risk knowing that, at least historically, this risk should provide you with a greater reward over the long term. Based on these parameters, your retirement accounts should be more heavily weighted toward stocks and bonds as opposed to cash and cash equivalents.

## Positioning

Once you have the necessary balance in your emergency fund, and you are contributing the maximum amount to your employer-provided retirement accounts, any additional excess income should be deposited into an investment account (your investment reservoir).

This is the point where you need to start thinking about asset allocation. In other words, you need to decide what portion of your excess income should be invested in cash and cash equivalents? What portion in stocks and what portion in bonds?

Your asset allocation will depend upon your particular facts and circumstances (e.g. your age, your goals). Typically, your asset allocation should be more heavily weighted toward cash and cash equivalents and bonds in the beginning—especially if you have a lot of short-term goals. As you accumulate more savings you will generally be able to invest a higher percentage in stocks.

# Quantify The Retirement Income Gap

You have established a long-term goal that you want to retire at age 65 and that you want to maintain the same standard of living in retirement as you have now. If your ordinary living expenses are currently $40,000 per year, you will have to make an assumption as to whether this amount, adjusted for inflation, is the amount you want to project to retirement. You may not have certain expenses (work clothing or home mortgage) but you may have others (travel). Financial planners frequently assume that you will need 70% to 100% of your current ordinary living expenses adjusted for inflation at retirement.

For example, if you need $40,000 in today's dollars when you retire in twenty years, and the assumed inflation rate is 4%, you will need approximately $88,000 to cover your ordinary living expenses in the year you retire. You have now quantified your retirement goal: you want sufficient resources (retirement income, savings) to spend $88,000 (adjusted for inflation) during each of your retirement years.

Now you have to determine whether you have a retirement gap. A retirement gap is the projected annual shortfall you would have when you retire because your projected retirement savings and income are insufficient.

Remember, all retirement income sources must be converted to an annual income stream. For example, let's assume that your projected annual income stream in retirement was $85,000. Since we have projected your annual retirement income ($85,000) and your annual retirement expenses ($88,000), we now know that you have a retirement gap of $3,000.

Because you have a projected annual retirement gap of $3,000, you need to do one or more of the following actions:

- Reevaluate your retirement needs to consider which, if any, projected costs can be reduced.

- Modify your current cash flow to build additional savings in company plans or on your own.

- Adjust your investment mix to try to increase the return on the assets you have available for retirement.

- Delay your projected retirement date.

- Work part-time during the early years of retirement.

The inflation rate is beyond your control. If the actual inflation rate is less than the projected inflation rate, you may also avoid the retirement gap.

If you do not project a retirement gap, you will need to evaluate whether you have a sufficient cushion to add short-term or long-term goals or to "leave well enough alone" and continue with the same assumptions until you update your projections. Generally, the farther you are from retirement, the more you should think of any excess income projected in retirement as cushion. Your projections should be updated, or at least verified, periodically to make sure that there have been no material changes in your retirement assumptions.

# Transition To Retirement

## Develop A Budget For Post-Retirement Income And Expenses

If you are nearing retirement, you need to review your current situation and make a realistic inventory of your income sources and expense needs at retirement. Retirement income can come from four broad sources:

- Company pension or retirement plans

- Employee savings plans and IRAs

- Social Security benefits

- Personal savings and earnings.

Reviewing these sources within a few years of retirement is important for two reasons. First, you can develop a specific projection of your total retirement income. Second, you can begin to determine your level of involvement in the management of your funds after retirement.

Your retirement needs fall into several categories of expenses:

**Fixed expenses,** such as housing, loans, insurance premiums, and taxes.

**Recurring basic living costs,** which are subject to some control, such as expenses for food and utilities.

**Discretionary expenses,** which are incurred voluntarily and include items such as gifts, travel, and recreation.

As you prepare your projected budget, focus on your fixed and basic living expenses and challenge the amounts as you project your needs into retirement. Many costs during your employment years have a habit of becoming fixed or recurring. It's a good idea to review each expense in order to eliminate or reduce costs whenever possible. This budget review should be completed before your actual retirement—otherwise, too many expenses will become "fixed."

## Projected Retirement Budget

**Sources:**

- Company pension or retirement plans

- Employee savings plans and IRAs

- Social Security benefits

- Other savings and earnings.

**Expenses:**

- Fixed: mortgage payment, loans

- Basic living expenses: food, clothing

- Discretionary: travel, gifts to family.

# Determine Specific Retirement Income Gap

At lease five years before your retirement, you should again complete the process of calculating whether you have a retirement income gap. However, the focus at this point is on fine-tuning and understanding what your retirement funds will provide rather than how you can significantly affect the accumulation of funds. Several strategies or alternatives should be examined:

- If you have a projected shortfall, you need to look at the impact of delaying your retirement for one or two years.

- Request a specific projection of your Social Security benefits and determine if altering the timing of these benefits can help close your retirement shortfall.

- If your retirement calculations indicate that you may have excess funds, at least during some years, you should begin to develop a plan for investing those funds.

## Review Your Role In Investment Decision Making

An understanding of investing is important throughout the retirement planning process. However, your role with respect to investment choices will increase in retirement. First, and perhaps most important, you must become at least somewhat knowledgeable about investing and investment alternatives. You should at least begin to learn about various types of investments, even if you don't intend to make the final decisions about specific investments.

You must also strike a balance between the desire to focus your investment plan on the immediate years after retirement and the need to plan for your entire retirement period that could span many years. You should review your retirement portfolio mix to ensure that funds will be available at retirement with the least possible risk of loss. In retirement, avoiding risk is crucial because you cannot simply save and make up for a loss. However, you must also define the time frame over which you are trying to avoid loss.

Again, retirement is a period of time not a point in time. The key issue is to determine when you will need your funds and then make your investments accordingly.

## Plan For Other Company Compensation Benefits

As you near retirement, you should also consider the consequences of receiving other forms of company benefits, such as stock options, deferred compensation, or restricted stock. You should plan for the income tax consequences of bunching these payments into the year of retirement and determine if spreading the payments over several years can result in a reduced tax liability. In addition, you will need to invest these funds. Your resulting investment decisions can affect how you approach any adjustment to your overall investment mix.

# Review Estate Planning Needs

Many people who are approaching retirement have not reviewed their estate planning needs for many years. Making the transition to retirement provides an excellent opportunity to review and revise your estate plans. This review includes an analysis of your planning documents (such as wills, trusts, and powers of attorney) to determine if they still adequately carry out your wishes.

In addition, the estate planning review should focus on whether the beneficiary you have designated to receive your retirement and life insurance benefits is still appropriate.

Finally, you may want to consider alternative ways to transfer property from your generation to your children or grandchildren. Determining your retirement income sources and needs can provide the foundation for determining when and if it is possible to transfer property to family members or other third parties.

# The First Year Of Retirement

## Understanding Retirement Distribution Options

In the year you retire, your overall planning focus should be on understanding your distributions and what you have to do to receive them. This focus begins with an analysis of the possible ways that retirement benefits can be paid or distributed.

### Definition Of Distribution Options

#### Single Life
A monthly annuity will be paid to the retired employee for life. This is usually the basic form of benefit under a pension plan.

#### Joint and Survivor
A reduced monthly annuity will be paid to the retired employee for life, with a percentage of that reduced benefit (e.g., 50%, 75%, or 100%) paid to the surviving spouse. The larger the continuing percentage, the smaller the initial benefit.

164

## Term Certain

Based on a single life or joint life annuity, a reduced monthly annuity will be paid for life (or joint life), coupled with a guaranteed minimum payment period such as 5, 10, or 15 years.

## Lump Sum

A single sum, rather than an annuity, will be paid to the retired employee. This amount is a present-value equivalent of the stream of otherwise available annuity payments in a pension plan or, in the case of a defined contribution plan, simply the balance accumulated.

Pension plans generally provide monthly retirement benefits. However, you may have choices regarding the period of time over which your benefits will be paid. The payments can be for your life, or for the joint life of you and your spouse. In addition, some retirement plans may allow you or your beneficiary to receive payments for a guaranteed period of time.

If you choose to receive payments over a joint life period, you will have a second set of choices involving whether the monthly payments will remain constant or be reduced by a specified amount when you die. A constant payment amount can maximize the financial security of your survivor. However, there is a cost because your initial pension payments will be smaller.

Employee savings plans, such as 401k plans and some pension plans may distribute your benefits in a lump sum payment. A retiree should consider several issues when evaluating whether to take a lump-sum distribution. First, the payment will have tax consequences and choices. Second, you must plan for the receipt and investment of the funds. Hundred of thousands of dollars may be received. Will you receive a check? Will the funds be wire-transferred to your bank? Do you want such a large amount in your checking account? How will you transfer funds into an investment account?

A final issue regarding distribution options can arise if you have a choice between a lump-sum and periodic monthly payments. The periodic payment alternative means the pension plan administrator continues to be involved in the investment of the funds, which may be beneficial. However, the monthly payments cannot be changed if your needs in retirement change. Your choice should be based upon the amount and predictability of your needs, your and your spouse's present health, and family history.

# Taxation Of Retirement Distributions

The taxation of retirement distributions depends on whether they are paid in a annuity, a monthly installment, or a single lump-sum distribution. Annuity or monthly payments are taxed as ordinary income as they are received. If any after-tax contributions were made to the retirement plan while you were actively employed, a portion of each monthly retirement payment will be treated as a return of the investment and will not be taxed. A single lump-sum distribution may either be taxed at the time it is received or it may be transferred to a tax-deferred individual retirement account (an IRA rollover).

If you decide to make an IRA rollover, you must transfer the distribution into an IRA within 60 days of the date the distribution is received. To avoid a 20% income tax withholding, this rollover must be accomplished through a "trustee-to-trustee" transfer. This choice allows you to defer the tax on the single-sum distribution until you begin to withdraw your retirement funds. In the meantime, your money will continue to grow in a tax-deferred account.

If you are considering retirement prior to age 59½, you must also consider the 10% excise tax that generally applies to early distributions from retirement accounts. There are very limited exceptions to this excise tax, which you should explore with your tax advisor. In addition, large retirement plan distributions (amounts in excess of $150,000) may be subject to an additional 15% excise tax. This, too, can be addressed with your tax advisor.

If you receive a single-sum distribution and choose to pay taxes in the year received, you may be able to calculate your tax liability using a special five or ten-year forward-averaging ("lump-sum distribution") election. Special averaging reduces the effective tax rate on qualifying distributions by calculating the tax as if the taxable income were spread over several years. Although the special averaging calculation assumes that the income is received over several years, the full amount of the tax is payable for the tax year in which the distribution is received.

Most taxpayers need to project the consequences of the IRA rollover versus the lump-sum distribution decision, taking into account their personal circumstances. Consider the following example:

A married individual has a retirement accumulation of $200,000 and is going to make a decision between a special averaging election for a lump-sum distribution and an IRA rollover. If five-year special averaging

166

is elected, the tax will be $43,945 - leaving $156,055 to be invested at 9% (fully taxable). The IRA will be invested at 9% as well, but in a tax-deferred environment. The tax rate outside the IRA is a constant 28% throughout the entire projection period.

Considering the other financial resources available, the taxpayer does not need to withdraw any of the retirement funds during the projection period under either scenario.

In this example, the after-tax accumulation within the IRA exceeds the accumulation outside the plan between years three and four. Of course, the crossover point will vary with each specific taxpayer and set of assumptions. The calculations also suggest that in year 10 the tax rate must exceed approximately 38% before the after-tax IRA accumulation would be less than the accumulation outside the IRA. Again, the break-even tax rate in a particular year will vary with each situation. Consultation with your tax and financial advisors can clarify your personal circumstances.

Choosing between an IRA rollover and lump sum taxation is basically a function of how much and how soon the retirement funds will be needed. For many taxpayers who expect to withdraw their retirement funds gradually over their retirement years, making an IRA rollover will enhance their overall financial position. The benefits of lump sum distributions are generally greatest if significant amounts will be needed within a few years of retirement.

## **Continuing Or Replacing Company Benefits**

When you retire, some of your company benefits may end or be significantly reduced while others may be available on a continuing basis at your choice and expense. You will need to evaluate each of these benefits to determine if you still need them as a part of your overall financial plan. For example, if group life insurance can be continued, is it necessary? If so how much? Is it cost competitive with other policies? How much insurance is available and for how long? Again, you should apply the planning process by first defining the goal, then quantifying the resources available, and finally determining the best strategy or alternative to ensure the achievement of the goal.

This same process should be applied to other company benefits such as health insurance and dental coverage. As a retiree, you must determine your health insurance needs by analyzing your health related risk exposure.

During your retirement years, your basic health needs such as doctors visits and simple surgery will continue, while your risk of major medical expenses will generally increase. How much of the cost of these risks can be absorbed or taken on individually?

While you may have an adequate retirement income to meet relatively small recurring expenses, a serious illness could put retirement funds in jeopardy. You should also look at your medical history as well as that of other family members to assess your total exposure to medical costs.

Finally the retiree should ensure that all risk exposures are considered. While you may have a good understanding of doctor, hospital and dental care, you may be faced with new and additional issues related to health care. For example, insurance coverage may change from a single employer-sponsored policy to a series of coverages.

When your individual health coverage needs have been identified, you should gather information on all available sources of insurance coverage. Start by looking at your company's post retirement group medical coverage. What is the cost of this coverage?

During your working years, the cost of group insurance is generally shared with the employer. After you retire, you may be solely responsible for the cost. You should compare benefits provided by the group policy against any additional premium expense. Also consider the fact that you generally are not subject to waiting periods of limitations for pre-existing conditions when covered by a group policy.

You should prepare an outline which details all coverage options and the premium cost. This outline should first be used to determine if any benefits are unnecessary or can be self-insured. Then the outline should be used to determine whether there are gaps in your coverage that should be addressed with supplemental insurance.

Another form of insurance coverage is Medicare. Medicare is a federally-administered health insurance program designed to help cover some, but not all, medical expenses. In general, Medicare is available to individuals who are 65 or older, people of any age who have permanent kidney failure, and some disabled individuals. Medicare is divided into two types of protection-Part A is hospital insurance coverage, and Part B is medical insurance coverage. The Medicare protection package is compulsory, and is funded primarily through Social Security payroll tax deductions. The Social Security Administration can provide additional information and publications to help answer questions regarding Medicare requirements and benefits.

A final health care issue to consider is whether you need to purchase long-term care coverage. Long-term care can be very expensive, ranging in cost from $5,000 annually for occasional in-home care, to tens of thousands of dollars for nursing home care. It is easy to see that the cost of long-term care could quickly deplete one's assets and savings. For this reason and because Medicare and Medigap policies do not cover the costs of long-term custodial care, a long-term care plan should be considered. Individual policy benefits vary, but generally help cover the day-to-day costs of nursing home care, home care, and adult day care. Benefits may be limited as to the length of coverage time and the dollar amounts paid. As with most insurance policies, there may be a waiting period between the time long-term care needs arise and the onset of policy benefit payments.

You should carefully consider the relationship of the benefit amount, waiting period, and premium cost. By choosing a longer elimination period, the premium cost can be lowered or, alternatively, the benefit can be increased. You should select an elimination period that considers your ability to pay a portion of the cost from your own funds. If you have assets that can fund the first three or six months' cost, it is usually expensive and unnecessary to also insure the same costs.

In summary, careful planning at retirement can result in a combination of policies which are tailored to provide adequate medical and long-term care coverage within your budget.

## __Consider Medigap Insurance Coverage__

Medicare provides basic health care coverage but cannot pay for every type of medical expense the retiree may incur. Many private insurance companies provide "Medigap" policies, or Medicare Supplemental insurance. There are various Medigap plan levels which provide coverages ranging from basic hospital care coinsurance to skilled nursing home care, prescription drugs, and preventive care.

Before purchasing any Medigap coverage, you should compare several policies and ask the following questions:

- Does the policy cover the Part A hospital deductible?

- Does the policy cover skilled nursing care facility daily coinsurance?

- Can the insurance company cancel or non-renew the policy?

- How often can the company raise premiums?

- How are pre-existing conditions treated and is there is a waiting period before benefits will be paid?

Be sure to look at all of these areas, and then compare the proposed Medigap coverage with your existing coverage and risk exposures. Medigap premiums can range from $400 annually for basic coverage, to $1,800 or more a year for comprehensive coverage.

In addition, some companies provide for medical benefits for retirees. However, as the health care environment is being drastically reshaped in the 2000's, these benefits may substantially change. If you are paying for your own medical insurance, or find that you must begin paying for more of your insurance, investigate whether or not you can join with other individuals (such as church groups, professional, or fraternal organizations) and obtain group insurance rates. You will still be responsible for paying the premium, but the costs may be cheaper than single policies.

# Social Security

On October 1, 1999, the Social Security Administration (SSA) began mailing new annual Social Security Statements of estimated benefits to over 125 million workers. More than 300,000 statements are expected to be mailed each day. If you are age 25 or older and are not currently receiving Social Security benefits, you can expect to receive your statement near your birthday.

Check your statement carefully to ensure that your earning history is accurately reflected and contact the SSA to correct errors. Note that your previous years' earnings, however, may not be up-to-date, due to delays in receiving and processing information at the SSA. No correction is required for missing information for the previous year unless you have reason to believe that information may not have been properly provided to the SSA by your employer.

The SSA has also posted an online, interactive calculator on its Internet site. You can use this calculator to estimate your Social Security benefits. This calculator is available at the Social Security Web site at www.ssa.gov.

## Social Security, Just One Piece Of The Retirement Pie

Many people may not realize that Social Security benefits will likely provide only a *portion* of the income they will need each year in retirement. The rest must come from other sources, such as company pension plans, personal savings, and perhaps part-time earnings. Your individual Social Security Statement of estimated benefits could help you assess whether you are adequately preparing for retirement.

The information in your statement includes estimates of your future retirement, and disability and survivor benefits. The statement offers you an opportunity to determine whether your earnings are accurately posted on your Social Security records. Because Social Security benefits are based on an individual's career record, this is an important feature.

When you receive your statement, you'll want to check to see that your record of earnings is correct. For example, if you have begun using a different name on your employment records and have not notified the SSA of the name change, some of your earnings may not have been posted to your Social Security account. If there are errors in your earnings record, follow the instructions included in the statement to notify the SSA of discrepancies.

## Applying For Social Security Benefits

Several months before your actual retirement date, you should go to your nearest Social Security Administration office to begin the process of applying for benefits. This process should include an understanding of several areas. What paperwork or documents are needed? How soon will benefits begin and how will they be paid? If you are married, what spousal benefits will be paid? How and when do you qualify for Medicare coverage? What is the financial impact of receiving retirement income benefits prior to age 65 or delaying benefits beyond normal retirement?

# Assess Your Retirement Readiness

Your Social Security statement will provide an estimate of your retirement benefits if you have already earned at least 40 "credits" during your working life. Each year, the SSA calculates the number of credits that you earned that year based on your reported income. For example, in 1999, you earned one credit for each $740 in earned income, up to a maximum of four credits.

Your statement also includes the following: a yearly breakdown of your recorded earnings to date; the total amount of Social Security taxes paid by you and your employers over your career; and an estimate of the monthly benefit you could receive if you should become disabled.

You can use your estimated monthly retirement benefit (if provided) to calculate a rough estimate of how much of your monthly retirement income you may need to provide from your personal retirement plans and savings.

Keep in mind that your estimated monthly benefit is based on your current wages. If your income increases in future years, your estimated Social Security benefits may also increase. In addition, Social Security benefits increase automatically annually based on the rise in the Consumer Price Index (CPI) from the third quarter of one year to the third quarter of the next year. In January 2000, Social Security benefits increased by 2.4%. For Social Security beneficiaries, that meant an average monthly payment increase from $785 to $804, and for couples, from $751 to $769.

# Can You Count On Your Benefits?

According to the SSA, your benefits will be there for you when you retire. However, the SSA acknowledges that some changes to the present system may be required. Most people today are living longer, healthier lives, but when Social Security was created the average life span was less than 65 years. In the next decade, 76 million Baby Boomers will start retiring, and, in about 30 years, there will be nearly twice as many older Americans as there are today.

Currently, Social Security takes in more in taxes each year than it pays out in benefits. But in 2015, according to estimates by the SSA, the amount of benefits paid out will begin to exceed the amount collected in taxes. Based on SSA projections, by 2037 the Social Security trust fund will be exhausted and payroll taxes collected will be enough to pay only about 72% of benefits owed. Recognition of these issues is growing and legislators are now looking at funding and investment options to resolve them.

Your Social Security benefits are an important piece of the retirement income pie. However, you should not rely solely on Social Security for your retirement income. Your employer-sponsored retirement savings plans, company pensions, and personal savings will likely provide the major portion of your income in retirement.

## Effect Of Converting Non-Retirement Assets Into Retirement Funds

When you assess your current situation in relation to specific, defined retirement goals, you may want to analyze the tax consequences of converting non-retirement assets into additional retirement funds. One of these assets is your personal residence.

Where will you live when you retire? Will you remain in your current home or purchase or lease a different home? If you decide to sell your current residence and use some or all of the funds to supplement your retirement income, you must consider the tax consequences.

Retirees often consider moving to different locations upon retirement. Moving to a different state raises several tax issues that will impact your projected living expenses. First, what are the differences in state income tax rates from the current state of residence? Second, states tax retirement pensions differently by allowing varying amounts to be received tax-free. In addition, some states provide property tax relief for individuals over age 65. You should also consider the state sales tax rate. Finally, states vary on the taxation of Social Security benefits.

## The Retirement Years

### Understand The Effects Of Part-Time Work

As a valuable supplement to retirement income, many retirees re-enter the work force on a part-time or full-time basis. Other retirees may re-enter for non-financial reasons (to provide something to occupy their time).

A retiree can continue to work and still receive retirement benefits. The earnings after you reach your full retirement age will not affect your Social Security benefits. However, your benefits will be reduced if your earnings exceed certain limits for the months before you reach your full retirement age (65 for persons born before 1938 and gradually increasing to 67 for persons born in 1960 or later).

Here's how it works:

If you're under full retirement age, $1 in benefits will be deducted for each $2 in earnings you make above the annual limit ($10,680 in 2001).

In the year you reach your full retirement age, your benefits will be reduced $1 for every $3 you earn over a different limit ($25,000 in 2001) until the month you reach full retirement age. Then you can work without any reduction in the amount of your monthly benefit, no matter how much you earn.

There's another way that working may increase your Social Security benefit. Your benefit is based on a percentage of your earnings averaged over most of your working lifetime. If any income you make after signing up for Social Security increases your overall average earnings, your benefit probably will increase.

## Remember The 70½ Rule

Minimum distributions must begin by April 1 of the year after you reach age 70½ whether or not you have actually retired. The amount of the minimum distribution is calculated based on your life expectancy or the joint and last survivor life expectancy of you and your designated beneficiary. If the amount distributed is less than the minimum required amount, an excise tax equal to 50% of the amount of the shortfall is imposed.

## Stay Educated And Use Professional Advisors

Estate planning for changes in your family (birth of a grandchild or death of a parent or spouse), changes of the investment mix in your portfolio, and the need for assistance with general money management or specific help with monthly bill paying are all examples of issues which you may face during your retirement years. Stay educated by reading financial publications or other magazines aimed specifically to retirees. Consult with competent advisors in the area of financial planning, estate planning, and income tax planning as needed.

In later years, it is crucial to have a relationship with financial professionals you can trust. Health conditions and dementia can cause a senior to make wrong financial decisions or to fall between the cracks.

# Chapter 9

---

# Investing for Retirement

This chapter discusses different plans for investing money and deferring the taxes on investment earnings until a later date. Tax reduction is not the primary criterion for choosing investments, but it certainly is an important one. Tax-exempt or tax-deferred refers to the tax status of the earnings on an investment. Although these terms sound similar, they are quite different. Understanding how taxes affect different investments will help you choose the investments that are best for you.

If no taxes are owed on money you earn from an investment, it is in the tax-exempt category (a.k.a. tax-free). Examples of tax-exempt investments are municipal bonds and Roth IRAs. The income from these investments is free of income taxes.

With a tax-deferred investment, taxes are not owed on the investment until it is sold (i.e., taxes are deferred until that time). This chapter focuses on the plans available for investing on a tax-deferred basis.

One of the best ways to save for retirement is through tax-deferred investments. Contributions (money added) to employer retirement plans and some IRAs can be made with pre-tax dollars (i.e., income you don't have to pay tax on), allowing you to defer taxes until you start making withdrawals. Tax-deferred investing allows you to keep money that would have been paid in taxes at the time you earned the money, leaving a greater amount available for investing.

# Common Advantages Of Retirement Accounts

A major advantage of tax-deferred investing is making contributions to a retirement account with pre-tax dollars. In many instances (e.g., 401k plans), the government allows taxable income to be reduced by the amount of the contribution to a tax-deferred retirement plan.

As a result, you can have the same amount of money in your pocket and invest what you would have paid the government. For instance, if you are in the 28% marginal income tax bracket and you contribute $1,000 to a tax-deferred retirement plan, you would lower your federal income taxes by $280 (0.28 times $1,000). The savings is based on your marginal tax rate, i.e., the rate you pay on the highest dollar of earnings.

A second advantage of tax-deferred investing is that earnings grow faster because they aren't taxed until withdrawn. Instead of paying tax on the interest earned, it continues to compound until the investment is sold. Over time, the gap between the value of a taxable and a tax-deferred account, earning the same rate of interest, increases sharply.

## Penalties for Early Withdrawal

All tax-deferred accounts carry a penalty for withdrawing the money before age 59½. However, some types of accounts have exceptions, such as money withdrawn to be used to buy a first home, or if the owner of the account becomes disabled or dies. In addition, for some accounts, the penalty may not apply if the individual is taking equal periodic payments over his or her life expectancy for at least five years or until age 59½, whichever comes later, or for college expenses, and certain medical expenses. The penalty is usually 10% of the amount withdrawn and then, of course, federal and state income taxes also have to be paid on the withdrawal.

# Types of Retirement Plans

The government allows several different types of tax-deferred retirement programs. Among these are employer-sponsored plans, plans for self-employed persons, and individual retirement accounts (IRAs). Many of the plans are named for sections of the tax code that establish these plans, (e.g., 401k and 403b). These plans differ in who is eligible to participate, administrative responsibilities, allowable contribution limits, the types of investments available in the plan, and tax consequences and penalties for early withdrawal.

# Employer-Sponsored Retirement Plans

Salary-reduction plans allow employees to deposit, through payroll deduction, part of their salary into a retirement account. There are a number of ways you, as an employee, can invest on a tax-deferred basis so your investment will grow free of taxes and will not be taxed until you start making withdrawals. Types of employer-sponsored retirement plans include:

## 401k

A retirement plan for employees in private corporations which defers the taxes on employee contributions and earnings on these contributions until retirement withdrawals are made. Usually only companies with over 25 employees are eligible to participate. You can contribute up to 20% of your earnings up to a set maximum. In the year 2000, the limit on the amount which can be contributed from income before taxes is $10,500. Contributions are deducted directly from your paycheck (e.g., 5% of your salary).

Some employers contribute a match or a percentage of your contribution. Many companies also allow their employees to borrow up to one-half of the funds from their 401k plan for any reason. Interest paid by the employee on the money that is borrowed from his 401k is paid into the employee's own account.

## 403b

A tax-deferred retirement plan that is similar to corporate 401k plans. A big difference is fewer employers match contributions because participants are often public (read: taxpayer-funded) employees. 403b plans are also available to employees of schools and charitable organizations. The year 2000 limit for contributions is $10,500. The mix of available investment choices differs among institutions. Many allow participants to borrow from their account and have a catch-up provision if you have not contributed fully in the past.

## Section 457

This plan is similar to the 401k and 403b but is for state and local government employees and employees of tax-exempt organizations. With Section 457 plans, employer matching is virtually non-existent. The year 2000 contribution is $8,000.

## Self-Employed Or Small Business Retirement Plans

There also are tax-deferred plans available to individuals who are self-employed or employees of small businesses. These include:

## Keogh Plan

Named after U.S. representative Eugene James Keogh, who first introduced the idea in 1962, this plan is available to anyone who has self-employed income. This is generally income from any unincorporated business that you conduct, whether it is your primary job or a business "on the side." Self-employed persons may contribute as much as 25% of their net self-employment income, up to a maximum amount of $30,000 per year. For purposes of a Keogh, the definition of earned income is net profit (i.e., net income after subtracting business expenses).

The money contributed to a Keogh plan is not taxed and grows in value until it is withdrawn. You may have both a Keogh plan and an IRA. If you work for an employer and are self-employed on the side, you may pay into a Keogh and also belong to the employer's retirement plans. In addition, if you have employees, you can enroll others who work for you.

To set up a Keogh plan, you must first select a brokerage, mutual fund, or other financial institution. Usually they will supply the needed paperwork and provide you with a prototype plan. You will be asked to choose a defined-contribution and/or a defined-benefit Keogh plan. These two options are not mutually exclusive—your plan can include both.

There are three forms of defined-contribution Keogh plans:

1. A **money-purchase** Keogh requires you to choose a fixed percentage of your earnings and contribute that percentage every year to the plan.

2. A **profit-sharing** Keogh allows you to contribute a fixed percentage of your profits, up to $30,000 a year. However, you can contribute the full amount one year and less or nothing the next, depending on how the business does.

3. A **combination of money-purchase and profit sharing** offers the option of contributing up to the maximum of $30,000, but doesn't lock a business owner into high payments.

179

Under a defined benefit plan, rather than contribute a percentage of your earnings, you are allowed to contribute more than the $30,000 limit imposed on defined-contribution plans. Also, the amount contributed each year can vary greatly. These plans can be complicated and costly to set up and administer because a professional actuary is required to oversee the plan. Generally, defined-benefit Keogh plans are used as a catch-up strategy by older business owners who have put off setting up a retirement plan.

## SEP or SEP-IRA

Although SEP-IRAs are aimed at the self-employed, employers also can establish SEP-IRAs for their employees. Contributions to a SEP-IRA are excluded from the employee's taxable income. A SEP plan allows you to contribute to a special type of IRA more than is allowed under the regular IRA rules.

The contribution limits are set at 15% of earned income for the employee and 13.04% for the employer, up to a maximum of $24,000 in 2001. Employers must contribute the same percentage to their employees' IRA as they do to their own.

One advantage to the employer or self-employed person is that contributions do not have to be made every year. Little paper work is required, it is much simpler than setting up a Keogh plan, and does not have the reporting requirements of a Keogh.

A disadvantage is that you cannot contribute as much to a SEP-IRA as you can to a Keogh plan. Generally, contributions are made by the employer and are tax-deductible to the employer.

## SIMPLE Plans

This is a tax-deferred savings plan that can be set up by owners of a business that employs 100 or fewer employees to cover all employees and themselves. As of 1997, small employers can establish SIMPLE-IRAs or SIMPLE 401k plans. To be covered, employees must earn at least $5,000 a year.

The maximum contribution is $7,000, and the employer can match up to 3% of the employee's compensation. The employee's contribution reduces taxable income and the employer's contribution reduces the business' taxable income. A SIMPLE-IRA is owned by the employee and belongs to the employee, even if employment is terminated. The employer can't sponsor another retirement plan in addition to a SIMPLE. Like SEPs, SIMPLE-IRAs have low administrative responsibilities and costs compared to Keogh plans.

# Individual Retirement Accounts (IRAs)

For individuals who qualify, another smart way to build a retirement nest egg is to take advantage of the tax-deferred growth offered by an Individual Retirement Account (IRA). An IRA is a personal retirement savings plan, which may be set up with banks, mutual fund companies, brokerage firms, or similar investment organizations.

IRAs described here are called "Traditional IRAs" to distinguish them from the new "Roth IRAs," first available starting in 1998. Contributions to a Roth IRA are not deductible (regardless of your AGI), but withdrawals that meet certain requirements are not subject to federal income tax, so dividends and investment growth on amounts held in the Roth IRA can escape federal income tax.

Traditional IRAs described in this chapter may be used as part of a simplified employee pension (SEP) plan maintained by your employer. Under a SEP, your employer may make contributions to your Traditional IRA and these contributions may exceed the normal limits on Traditional IRA contributions.

### Advantages Of A Traditional IRA

A Traditional IRA gives you several tax benefits. Earnings on the assets held in your Traditional IRA are not subject to federal income tax until withdrawn by you. And, in addition, you may be able to deduct all or part of your Traditional IRA contribution on your federal income tax return. State income tax treatment of your Traditional IRA may differ from federal treatment; ask your state tax department or your personal tax advisor for details.

### Eligibility Requirements For A Traditional IRA

You are eligible to establish and contribute to a Traditional IRA if:

1. You received compensation (or earned income if you are self-employed) during the year for personal services you rendered. If you received taxable alimony, this is treated like compensation for IRA purposes.

181

2. You did not reach age 70½ during the tax-filing year.

## Spousal IRA

For each year before the year your spouse attains age 70½, you may contribute to a separate Traditional IRA for your spouse, regardless of whether your spouse had any compensation or earned income in that year. This is called a "spousal IRA." For a spousal IRA, your spouse must set up a Traditional IRA, separate from yours, to which you contribute. To make a contribution to a Traditional IRA for your spouse, you must file a joint tax return for the year with your spouse.

## Contribution Rules

You may make a contribution to your existing Traditional IRA or establish a new Traditional IRA for a taxable year by the due date (not including any extensions) for your federal income tax return for the year. Usually this is April 15 of the following year.

For each year that you are eligible, you can contribute up to the lesser of $3,000 (for 2002, and increases up to $5000 in 2008) or 100% of your compensation (or earned income, if you are self-employed). However, under the tax laws, all or a portion of your contribution may not be deductible.

If you and your spouse have spousal Traditional IRAs, each spouse may contribute up to $3,000 (for 2002, increases up to $5,000 in 2008) per year to his or her IRA as long as the combined compensation of both spouses for the year (as shown on your joint income tax return) is at least $6,000. If the combined compensation of both spouses is less than $6,000, the spouse with the higher amount of compensation may contribute up to that spouse's compensation amount, or $3,000, if less.

If you (or your spouse) make contributions to both your Traditional IRA and a Roth IRA, the combined limit on contributions to both your (or your spouse's) Traditional IRA and Roth IRA for a single calendar year is $3,000.

## Tax Deductibility

The deductibility of your contribution depends upon whether you are an active participant in any employer sponsored retirement plan. If you are not an active participant, the entire contribution to your Traditional IRA is deductible.

If you are an active participant in an employer-sponsored plan, your Traditional IRA contribution may still be completely or partly deductible on your tax return. This depends on the amount of your income.

Similarly, the deductibility of a contribution to a Traditional IRA for your spouse depends upon whether your spouse is an active participant in any employer-sponsored retirement plan. If your spouse is *not* an active participant, the contribution to your spouse's Traditional IRA will be deductible. If your spouse *is* an active participant, the Traditional IRA contribution will be completely, partly, or not deductible depending upon your combined income.

An exception to the preceding rules applies to high-income married taxpayers, where one spouse is an active participant in an employer-sponsored, retirement plan and the other spouse is not. A contribution to the nonparticipant spouse's Traditional IRA will be only partly deductible at an adjusted gross income level on the joint tax return of $150,000, and the deductibility will be phased out as described below over the next $10,000 so there will be no deduction at all with an adjusted gross income level of $160,000 or higher.

## Active Participant

Your (or your spouse's) Form W-2 should indicate if you (or your spouse) were an active participant in an employer sponsored retirement plan for a year. If you have a question, you should ask your employer or the plan administrator.

In addition, regardless of income level, your spouse's "active participant" status will not affect the deductibility of your contributions to your Traditional IRA if you and your spouse file separate tax returns for the taxable year and you lived apart at all times during the taxable year.

If you (or your spouse) are an active participant in an employer plan during a year, the contribution to your Traditional IRA (or your spouse's Traditional IRA) may be completely, partly, or not deductible depending upon your filing status and your amount of adjusted gross income (AGI). If AGI is any amount up to the lower limit, the contribution is deductible. If your AGI falls between the lower limit and the upper limit, the contribution is partly deductible. If your AGI falls above the upper limit, the contribution is not deductible.

The AGI is your gross income minus those deductions that are available to all taxpayers even if they don't itemize. Instructions to calculate your AGI are provided with your income tax form.

## Excess Contributions

The maximum contribution you can make to a Traditional IRA generally is $3,000 (for 2002 and increases up to $5,000 in 2008) or 100% of compensation or earned income, whichever is less. Any amount contributed to the IRA above the maximum is considered an "excess contribution." The excess is calculated using your contribution limit, not the deductible limit. An excess contribution is subject to excise tax of 6% for each year it remains in the IRA.

Excess contributions may be corrected without paying a 6% penalty. To do so, you must withdraw the excess and any earnings on the excess before the due date (including extensions) for filing your federal income tax return for the year for which you made the excess contribution. A deduction should not be taken for any excess contribution. Earnings on the amount withdrawn must also be withdrawn. The earnings must be included in your income for the tax year for which the contribution was made and may be subject to a 10% premature withdrawal tax if you have not reached age 59½.

Any excess contribution withdrawn after the tax filing due date (including any extensions) for the year for which the contribution was made will be subject to the 6% excise tax. There will be an additional 6% excise tax for each year the excess remains in your account.

Under limited circumstances, you may correct an excess contribution after tax filing time by withdrawing the excess contribution (leaving the earnings in the account). This withdrawal will not be includable in income nor will it be subject to any premature withdrawal penalty if (1) your contributions to all Traditional IRAs do not exceed $3,000, and (2) you did not take a deduction for the excess amount (or you file an amended return, Form 1040X, which removes the excess deduction).

You may be able to take an income tax deduction for the amount of excess that was reduced or eliminated, depending on whether you would be able to take a deduction if you had instead contributed the same amount.

## IRA Rollover

Almost all distributions from employer plans are eligible for rollover to a Traditional IRA. The main exceptions are:

- Payments over the lifetime or life expectancy of the participant (or participant and a designated beneficiary).

- Installment payments for a period of 10 years or more.

- Required distributions (generally the rules require distributions starting at age 70½ or for certain employees starting at retirement, if later).

- Payments of employee after-tax contributions.

- Starting in 1999, hardship withdrawals from a 401k plan or a 403b arrangement.

- If you are eligible to receive a distribution from a tax qualified retirement plan as a result of, for example, termination of employment, plan discontinuance, or retirement, all or part of the distribution may be transferred directly into your Traditional IRA. This is a called a "Direct Rollover." Or, you may receive the distribution and make a "Regular Rollover" to your Traditional IRA within 60 days. By making a Direct Rollover or a Regular Rollover, you can defer income taxes on the amount rolled over until you subsequently make withdrawals from your IRA.

- The maximum amount you may roll over is the amount of employer contributions and earnings distributed. You may not roll over any after-tax employee contributions you made to the employer retirement plan. If you are over age 70½ and are required to take minimum distributions under the tax laws, you may not roll over any amount required to be distributed to you under the minimum distribution rules. Also, if you are receiving periodic payments over your, or your and your designated beneficiary's life expectancy, or for a period of at least 10 years, you may not roll over these payments. A rollover to a Traditional IRA must be completed within 60 days after the distribution from the employer retirement plan to be valid.

- A qualified plan administrator or 403b sponsor MUST WITHHOLD 20% OF YOUR DISTRIBUTION for federal income taxes UNLESS you elect a Direct Rollover. Your plan or 403b sponsor is required to provide you with information about direct and Regular Rollovers and withholding taxes before you receive your distribution and must comply with your directions to make a Direct Rollover.

The rules governing rollovers are complicated. Be sure to consult your tax advisor or the IRS if you have a question about rollovers.

Rollovers, if properly made, do not count toward the maximum contribution. Also, rollovers are not deductible and they do not affect your deduction limits as described above.

## Withdrawals

You may withdraw from your Traditional IRA at any time. However, withdrawals before age 59½ may be subject to a 10% penalty tax in addition to regular income taxes.

## Minimum Distribution

If you have not withdrawn your entire IRA by the April 1 following the year in which you reach 70½, you must make minimum withdrawals in order to avoid penalty taxes. The rule allowing certain employees to postpone distributions from an employer qualified plan until actual retirement (even if this is after age 70½) does not apply to Traditional IRAs.

The minimum withdrawal amount is determined by dividing the balance in your Traditional IRA (or IRAs) by your life expectancy or the combined life expectancy of you and your designated beneficiary. The minimum withdrawal rules are complex. Consult your tax advisor or financial advisor for assistance.

The penalty tax is 50% of the difference between the minimum withdrawal amount and your actual withdrawals during a year. The IRS may waive or reduce the penalty tax if you can show that your failure to make the required minimum withdrawals was due to reasonable cause and you are taking reasonable steps to remedy the problem.

## Taxation

Amounts withdrawn by you are includable in your gross income in the taxable year that you receive them, and are taxable as ordinary income. Amounts withdrawn may be subject to income tax withholding by the custodian unless you elect not to have withholding.

Lump sum withdrawals from a Traditional IRA are not eligible for averaging treatment currently available to certain lump sum distributions from qualified employer retirement plans.

Since the purpose of a Traditional IRA is to accumulate funds for retirement, your receipt or use of any portion of your Traditional IRA before you attain age 59½ generally will be considered an early withdrawal and subject to a 10% penalty tax.

The 10% penalty tax for early withdrawal will not apply if:

- The distribution was a result of your death or disability.

- The purpose of the withdrawal is to pay certain higher education expenses for yourself or your spouse, child, or grandchild. Qualifying expenses include tuition, fees, books, supplies, and equipment required for attendance at a post-secondary educational institution. Room and board expenses may qualify if the student is attending at least half-time.

- The withdrawal is used to pay eligible first-time homebuyer expenses. These are the costs of purchasing, building, or rebuilding a principal residence (including customary settlement, financing, or closing costs). The purchaser may be you, your spouse, or a child, grandchild, parent, or grandparent of you or your spouse. An individual is considered a "first-time homebuyer" if the individual (or the individual's spouse, if married) did not have an ownership interest in a principal residence during the two-year period immediately preceding the acquisition in question. The withdrawal must be used for eligible expenses within 120 days after the withdrawal.

- There is a lifetime limit on eligible first-time homebuyer expenses of $10,000 per individual.

- The distribution is one of a scheduled series of substantially equal periodic payments for your life or life expectancy (or the joint lives or life expectancies of you and your beneficiary).

- If there is an adjustment to the scheduled series of payments, the 10% penalty tax may apply. The 10% penalty will not apply if you make no change in the series of payments until the end of five years or until you reach age 59½, whichever is later. If you make a change before then, the penalty will apply. For example, if you begin receiving payments at age 50 under a withdrawal program providing for substantially equal payments over your life expectancy, and at age 58 you elect to receive the remaining amount in your Traditional IRA in a lump sum, the 10% penalty tax will apply to the lump sum and to the amounts previously paid to you before age 59½.

- The distribution does not exceed the amount of your deductible medical expenses for the year (generally speaking, medical expenses paid during a year are deductible if they are greater than 7½ % of your adjusted gross income for that year).

- The distribution does not exceed the amount you paid for health insurance coverage for yourself, your spouse, and dependents. This exception applies only if you have been unemployed and received federal or state unemployment compensation payments for at least 12 weeks; this exception applies to distributions during the year in which you received the unemployment compensation and during the following year, but not to any distributions received after you have been reemployed for at least 60 days.

- Starting in the year 2000, the distribution is made pursuant to an IRS levy to pay overdue taxes.

## Roth IRAs

Roth IRAs are a new IRA that became effective January 1, 1998. Contributions to a Roth IRA are not tax-deductible, but withdrawals that meet certain requirements are not subject to federal income taxes. This makes the dividends on and growth of the investments held in your Roth IRA tax-free for federal income tax purposes if the requirements are met.

The Roth IRA gives you several tax benefits. While contributions to a Roth IRA are not deductible, dividends on and growth of the assets held in your Roth IRA are not subject to federal income tax and withdrawals by you from your Roth IRA are excluded from your income for federal income tax purposes if certain requirements are met. State income tax treatment of your Roth IRA may differ from federal treatment; ask your state tax department or your personal tax advisor for details.

## Eligibility Requirements

You are eligible to establish and contribute to a Roth IRA if you received compensation (or earned income if you are self-employed) during the year for personal services you rendered. If you received taxable alimony, this is treated like compensation for IRA purposes.

In contrast to a Traditional IRA, with a Roth IRA you may continue making contributions after you reach age 70½.

## Spousal Roth IRA

If you meet the eligibility requirements you can not only contribute to your own Roth IRA, but also to a separate Roth IRA for your spouse out of your compensation or earned income, regardless of whether your spouse had any compensation or earned income in that year. This is called a "spousal Roth IRA." For a spousal Roth IRA, your spouse must set up a different Roth IRA, separate from yours, to which you contribute. To make a contribution to a Roth IRA for your spouse, you must file a joint tax return for the year with your spouse.

Of course, if your spouse has compensation or earned income, your spouse can establish his or her own Roth IRA and make contributions to it.

## Roth IRA Contributions

You may make a contribution to your Roth IRA or establish a new Roth IRA for a taxable year by the due date (not including any extensions) for your federal income tax return for the year. Usually this is April 15 of the following year. For example, you will have until April 15, 2002, to establish and make a contribution to a Roth IRA for 2001.

For each year when you are eligible, you can contribute up to the lesser of $3,000 (for 2002, and increases up to $5,000 in 2008) or 100% of your compensation (or earned income, if you are self-employed).

If you and your spouse have spousal Roth IRAs, each spouse may contribute up to $3,000 to his or her Roth IRA for a year as long as the combined compensation of both spouses for the year (as shown on your joint income tax return) is at least $4,000. If the combined compensation of both spouses is less than $4,000, the spouse with the higher amount of compensation may contribute up to that spouse's compensation amount, or $2,000, if less.

As noted above, the spousal Roth IRA limits are reduced by any contributions for the same calendar year to a Traditional IRA maintained by you or your spouse.

For taxpayers with high-income levels, the contribution limits may be reduced.

Contributions to a Roth IRA are not deductible. This is a major difference between Roth IRAs and Traditional IRAs. Contributions to a Traditional IRA may be deductible on your federal income tax return depending on whether or not you are an active participant in an employer-sponsored plan, and on your income level.

Taxpayers with very high income levels may not be able to contribute to a Roth IRA at all, or their contribution may be limited to an amount less than $3,000. This depends upon your filing status and the amount of your adjusted gross income (AGI).

Rollovers, if properly made, do not count toward the maximum contribution. Also, you may make a rollover from one Roth IRA to another even during a year when you are not eligible to contribute to a Roth IRA (for example, because your AGI for that year is too high).

## Taxation

Any dividends on or growth of investments held in your Roth IRA are generally exempt from federal income taxes and will not be taxed until withdrawn by you, unless the tax-exempt status of your Roth IRA is revoked. If the withdrawal qualifies as a tax-free withdrawal, amounts reflecting earnings or growth of assets in your Roth IRA will not be subject to federal income tax.

## Excess Contributions

The maximum contribution you can make to a Roth IRA generally is $3,000 (for 2002, and increases up to $5,000 in 2008) or 100% of compensation or earned income, whichever is less. As noted above, your maximum is reduced by the amount of any contribution to a Traditional IRA for the same year and may be further reduced if you have high AGI. Any amount contributed to the Roth IRA above the maximum is considered an "excess contribution."

An excess contribution is subject to excise tax of 6% for each year it remains in the Roth IRA.

## Correcting An Excess Contribution

Excess contributions may be corrected without paying a 6% penalty. To do so, you must withdraw the excess and any earnings on the excess before the due date (including extensions) for filing your federal income tax return for the year for which you made the excess contribution. Earnings on the amount withdrawn must also be withdrawn. The earnings must be included in your income for the tax year for which the contribution was made and may be subject to a 10% premature withdrawal tax if you have not reached age 59½ (unless an exception to the 10% penalty tax applies).

Any excess contribution withdrawn after the tax return due date (including any extensions) for the year for which the contribution was made will be subject to the 6% excise tax. There will be an additional 6% excise tax for each year the excess remains in your account.

Unless an excess contribution qualifies for the special treatment outlined above, the excess contribution and any earnings on it withdrawn after tax filing time will be includable in taxable income and may be subject to a 10% premature withdrawal penalty.

You may reduce the excess contributions by making a withdrawal equal to the excess. Earnings need not be withdrawn. To the extent that no earnings are withdrawn, the withdrawal will not be subject to income taxes or possible penalties for premature withdrawals before age 59½. Excess contributions may also be corrected in a subsequent year to the extent that you contribute less than your Roth IRA contribution limit for the subsequent year. As the prior excess contribution is reduced or eliminated, the 6% excise tax will become correspondingly reduced or eliminated for subsequent tax years.

## Converting An Existing Traditional IRA Into A Roth IRA

You can convert an existing Traditional IRA into a Roth IRA if you meet the eligibility requirements described below. Conversion may be accomplished in two ways:

First, you can withdraw the amount you want to convert from your Traditional IRA and roll it over to a Roth IRA within 60 days.

Second, you can establish a Roth IRA and then direct the custodian of your Traditional IRA to transfer the amount in your Traditional IRA you wish to convert to the new Roth IRA.

You are eligible to convert a Traditional IRA to a Roth IRA if, for the year of the conversion, your AGI is $100,000 or less. The same limit applies to married and single taxpayers. Married taxpayers are eligible to convert a Traditional IRA to a Roth IRA only if they file a joint income tax return; married taxpayers filing separately are not eligible to convert. However, if you file separately and have lived apart from your spouse for the entire taxable year, you are considered not married, and the fact that you are filing separately will not prevent you from converting.

If you accomplish a conversion by withdrawing from your Traditional IRA and rolling over to a Roth IRA within 60 days, the requirements in the preceding paragraph apply to the year of the withdrawal (even though the rollover contribution occurs in the following calendar year).

## Recharacterization

You can undo a conversion by notifying the custodian or trustee of each IRA (the custodian of the first IRA—the Traditional IRA you converted—and the custodian of the second IRA—the Roth IRA that received the conversion).

The amount you want to unconvert by transferring back to the first custodian is treated as if it had not been converted. This is called "recharacterization."

If you want to recharacterize a converted amount, you must do so before the due date (including any extensions you receive) for your federal income tax return for the year of the conversion. Any net income on the amount recharacterized must accompany it back to the Traditional IRA.

Under current IRS rules, you can recharacterize for any reason. For example, you would recharacterize if you converted early in a year and then turned out to be ineligible because your income was over the $100,000 limit. Also, if you convert and then recharacterize during a year, you can then convert to a Roth IRA a second time if you wish.

There is no limit to the number of times you can convert, recharacterize, and then convert again during a year, and no restrictions on the reasons for doing so. However, if you convert an amount more than twice in a year, any additional conversion transactions will be disregarded when determining the amount of income taxes you have to pay because of the conversion.

For example, suppose you converted a Traditional IRA with $100,000 in it to a Roth IRA early in 1998. You will owe income taxes on $100,000 (assuming the Traditional IRA held all taxable amounts). The market value of your Roth IRA declines to $80,000, so you recharacterize it back to a Traditional IRA, and then convert the Traditional IRA a second time to a Roth IRA. You will have to pay income taxes on $80,000 for the second conversion, rather than on $100,000. The value of the Roth IRA declines further and, in late 1998 the Roth IRA is worth $60,000, so you recharacterize back to a Traditional IRA and then convert it to a Roth IRA a third time. This last conversion is disregarded for income tax purposes, and you will still have to pay income taxes on $80,000 under this example.

Under current IRS rules, recharacterization is not restricted to amounts you converted from a Traditional IRA to a Roth IRA. You can, for example, make an annual contribution to a Traditional IRA and recharacterize it as a contribution to a Roth IRA, or vice versa. You must make the election to recharacterize by the due date for your tax return for the year and follow the procedures summarized above.

## The Tax Results From Converting

The taxable amount in the Traditional IRA you convert to a Roth IRA will be considered taxable income on your federal income tax return for the year of the conversion. All amounts in a Traditional IRA are taxable except for your prior nondeductible contributions to the Traditional IRA.

If you convert a Traditional IRA to a Roth IRA, under IRS rules, income tax withholding will apply unless you elect not to have withholding. However, withholding income taxes from the amount converted (instead of paying applicable income taxes from another source) may adversely affect the anticipated financial benefits of converting. Consult your financial advisor for more information.

### Reasons To Convert My Traditional IRA To A Roth IRA

Conversion may be advantageous if you expect to leave the converted funds on deposit in your Roth IRA for at least five years and to be able to withdraw the funds under circumstances that will not be taxable. The benefits of converting will also depend on whether you expect to be in the same tax bracket when you withdraw from your Roth IRA as you are now.

### Rollover From One Roth IRA To Another Roth IRA

You may make a rollover from one Roth IRA to another Roth IRA you have or establish to receive the rollover. Such a rollover must be completed within 60 days after the withdrawal from your first Roth IRA. After making a rollover from one Roth IRA to another, you must wait a full year (365 days) before you can make another such rollover. However, you can instruct a Roth IRA custodian to transfer amounts directly to another Roth IRA custodian; such a direct transfer does not count as a rollover.

### Roth IRA Withdrawals

You may withdraw from your Roth IRA at any time. If the withdrawal meets certain requirements below, it is tax-free.

There are no rules on when you must start making withdrawals. Unlike Traditional IRAs, you are not required to start making withdrawals from a Roth IRA by the April 1 following the year in which you reach age 70½.

### Distributions After Death

After your death, there are IRS rules on the timing and amount of distributions. In general, the amount in your Roth IRA must be distributed by the end of the fifth year after your death. However, distributions to a designated beneficiary that begin by the end of the year following the year of your death, and that are paid over the life expectancy of the beneficiary, satisfy the rules. Also, if your surviving spouse is your designated beneficiary, the spouse may defer the start of distributions until you would have reached age 70½, had you lived.

## The Requirements For A Tax-Free Withdrawal

To be tax-free, a withdrawal from your Roth IRA must meet two requirements:

First, the Roth IRA must have been open for five or more years.

Second, at least one of the following conditions must be satisfied:

1.  You are age 59½ or older when you make the withdrawal.

2.  Your beneficiary makes the withdrawal after you die.

3.  You are disabled (as defined by IRS rules) when you make the withdrawal.

4.  You are using the withdrawal to cover eligible first-time homebuyer expenses. These are the costs of purchasing, building, or rebuilding a principal residence (including customary settlement, financing or closing costs). The purchaser may be you, your spouse, or a child, grandchild, parent, or grandparent of you or your spouse. An individual is considered a "first-time homebuyer" if the individual (or the individual's spouse, if married) did not have an ownership interest in a principal residence during the two-year period immediately preceding the acquisition in question. The withdrawal must be used for eligible expenses within 120 days after the withdrawal.

## Summary Of Tax Rules For Withdrawals

If your beneficiary is not your surviving spouse, withdrawals by the beneficiary will be subject to income taxes depending on the type of contribution withdrawn. A beneficiary will not be subject to the 10% premature withdrawal penalty because withdrawals following the original owner's death are an exception to the 10% penalty tax.

If your surviving spouse is the beneficiary, the spouse can elect either to receive withdrawals as beneficiary, or to treat your Roth IRA as the spouse's Roth IRA.

If the spouse treats the Roth IRA as the spouse's own, there are a couple of special rules. First, the spouse will be treated as having had a Roth IRA for five years (one of the requirements for tax-free withdrawals) if either your Roth IRA or any of the spouse's Roth IRAs has been in effect for a least five years. Second, withdrawals will be subject to the 10% penalty tax unless an exception applies. Since the spouse has elected to treat your Roth IRA as the spouse's own Roth IRA, the exception for payments following your death will not apply.

## IRA Requirements

All IRAs must meet certain requirements. Contributions generally must be made in cash. The IRA trustee or custodian must be a bank or other person who has been approved by the Secretary of the Treasury. Your contributions may not be invested in life insurance or collectibles, or be commingled with other property, except in a common trust or investment fund. Your interest in the account must be nonforfeitable at all times.

## Investing IRA Contributions

You control the investment and reinvestment of contributions to your Traditional or Roth IRA. Investments must be in one or more of the fund(s) available from the custodian. Since you control the investment of your Traditional or Roth IRA, you are responsible for any losses; neither the custodian, nor the service company, has any responsibility for any loss in value of your account.

Before making any investment, read carefully the current prospectus for any fund you are considering as an investment for your Traditional IRA or Roth IRA. The prospectus will contain information about the fund's investment objectives and policies, as well as any minimum initial investment or minimum balance requirements and any sales, redemption or other charges.

Because you control the selection of investments for your Traditional or Roth IRA and because mutual fund shares fluctuate in value, the growth in value of your Traditional or Roth IRA cannot be guaranteed or projected.

## Which is Better, a Roth IRA or a Traditional IRA?

This will depend upon your individual situation. A Roth IRA may be better if you are an active participant in an employer-sponsored plan and your adjusted gross income is too high to make a deductible IRA contribution (but not too high to make a Roth IRA contribution).

The benefits of a Roth IRA vs. a Traditional IRA may depend upon a number of other factors including: your current income tax bracket vs. your expected income tax bracket when you make withdrawals from your IRA, whether you expect to be able to make nontaxable withdrawals from your Roth IRA, how long you expect to leave your contributions in the IRA, how much you expect the IRA to earn in the meantime, and possible future tax law changes.

Consult a qualified tax professional or financial advisor for assistance.

# Chapter 10

---

# Understanding Taxes

Taxes are an important consideration for all investors. Unless you pay careful attention to the tax implications of your investments, taxes can sharply reduce the earnings you are actually able to keep. Fortunately, you don't need an accounting or law degree to understand the basics of taxes and investments.

The focus is on investments in taxable accounts, but we will also note how you can delay or even completely avoid taxes by using tax-deferred or tax-exempt accounts.

Though this chapter is not meant to serve as a complete guide for all tax questions, it can help you make sound investment decisions, choose funds that are appropriate for you, and minimize the impact of taxes on your investment returns.

## How Your Mutual Fund Investments Are Taxed

Since your goal as an investor should be to keep as much as possible of what you earn from mutual fund investments, you can't look past the inescapable reality that taxes take a big bite out of bottom-line returns.

As a mutual fund investor, you can incur income taxes in three ways:

1. When the fund distributes income dividends.
2. When the fund distributes capital gains from a sale of securities.
3. When you sell or exchange fund shares at a profit.

We'll explain how a fund's earnings are taxed—then we'll show how your sales or exchanges of shares can trigger taxes.

## Owning Shares And Paying Taxes

A mutual fund is not taxed on the income or profits it earns on its investments as long as it passes those earnings along to shareholders. The shareholders, in turn, pay any taxes due. The two types of distributions that mutual funds make are income distributions and capital gains distributions:

**Income distributions** represent all interest and dividend income earned by securities—whether cash investments, bonds, or stocks—after the fund's operating expenses are subtracted.

**Capital gains distributions** represent the profit a fund makes when it sells securities. When a fund makes such a profit, a capital gain is realized. When a fund sells securities at a price lower than it paid, it realizes a capital loss. If total capital gains exceed total capital losses, the fund has net realized capital gains, which are distributed to fund shareholders. Net realized capital losses are not passed through to shareholders but are retained by the fund and may be used to offset future capital gains.

Occasionally distributions from mutual funds may include a return of capital. Returns of capital are not taxed (unless they exceed your original cost basis) because they are considered a portion of your original investment being returned to you.

Generally, all income dividend and capital gains distributions are subject to federal income taxes (and often state and local taxes as well). You must pay taxes on distributions regardless of whether you receive them in cash or reinvest them in additional shares. The exceptions to the general rule are:

1. U.S. Treasury securities, whose interest income is exempt from state income taxes.

2. Municipal bond funds, whose interest income is exempt from federal income tax and may be exempt from state taxes as well. However, any capital gains on U.S. Treasury securities or municipal bond funds are generally taxable.

199

While the amount of income and capital gains you receive from a mutual fund affects the taxes you pay, another important factor is the holding period—that is, how long the fund held the securities before they were sold. Securities held for one year or less before being sold are categorized as short-term capital gains (or losses). Short-term capital gains are taxed at your ordinary income tax rate. But long-term capital gains—gains on securities the fund held for more than one year before they were sold—are taxed at a maximum rate of 20%. (The long-term capital gains rate is 10% for taxpayers in the lowest income tax bracket.)

## Income Is Taxed At Varying Rates

The federal income tax system is graduated, which means that people with higher incomes pay a higher percentage of taxes on what they earn. For tax purposes, income includes your salary, bonuses, tips, business profits, and earnings from investments, minus any tax deductions you may be able to claim.

Here's how the graduated part works: If you're single and have taxable income of $22,000, you're in the 15% tax bracket. But if you're single and you earn $35,000, you pay 15% on the first $26,250 of taxable income and 28% on the rest. In this case, 28% is your marginal tax rate, the highest level at which your income is taxed. When calculating taxes on investment income, it's the marginal rate that matters.

Your mutual fund will tell you the category of any capital gains it distributes. This is determined by how long the fund held the securities it sold, not by how long you have owned your shares. For example, say you first bought shares in a fund last month and today the fund is making a capital gains distribution as a result of selling securities it owned for five years. That distribution is a long-term capital gain because the fund's holding period was longer than one year. On the other hand, say you bought shares in a mutual fund 10 years ago. The fund makes a capital gains distribution because it sold securities it had held for six months. That distribution is a short-term capital gain for you because the fund's holding period was less than one year.

These are key distinctions simply because not all investment income is treated equally. Income (such as interest and dividends) and short-term capital gains are taxed as ordinary income at your marginal tax rate. Net capital gains on securities held more than one year are taxed at 20% (10% for taxpayers in the lowest tax bracket).

Internal Revenue Service (IRS) Form 1099-DIV, which your mutual fund usually sends in January for the previous tax year, details fund distributions you must report on your federal income tax return, including income distributions and capital gains distributions from your funds. You won't receive a Form 1099-DIV for mutual funds that distribute tax-exempt interest dividends (such as municipal bond funds) or for funds on which you earned less than $10 in dividends. However, you still owe taxes on all distributions, regardless of their size.

## Taxes On Sales Or Exchanges Of Shares

You can trigger capital gains taxes on mutual fund investments by selling some or all of your shares at a profit, or by exchanging shares of one fund for shares of another. The length of time you hold shares and your tax bracket determine the tax rate on any gain.

### Three important notes:

1. All capital gains from your sale of mutual fund shares are taxable, even those from the sale of shares of a tax-exempt fund.

2. Exchanging shares between funds is considered a sale, which may lead to capital gains. (An exchange involves selling shares of one fund to buy shares in another.)

3. Writing a check against an investment in a mutual fund with a fluctuating share price (all funds except money market funds) also triggers a sale of shares and may expose you to tax on any resulting capital gains.

## Timing Affects Your Taxes

Here's an example of how timing may affect taxes on the sale of mutual fund shares: If you buy 100 shares of Mutual Fund ABC for $20 a share and sell them six months later for $22 a share, you owe taxes on your $200 short-term capital gain. If you're in the 31% marginal tax bracket, that's $62. However, if you hold on to the shares for more than 12 months after the original purchase, your profit is considered a long-term gain. Therefore, it is taxed at a maximum capital gains rate of 20% for a maximum total tax of $40 on the $200 capital gain.

## Don't Buy A Tax Bill With Your Fund Shares

The tax owed on mutual fund investments may also depend in part on when you buy the shares. Mutual fund distributions, whether from income or capital gains, are taxed in the year they are made. However, under certain circumstances, distributions declared during the last three months of a year and paid the following January are taxable in the year they were declared.

If you hold shares in mutual funds that declare dividends daily—such as money market and bond funds—you are entitled to a dividend for each day you own shares in the fund. For other funds, such as stock and balanced funds, dividend and capital gains distributions are not declared daily but according to a regular schedule (monthly, quarterly, semiannually, or annually).

When a mutual fund makes a distribution, its share price (or net asset value) falls by the amount of the distribution. For example, let's say you own 1,000 shares of Fund X worth $10,000, or $10 a share. The fund distributes $1 a share in capital gains, so its share price drops to $9 a share on the fund's reinvestment date (not counting market activity). You'll still have $10,000 (1,000 × $9 = $9,000, plus the $1,000 distribution). But now you'll owe tax on the $1,000 distribution, even if you reinvest it to buy more shares.

As a result, when considering whether to purchase a fund, you need to know when the fund plans to make its next distribution. If you own shares of a fund on the fund's record date, you will receive a distribution. (Most mutual fund companies can tell you the projected timing and amount of upcoming distributions.) If you buy shares shortly before a distribution, you are simply "buying the dividend"—exposing yourself to taxes on the distribution but gaining no added value for the shares.

## How A Fund's Investment Strategy Can Affect Taxes

The likelihood that a mutual fund will pass along taxable distributions is heavily influenced by two factors: the kinds of securities the fund invests in and the fund's investment policies.

# Security Holdings

## Money Market Funds

Money market funds pay dividends that are fully taxable. Some funds—those that invest in municipal securities—earn interest that is generally not subject to federal income tax and that often is exempt from state and local taxes as well. However, because these funds are designed to maintain a constant value of $1 per share, they do not ordinarily generate capital gains or losses, either within the fund or as the result of sales or exchanges you make. An investment in a money market fund is not insured or guaranteed by the Federal Deposit Insurance Corporation FDIC) or any other government agency. Although a money market fund seeks to preserve the value of your investment at $1 per share, it is possible to lose money by investing in such a fund.

## Bond Funds

Ordinarily, bond funds produce relatively high levels of taxable income. Over long periods, almost all the return from bond funds comes from dividend payments. However, because the prices of bonds and bond funds fluctuate in response to changing interest rates, it is possible to have taxable capital gains from investing in bond funds, even tax-exempt bond funds. Sometimes a fund will generate taxable capital gains distributions by selling bonds at a profit. Alternatively, a shareholder can trigger a capital gain by selling shares in a bond fund for a price higher than the original cost.

## Stock Funds

Stock funds may pass along income from dividends paid by stocks held in the fund as well as from capital gains from the sale of stocks. Over time, however, most of the return from stocks comes from appreciation in stock prices. Because stock prices fluctuate considerably, you are generally more likely to realize a capital gain or loss when selling shares of a stock mutual fund than when selling shares of bond funds or money market funds. If you sell shares that have fallen in value, you won't owe taxes on the transaction; indeed, you may be able to take a deduction for a capital loss.

But to gauge the tax impact, it's not enough merely to know that a fund owns stocks. You must know what kind of stocks it owns. Carefully study a stock fund's objective to learn whether it emphasizes income or capital appreciation. Also determine whether it concentrates on value stocks that generally pay higher dividend yields or growth stocks that seek long-term capital growth rather than current income. The annualized rate at which a stock earns income known as the dividend yield, which can be found in a fund's annual report serves as one indication of whether a fund takes a value or growth approach.

Large, well-established companies are more likely to pay dividends than smaller companies. Consequently, funds that emphasize large-company "blue chip" stocks tend to generate more taxable dividend income than funds that emphasize small-company stocks.

## Investment Policies

How a mutual fund's advisor manages the fund's securities can also affect the taxes of shareholders in the fund. Because capital gains distributions result from the profitable sale of securities in the fund, frequent selling within a fund makes the fund more likely to produce taxable distributions than a fund that follows a strategy of "buy and hold."

A common measure of a mutual fund's trading activity is its turnover rate, which is expressed as a percentage of the fund's average net assets. For example, a fund with a 50% turnover rate has over the course of a year sold and replaced securities with a value equal to 50% of the fund's average net assets. This means that, on average, the fund holds securities for two years. (The average turnover rate for U.S. stock mutual funds is about 113%, according to Lipper Inc.)

Turnover rates can't be used to forecast a fund's taxable distributions, but they can help you compare the trading policies between different funds. Assuming that a fund's holdings will increase in value over time, you need to consider how much of that increase in value will be passed along to you as a taxable capital gains distribution. The fund's turnover rate bears directly on this point.

A capital gain on the sale of securities is a realized gain. In contrast, an unrealized "paper" gain has not yet been locked in by the sale of securities. For example, a fund may have bought stock in XYZ Inc. for $5 per share three years ago. If the stock's price rises to $15, the fund has an unrealized capital gain of $10 per share on XYZ's stock. As long as the fund continues to hold the XYZ shares, there is no taxable gain. But if the fund actually sells the stock at $15 per share, shareholders will usually have to pay taxes on the $10 per share of realized capital gain, regardless of whether the shareholders owned their shares in the mutual fund for a month or for a decade. Thus, all unrealized capital gains have the potential to be converted eventually into realized capital gains.

This means that you should consider both a fund's realized and unrealized gains information that is available through your mutual fund company and also its turnover rate to determine the potential tax implications of your investment.

## When The Markets Move

The financial markets also play a part in determining the taxable distributions a fund may pass along to you. Generally, rising markets lead to bigger gains and higher tax liabilities. Rising markets are no cause for concern—after all, strong returns are undoubtedly the goal of every mutual fund investor.

All these factors—security holdings, investment policies, and market movements—cannot reliably predict your annual tax bill. Taken together, however, they should give you a sense of whether a fund may add to that bill.

## Calculating And Reporting Your Taxes

Your mutual fund will provide a variety of information to help you complete your tax returns accurately. Here is a list of the various reports and how they can be used.

IRS Form 1099-DIV, which is typically mailed by late January of each year, lists the ordinary dividends and capital gains distributed by each mutual fund you own. "Ordinary dividends" reported on Form 1099-DIV includes taxable dividends and any net short-term capital gains. Form 1099-DIV may also include return-of-capital distributions and foreign taxes paid. (Mutual funds that invest in foreign securities may elect to pass through foreign taxes paid by the fund to its shareholders. Shareholders may be able to claim a tax credit or deduction for their portion of foreign taxes paid).

IRS Form 1099-B serves as a record of all sales of shares. Mailed in January, this form lists all of your sales of shares, check writing activity, and exchanges between funds. It is essential to determining capital gains or losses. If you realize capital gains or losses from the sale or exchange of mutual fund shares or other capital assets, you must report them on your tax return.

IRS Form 1099-R summarizes all distributions from retirement accounts such as IRAs, 401(k) plans, and annuities. Mailed in January, this form lists total distributions, the taxable amount, and any federal taxes withheld.

If you own shares of funds that hold U.S. Treasury securities, you may receive a United States Government Obligation listing with your Form 1099-DIV. This provides the percentage of a fund's income that came from U.S. Government securities—and thus the percentage of income dividends that may be exempt from state income taxes.

If you own shares of a municipal bond fund, you may receive an Income by State listing that tells you the percentage of the fund's income that came from each state's obligations. You can use this information to exclude income from municipal bonds issued in the state where you live.

You may also receive other tax-related information, depending on the types of funds you own. For example, if you invest in an international mutual fund, you may receive information that you can use to take a credit for foreign taxes paid by the fund.

## Capital Gain Or Loss?

To determine the gain or loss when you sell or exchange mutual fund shares, you must know both the price at which you sold the shares and your cost basis—generally the original price you paid for the shares. The sales price is the easy part. Figuring your cost basis can be complicated, especially if you bought shares at different times and at different prices.

An important note: Always count reinvested dividend and capital gains distributions as part of your cost basis. This will raise your cost basis and thus reduce the amount of your taxable gain when you sell or exchange shares. Because the size of the taxable gain will be smaller, you will owe less in taxes.

When figuring your cost basis, keep in mind that any sales charge or transaction fee you pay when you buy shares is part of your cost basis. Any fees or charges paid when you sell shares reduce the proceeds of the sale. In general, fees paid when you buy or redeem shares reduce your taxable gain or increase your capital loss. Other fees charged by a mutual fund, such as account maintenance fees, do not affect your cost basis.

The IRS allows you to figure the gain or loss on sales or exchanges of mutual fund shares by using one of four methods, each of which has its own benefits and drawbacks. Once you begin using an average cost method for the sale of shares of a particular fund, the IRS prohibits a switch to another method without prior approval. However, you may employ different methods for different funds. To determine which method is best for you, you may wish to consult a tax professional.

## First-In, First-Out (FIFO)

This method assumes that the first shares you sold were the first shares you purchased. While fairly easy to understand, this method often leads to the largest capital gains, because the longer you hold shares, the more time they have to rise in value. If you do not specify a method for calculating your cost basis, the IRS assumes that you use the FIFO approach.

## Average Cost (Single Category)

This method considers the cost basis of your mutual fund investment to be the average basis of all the shares you own—a figure that changes as you continue investing in a fund. Most mutual fund companies use this method to calculate average cost. In determining whether a sale generated a short-term gain or a long-term gain, the shares sold are considered to be the shares acquired first.

## Average Cost (Dual Category)

This approach is similar to the single category method except that you must separate your shares into two categories—shares held for a year or less and shares held for more than a year.

Selling short-term shares means basing the gain that is taxed at ordinary income rates of up to 39.6% on the difference between the average short-term basis and the sales price. By contrast, the gain on the sale of long-term shares which is taxed at a maximum rate of 20% is based on the difference between the average long-term basis and the sales price. If you choose this method, you must notify the fund company in advance of which category of shares to sell.

## Specific Identification

This method provides the most flexibility and therefore the best chance to minimize taxable gains. The first step is to identify the specific shares you want to sell—in most cases, these would be the shares bought at the highest price so that you can minimize your gain. However, this method is not necessarily the best choice because it can be complex and also imposes the heaviest record-keeping burden on shareholders. In addition, the shares with the highest cost basis may be the ones you purchased most recently, which could mean your having to pay taxes at a higher rate if the resulting gains are short-term.

To use the specific identification method, notify your mutual fund company in writing and provide detailed instructions about which shares you are selling each time you sell or exchange shares.

## Making Losses Work For You

You can use losses on the sale of shares to offset other capital gains. You can also use up to $3,000 of net capital losses ($1,500 for people who are married and filing separately) to offset ordinary income such as salary, wages, or investment income in any year.

For example, if you have a net capital loss of $2,000 because of unprofitable sales of mutual funds, for instance, that loss can be used to reduce your taxable income. Losses that exceed $3,000 in one year can be carried forward for as long as you wish.

## Wash Sale Rule

If you redeem shares at a loss and purchase shares in the same fund within 30 days before, after, or on the day of the redemption, the IRS considers the redemption a "wash sale." This means that you may not be allowed to claim some or all of the loss on your tax return.

If you redeem shares at a loss from a tax-exempt municipal bond fund by selling shares held for six months or less, a portion of the loss may not be allowed. In this case, the realized loss must be reduced by the tax-exempt income you received from these shares.

If you realize a short-term capital loss on shares held six months or less in an account that received long-term capital gains distributions on those shares, the short-term loss you realize from a sale of shares (up to the amount of the capital gains distributions they earned) must be reported as a long-term loss.

You may wish to consult with a tax advisor or tax preparer for guidance in dealing with these situations.

# Record Keeping

Keeping complete, accurate records of your mutual fund investments helps ensure that you'll pay the taxes you owe—and no more. The statements you'll receive from most fund companies quarterly will serve to confirm transactions and show the share prices of your purchases and sales. Keep your quarterly statements until you receive your annual statement, which typically reports account activity for the entire year. Once you have confirmed that the annual statement is accurate, there's no need to hold on to the quarterly statements.

In some cases your account statements supply information not available on IRS-mandated forms. For example, Form 1099-DIV combines short-term gains and dividend income. But you may need to know the exact amount of dividend income you had from direct government obligations (such as U.S. Treasury securities) so you can reduce your state tax bill. In that case, refer to your year-end statement to separate dividends from short-term gains.

To illustrate, assume your 1099-DIV shows that you earned a total of $500 from short-term gains and dividends in a fund, and the United States Government Obligation listing shows that the fund received 50% of its income from U.S. Treasury securities. You would need to check your year-end statement to determine how much of the $500 reported on your 1099-DIV came only from dividends. You could then exclude half of the dividend income on your state tax return.

## The Impact Of Taxes On Your Investment Returns

Understanding how mutual fund investments are taxed prepares you for the critical next step, which is to understand the impact that taxes can have on the overall performance of your investment program. Ignoring their impact can be a serious error.

Along with such fundamental factors as risk, return, and cost, taxes should be considered when deciding whether to invest in a mutual fund. Here's why: minimizing taxes can substantially boost the net returns you receive from mutual fund investments, particularly if you're in a high tax bracket.

According to one recent analysis, a significant portion of the pretax return on domestic stock mutual funds ultimately goes to pay federal income tax on dividends and capital gains distributions—especially for investors in high tax brackets. Specifically, for the mutual funds included in the analysis, the average annual pretax return (for 10 years ended December 31, 1999) was 15.4%, but the after-tax annual return was only 12.9%. In other words, about one-sixth of the pretax returns was consumed by federal income tax. The amount lost to taxes for individual funds ranged from zero (the pretax and after-tax returns were equal) to 7.7 percentage points per year.

Over the long haul, efforts to minimize taxes can provide a handsome payoff. Figure 1 shows the growth of hypothetical taxable investments of $10,000 in two mutual funds. Both funds have total returns of 10% a year, but their after-tax returns are different. Investors in one fund paid taxes equal to 10% of their earnings for an after-tax return of 9% a year, and investors in the other fund paid taxes equal to 30% of their earnings for an after-tax return of 7% a year. Though the advantage is not dramatic at first, it becomes huge as earnings compound over time. After 30 years, the investment with the smaller tax bite grows to almost $133,000 after taxes—about 75% more than the $76,123 produced by the more heavily taxed fund.

Figure 1    **The Effect of Taxes Over the Long Term**

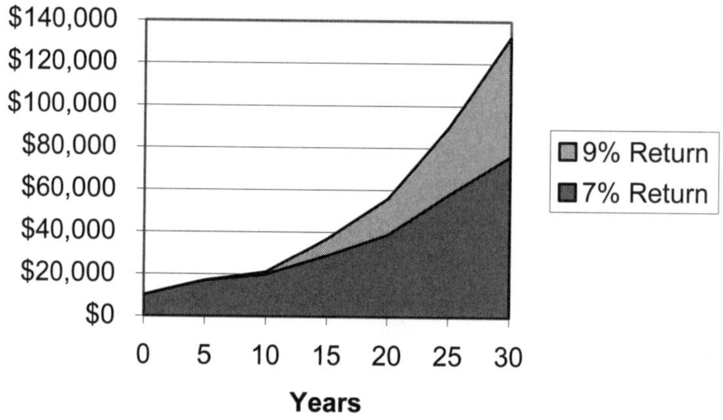

This example, which assumes original investments of $10,000 each, is for illustrative purposes only and does not imply returns available on any particular investment.

## What To Do About Taxes

Because most mutual fund managers focus on maximizing pretax returns within a fund's guidelines, the important task of considering the tax effect of mutual fund investments is up to you.

Several approaches can help in crafting an investment program that keeps taxes to a minimum:

1) Deferring taxes on your investments for as long as possible.

2) Selecting mutual funds that feature low turnover rates.

3) Choosing tax-exempt investments such as municipal bond funds (for people in high tax brackets).

## Seeking Low Turnover

Though most funds are not managed to keep taxes low, some types of mutual funds are tax-friendly by nature, especially those that keep turnover (the buying and selling of securities) low. A fund that buys and holds securities is likely to realize fewer gains than a fund that engages in active trading and is thus less likely to pass along taxable gains to investors. Such funds are sometimes called tax-efficient funds.

## Index Funds

The objective of an index fund is to match the performance and risk characteristics of a market benchmark, such as the Standard & Poor's 500 Index. Stock index funds—but not bond index funds—can reduce an investor's exposure to taxes.

Index funds buy and hold the securities in a specific index or a representative sample of the index. Because of this, the portfolio turnover of index funds is typically low. The chance that a security held in an index fund will be sold for a large gain, thus generating a large tax bill for shareholders, is much lower than a fund that employs an active management approach (buying and selling securities at the fund manager's discretion).

Nonetheless, index funds do sometimes realize gains—for example, when a stock is removed from a fund's target index and thus must be sold by the fund. An index fund could also be forced to sell securities in its portfolio if many investors decide to sell their shares—say, during a downturn in the stock market.

Bond index funds do not offer a tax-efficiency edge over actively managed bond funds because income—not capital gains—typically accounts for almost all of the long-term total return from bond funds.

## Tax-Managed Funds

Some funds are managed to keep taxable gains and income low. Among the strategies these funds employ are indexing to hold down turnover, carefully selecting which shares to sell, so capital losses offset most capital gains, and encouraging long-term investing. For example, by assessing fees on shareholders who redeem their shares soon after buying them.

## Investing For Tax-Exempt Income

Interest on most municipal bonds is exempt from federal income taxes and, in some cases, from state and local income taxes as well. However, municipal bond funds that pay lower yields than taxable bond funds as the trade-off for their tax advantage are not for everyone. Generally, investors in the 15% or 28% tax brackets do not benefit from owning municipal bond funds.

# Chapter 11

## Planning Your Estate

Because you've worked hard to create a secure and comfortable lifestyle for your family and loved ones, you'll want to ensure that you have a sound financial plan that includes trust and estate planning. With some forethought, you can minimize gift and estate taxes and preserve more of your assets for those you care about.

### A Needs Evaluation

Two key components of your initial needs evaluation are an estate analysis and a settlement cost analysis. The estate analysis includes an in-depth review of your present estate settlement arrangements. This estate analysis will also disclose potential problems in your present plan and provide facts upon which to base decisions concerning alterations in your estate plan.

For example, you may believe that your current arrangements are all taken care of in a will that leaves everything to your spouse. However, if you've named anyone else as a beneficiary on other documents such as life insurance policies, retirement or pension plans, and joint property deeds—those instructions will likely overrule anything set forth in a will.

You want to ensure that all your instructions work harmoniously to follow your exact wishes. In addition, you may want to consider leaving a portion of your assets to someone other than your spouse. The reason? While your spouse will receive your estate free of estate taxes, anything he or she receives above the estate tax exemption amount will be subject to estate taxes upon his or her death.

An estate settlement cost analysis summarizes the costs of various estate distribution arrangements. In estimating these costs, the analysis tests the effectiveness of any proposed estate plan arrangement by varying the estate arrangement, the inflation and date of distribution assumptions, as well as specific personal and charitable bequests.

Though a simple will may adequately serve your estate planning needs, you should contact an estate-planning attorney, who can assist you in developing a plan that works best for you.

## Estate Planning Checklist

Bring this checklist to your financial advisor to discuss how to make your plan comprehensive and up-to-date.

### Part 1 — Communicating Your Wishes

| Yes | No | |
|-----|----|---|
| Yes | No | Do you have a will? |
| Yes | No | Are you comfortable with the executor(s) and trustee(s) you have selected? |
| Yes | No | Have you executed a living will or health care proxy in the event of catastrophic illness or disability? |
| Yes | No | Have you considered a living trust to avoid probate? |
| Yes | No | If you have a living trust, have you titled your assets in the name of the trust? |

### Part 2 — Protecting Your Family

|  |  | |
|-----|----|---|
| Yes | No | Does your will name a guardian for your children if both you and your spouse are deceased? |
| Yes | No | If you want to limit your spouse's flexibility regarding the inheritance, have you created a Q-TIP trust in your will? |
| Yes | No | Are you sure you have the right amount and type of life insurance for both survivor income, loan repayment, capital needs and all estate-settlement expenses? |
| Yes | No | Have you considered an irrevocable life insurance trust to exclude the insurance proceeds from being taxed as part of your estate? |
| Yes | No | Have you considered creating trusts for family gift giving? |

## Part 3 — Reducing Your Taxes

| | | |
|---|---|---|
| Yes | No | If you are married, are you taking full advantage of the marital deduction? |
| Yes | No | Are both your estate plan and your spouse's plan designed to take advantage of each of your unified credit? |
| Yes | No | Do you and your spouse each individually own enough assets for each of you to qualify for the unified credit? |
| Yes | No | Are you making gifts to family members that take advantage of the $10,000 annual gift tax exclusion? |
| Yes | No | Have you gifted assets with a strong probability of future appreciation in order to maximize future estate tax savings? |
| Yes | No | Have you considered charitable trusts that could provide you with both estate and income tax benefits? |

## Part 4 — Protecting Your Business

| | | |
|---|---|---|
| Yes | No | If you own a business, do you have a management succession plan? |
| Yes | No | Do you have a buy/sell agreement for your family business interests? |
| Yes | No | Have you considered a gift program that involves your family-owned business, especially in light of recent estate rules? |

# Points To Remember

- A plan helps to determine the most advantageous means of owning family properties.

- Planning will minimize estate and income taxes, administrative expenses, executor's commissions, and attorney's fees.

- Your plan may help to provide adequate income to your survivors.

- By planning, you can preserve the assets you have worked hard to accumulate.

- Provide funds for debt repayment, if desired, and educational expenses.

- Provide adequate and available money to meet known and anticipated settlement expenses upon your death.

215

# Trust

A trust is a three-part agreement in which the owner of an estate, or the trust's "grantor," transfers the legal title to that estate to somebody else (the trustee) for the purpose of benefiting one or more third parties (the beneficiaries). Trusts may be revocable or irrevocable and may be included in a will to take affect at death.

Revocable trusts can be changed or revoked at any time. For this reason, the government considers the specified assets to still be included in the grantor's taxable estate. Therefore, you must pay income taxes on revenue generated by the trust and possibly estate taxes on those assets remaining after your death.

Irrevocable trusts cannot be changed once they are set up. The assets placed into an irrevocable trust are permanently removed from a grantor's estate and transferred to the trust. Income and capital gains taxes on assets in the trust are paid by the trust. Upon a grantor's death, the assets in the trust are not considered part of the estate and are therefore not subject to estate taxes. Most revocable trusts become irrevocable at the death or disability of the grantor.

## The Role Of A Trustee

The trust's grantor names a trustee to handle investments and manage the portfolio. The grantor can work with the trustee on major decisions, or the trustee can be assigned full authority to act on the grantor's behalf.

A trustee may be an individual such as an attorney or accountant, or it may be an entity that offers experience in such areas as taxation, estate law, and money management. Trustees have a responsibility—known as "fiduciary responsibility"—to act in the grantor's best interest according to professional standards.

## Benefits Of A Trust

Although trusts can be used in many ways for estate planning, they are most commonly used to:

- provide expert management of estates.

- provide security for both the grantor and the beneficiaries.

- protect real estate holdings or a business.

- provide for beneficiaries who are minors or require expert assistance managing money.

- avoid estate or income taxes.

- avoid probate expenses.

- maintain privacy.

Most people use trusts to benefit from the expertise of the trustee. They may be too busy to pay proper attention to their estate; they may face a serious illness; or they simply may not want to worry about financial matters.

## Trusts Offer Flexibility To Meet Your Needs

Different kinds of trusts are designed to meet different needs and objectives. For example, if your primary goal is to ensure privacy in the settlement of your estate and to provide expert management of your affairs should you become incapacitated, you might choose a living trust.

The living trust allows you to remain both the trustee and the beneficiary of the trust while you're alive. You maintain control of the assets and receive all income and benefits. Upon your death, a designated executor distributes the remaining assets according to the terms set in the trust, avoiding the probate associated with a common will. Should you become incapacitated during the term of the trust, your successor or co-trustee can take over its management.

A qualified personal residence trust (QPRT) allows you to remove a residence from your estate. For example, you can turn over your vacation home to a trust but still use it for a designated period of time, after which the home belongs to the trust or its beneficiaries, depending on mandates outlined in the trust. The benefit is that any gift tax you might incur from giving away the property is decreased because you still have rights to the house. The potential drawback is that if you die before the term of the trust ends, the home is considered part of your estate.

If you want to leave money to your grandchildren, you might consider a generation-skipping trust, which can help preserve your $1 million tax exemption on bequests to your grandchildren and avoid the tax on bequests exceeding that amount, which can be up to 55%. For example, even if you put $50,000 in a generation-skipping trust and allow it to accumulate earnings for many years, your lifetime exemption would be eroded by only the original $50,000.

To help benefit your favorite charity while serving your own trust purposes, you might consider a charitable lead trust. This trust lets you pay a charity income from a particular asset for a designated amount of time, after which the principal goes to the beneficiaries, with reduced estate taxes.

Another charitable option, the charitable remainder trust, allows you to leave assets to a charity and receive income and a tax deduction at the same time. Through this trust, the trustee will sell the donated property or assets, tax-free, and establish an annuity payable to you, your spouse, or your heirs for a designated period of time. Upon completion of that time period, the remaining assets go directly to the charity.

## Consider The Costs

Different types of trusts and trustees can require a variety of fees for administration and wealth management. As you develop your trust strategies, remember to consider the costs that may be involved and weigh them carefully in relation to the benefits.

## Is A Trust Right For You?

Although not quite as popular as wills, trusts are becoming more widely used among Americans, wealthy or not. Increasing numbers of people are discovering the potential benefits of a trust and how it can help protect their assets, reduce their tax obligations, and define the management of assets according to their wishes in a private, effective way. Your financial advisor can help you evaluate a certain type of trust to determine if it may be appropriate for your circumstances.

# Chapter 12

---

# Surrounding Yourself With Professionals

## Members Of A Professional Financial Team

Depending on your personal financial situation, and how much knowledge you have, your professional financial team can be as large as 10 people. Here are the possibilities:

**Bankers** (or their counterparts at credit unions) can help you choose appropriate accounts for your checking accounts, savings accounts, line of credit, and safety deposit boxes.

**Real estate agents** can help you make housing purchase decisions and help you make contact with mortgage lenders. (Note: You can often negotiate a lower sale price by employing a buyer's broker who works for you, not the seller. If the buyer's broker or the broker's firm also lists properties, there may be a conflict of interest, so ask them to tell you if a property is one of their listings.)

**Lawyers** can help you with certain legal implications of your investments, such as real estate or partnerships. They may also provide legal financial planning by drafting wills and trusts. Choose a lawyer that has the expertise you need (e.g., real estate, family law, estate planning).

**Accountants** (and some highly qualified tax preparers) can answer questions about the income tax consequences of your investments and help you submit your tax return to the Internal Revenue Service. Some prefer an accountant with a CPA designation (Certified Public Account) while others feel that a public accountant is sufficient.

**Employee benefit counselors** at your place of work can help you with decisions related to retirement accounts, if any, available through your employer.

**Life insurance agents** can sell you insurance products (e.g., variable life insurance, whole life insurance, universal life) which have an investment component. They can also offer a much less expensive product: term life insurance. Most life insurance agents are trained by the company whose products they sell and may not be knowledgeable about all investment options available to you.

If possible, try to employ a life insurance *broker* instead of an agent as the broker works for the client and the agent works for the company that employs them. This can benefit you more because the broker has more product selection and is more likely to be objective.

**Estate planners** can help with a strategy for management of your assets at the time of your death. Many estate planners hold the AEP (Accredited Estate Planner) designation, but they are not qualified to prepare legal documents, such as wills, trusts, and powers of attorney. Only a lawyer is qualified for that.

**Stockbrokers** may sell you a wide variety of investment products. Large national or regional firms may have special programs for the beginning investor. Brokers may be either full-service or discount. Full service brokers can provide good financial advice. Discount brokers, who get their name because sales commissions are discounted (sometimes as much as 70%), are useful if you know what you want to purchase. They generally do not offer advice.

Stockbrokers are licensed by the state(s) in which they buy and sell securities, and they must be registered with a company that is a member of the National Association of Securities Dealers (NASD) and pass NASD-administered securities exams. NASD maintains the Central Registration Depository (CRD), where you can check to see if your broker is registered to sell securities.

**Investment advisors** can give you advice on securities (e.g., stocks, bonds, mutual funds, and money markets) and must be registered with the Securities and Exchange Commission or a state securities agency. The registry designation is RIA (Registered Investment Advisor).

If possible, try to work with a fee-only investment advisor as the client pays the fee-only advisor while commissioned sales people such as stockbrokers tend to be more focused on making more trades.

**Financial planners** consider your total financial situation to develop a comprehensive plan. This involves taking a "snapshot" of where you are now with a net worth statement. This will help you in identifying where you want to be financially (e.g., buying a house, financing a child's college education, living comfortably in retirement), and developing recommendations to help close the gap between what you have now and what you need to meet your life's goals.

Financial planners look at meeting short-and long-term financial goals and managing risk with insurance, investments, tax planning, retirement planning, and estate planning. Making decisions about one area, such as saving for retirement, has implications for other areas, such as tax planning and investment choices. Working with someone who can give you the complete picture, and can call on specialized experts (e.g., lawyers, accountants) when needed, has its advantages for some people.

# How To Select A Financial Advisor

Many people feel comfortable making financial decisions on their own, perhaps with the help of books on personal finance, online calculators, or financial planning software. Others choose to meet their goals by seeking professional financial help.

A professional advisor can often help people who:

1. Lack the time to manage and monitor their own financial matters.

2. Does not have the expertise to make wise financial decisions.

3. Face changed circumstances—perhaps because of marriage, the birth of a child, an inheritance, a divorce, a new job, the sale of a business, or the receipt of a lump sum from a retirement plan.

4. Need explanations, advice, or reassurance from an expert to navigate through the complexities and risks of the financial markets.

5. Want a second opinion about a financial plan they have developed on their own (or that another advisor has proposed).

Finding expert help need not be difficult. But it's not a step to be taken lightly, so you should devote some effort to the search. This chapter frames the considerations involved by describing various types of advisors and their credentials, then explaining the importance of how an advisor is compensated. Finally, this chapter presents a method to help you choose, and then work with, a financial professional who's right for you.

# Preparing For Your Search

A professional advisor analyzes your financial circumstances, prepares a plan to meet your financial goals, and sometimes, manages your investment portfolio. He or she may be called a financial planner, an investment advisor (who may also be known as an asset manager or a money manager), a wealth manager, an accountant, a banker, an insurance agent, or a securities broker.

Because there are so many types of financial professionals to choose from, you should ask yourself two key questions before you begin a search for an advisor.

## What Are My Financial Goals?

You should define your financial goals, even if only in a general way. You might find, for example, that you need a comprehensive plan that will take into account cash management and budgeting, investments, taxes, insurance coverage, and estate planning. If so, you might consider a financial planner, a type of advisor who analyzes and coordinates the many aspects of your financial picture. Such a comprehensive planner often works with specialists such as lawyers, investment managers, and tax and insurance experts. These specialists may be either on the planner's staff or with outside firms (including, for example, your own lawyer or accountant).

By contrast, the exercise of defining your goals might show that your focus can be much narrower. Perhaps you need help only in one or two areas such as selecting investments, managing your portfolio, developing a retirement plan, minimizing estate taxes, investing an inheritance, or handling a large distribution from a retirement plan. A financial planner can help with any of these. Or you can go to a specialist, such as an investment advisor, for your investing needs or an accountant or tax lawyer for tax planning.

## What Do I Expect From An Advisor?

An advisor can help you achieve your financial goals in several ways. So ask yourself whether you want one-time advice—or whether you'll require ongoing financial planning and guidance.

Also decide whether you want to handle some parts of your finances yourself. For example, your advisor may recommend an investment plan and then carry it out for you or recommend another firm that can execute your plan. But you may decide to implement the investment plan yourself (and save on fees).

Being clear about your financial goals and the role you expect an advisor to play will help you stay on track as you search for, and then work with, an advisor. As you gather information, you'll want to make sure you have a good understanding of each advisor's expertise and compensation arrangements.

# How To Find A Competent Advisor

## Developing An Initial List

Now you are in a good position to start the actual search. Begin by creating a list of possible advisors. One approach is to ask for recommendations from friends and relatives. But don't ask only for names: find out whether their financial goals are similar to yours, how they use their advisors, and why they chose them.

But friends and relatives may lack the expertise needed to accurately judge the quality of an advisor's work, so consider checking with professionals such as attorneys and accountants, too. Because they are concerned about their reputations, their recommendations could well prove to be more reliable.

Additional sources are available but should be used with caution:

## Other Referral Services

Various private organizations make available lists of advisors. In addition, some personal finance magazines publish lists. Check the requirements for listing by asking, for example, whether anyone who pays can be listed and what standards, if any, have to be met.

## Seminars

Many financial services organizations host seminars. Some of these seminars are education-oriented, but many are simply a way for the sponsoring individual or company to generate lists of potential customers. Attendees do, however, get the chance to sample the style and credibility of the advisor.

This is a great opportunity to get some of your financial questions answered without scheduling a meeting with the advisor.

## Articles Or News Appearances

A financial professional who is featured in a publication or on a news clip may be excellent—or may simply be quotable. Always check to ensure that he or she can meet your particular needs.

# Looking Beyond Titles And Credentials

In your search for expert help, you will come across a variety of job titles, including not only the title "financial advisor" but also titles such as financial planner, financial consultant, or even account executive. However, it's important to keep in mind that anyone can use generic titles such as these, regardless of his or her training or education.

You may also find yourself adrift in what has been called an "alphabet soup" of credentials—CFP, CPA, CFS, and CSA, for example. Focusing on advisors who have credentials is usually a good idea because having a professional designation suggests a commitment to the field based on some combination of work experience, formal study (including passing qualifying exams in their field), and continuing education.

No professional credential or job title can guarantee the quality of an advisor's services or ensure that your needs will be met. Moreover, the primary interest of some advisors may be to sell you a particular financial product rather than to provide impartial guidance. So, in your search, look beyond job titles or credentials by gathering other information to ensure that the advisor you choose will be the right one for you.

Most financial advisors come to planning from a sales job. One of the first things the good ones learn is to leave their sales hat at the door.

The following explanations will help you thread your way through the best-known professional credentials and the types of advisors who may hold them (and some may hold more than one):

## Certified Financial Planner (CFP)

This designation is awarded by the Certified Financial Planner Board of Standards to individuals who have had at least three years of work experience in the financial planning field, completed an approved course of study, and passed an exam. The training of CFPs, which focuses on financial planning, includes taxes, investments, retirement planning, estate planning, and insurance.

## Certified Funds Specialists (CFS)

This designation is for financial planners and investment advisors who focus more on investments using mutual funds. The CFS designation indicates advisors who are qualified to consult with clients on the advisability and costs of acquiring or retaining mutual funds in their investment portfolio. To qualify for the designation they must complete six ten-hour educational modules provided by the Institute of Business and Finance on: Investment Companies; Fixed-Rate & Variable Annuities; Wealth Management & Performance Measurement; The Planning Cycle; Strategies; and Asset Allocation.

## Certified Public Accountant (CPA)

Business accountants, some of who specialize in personal tax planning and preparation, hold this designation. To qualify for the CPA credential, they must pass a two-day examination administered by the American Institute of Certified Public Accountants (AICPA) and meet state licensing requirements relating to work experience and, in most states, special academic work.

## Certified Senior Advisor (CSA)

The Society of Certified Senior Advisors offers this designation. The Society is dedicated to providing initial and continuing education about key senior issues to professionals serving the senior market. This program provides participants with the tools they will need to communicate more successfully with their senior clients.

Advisors serving seniors need a credible source of information and access to training from recognized experts in senior issues. Senior citizens require advice and services from professionals who are thoroughly educated about issues that are important to seniors. Certification is awarded upon successful class completion (21 instruction hours) followed by an exam.

## Chartered Financial Analyst (CFA)

This designation is awarded by the Association for Investment Management and Research to investment professionals who have worked in the investment industry for three years and have passed each of three yearly exams involving security analysis and professional money management.

Many mutual fund managers and security analysts have this designation.

## Registered Investment Advisor (RIA)

This designation is neither an indication of expertise nor a license to buy or sell securities. It merely indicates that an individual, or his or her employing firm, was required under federal securities laws to file (for a nominal fee) with the Securities and Exchange Commission or a state securities commission for a license to dispense investment advice.

## Registered Representative

Securities brokers who have passed mandatory basic exams given by the National Association of Securities Dealers, a regulatory body for the securities industry, hold this designation. Securities brokers recommend investments for clients and execute client orders to buy and sell securities such as stocks, bonds, options, and mutual funds. In other words, it's a sales license to sell variable insurance and mutual funds.

# Understanding How You'll Be Charged

To judge the value of an advisor's services, it's important to understand how the advisor is compensated and what the total costs are that you're likely to pay.

Some costs may not be obvious—leading some advisors to promote their services as "free." Because almost nothing is free, it's prudent to always ask for a detailed explanation. If you don't fully understand the compensation arrangement, probe for more information until all the details are clear to you. A reputable advisor will be completely open and forthright when discussing compensation.

Always ask what an advisor charges, what the fees are based on, and how much your specific job is likely to cost. There's nothing indelicate about these questions; no professional will blush at them.

An advisor that is a Registered Investment Advisor under the Securities Exchange Commission is required to provide an ADV Part II Disclosure Statement prior to commencing services for each client.

Generally speaking, advisors are compensated through either fees or commissions.

**Commission-Only Advisors** earn their income by selling financial products such as insurance or certain types of mutual funds, or by executing securities trades.

**Fee-Only Advisors** earn their income through—as their name implies—fees (based, for example, on an hourly rate, a flat annual or single-project amount, or an annual percentage of assets).

But some advisors may receive income from both commissions and fees. (Some of these advisors may therefore say their compensation arrangement is "fee-based," not to be confused with "fee-only" arrangements.) Other advisors will reduce their fees by the amount of investment commissions they receive on products you buy from them. Advisors may even be compensated through non-cash sales incentives, such as free vacation trips.

Moreover, some compensation arrangements are subtle. Commissions on mutual fund purchases, for example, aren't always paid from a visible up-front sales charge (load). Instead, a fund may use a portion of operating expenses to pay commissions—which investors never see—to financial advisors. That's why you should review the expense ratio section of a fund's prospectus. There, the prospectus discloses whether the fund charges a 12b-1 fee, which it uses to recoup marketing and distribution costs, such as commission payments to advisors.

In the case of insurance products, you typically won't be told how much commission—also called a load—the agent or broker will receive from the premium payments you make—you'll have to ask!

There may be other types of expenses as well—commissions on the purchases and sales of stocks and bonds, for example, or legal fees for the drafting of documents in an estate plan. When you talk to potential advisors, therefore, ask about all the fees, sales charges, and other costs that you will have to pay, both directly and indirectly.

# Fee Arrangements

Fee arrangements will differ depending on whether an advisor works with you for a short period on a specific aspect of your financial situation, or works with you on an ongoing basis.

## One-Time Fee

A one-time fee can be useful for clients requiring a specific need such as a retirement plan, estate plan, or an investment review. An advisor can provide an analysis of your income and insurance needs based on your financial goals for your financial plan.

The costs of these analyses typically range from $500 to $7,500, although they could run higher or lower. (Such plans will have to be updated from time to time, especially if your circumstances change.)

## Ongoing Fees

Advisors can also provide ongoing planning and guidance, including managing money for you. Yearly fees, often based on a percentage of assets under management, may be as low as 0.75% ($750 per $100,000) or as high as 2% ($2,000 per $100,000) and may be based on a sliding scale (the more assets managed, the lower the percentage charged).

Keep the following points in mind as you evaluate advisor fees. Many advisors charge minimum fees, which may simply be too high when you consider the value of the assets you'll be asking the advisor to handle for you. Some advisors may even decline your business if your assets aren't high enough in value. And importantly, paying higher fees doesn't necessarily get you better service. A competent and trustworthy advisor whose fees are at the lower end of the scale may be as good as or better than a more expensive advisor.

# Commissions Versus Fees: Cautions

Commissions inevitably come with potential conflicts of interest. A commission-based advisor, for example, might be motivated to earn income by:

1. Recommending mutual funds or annuities with sales charges (loads) when equivalent funds that don't charge loads to advisors (no-load funds) are available.

2. Encouraging frequent buying and selling of securities to generate commissions (churning), even though a buy-and-hold approach is usually in an investor's long-term interest.

3. Recommending specific investment or insurance products over others primarily because of commission levels.

# Fees Versus Commissions: Advantages

Fee-only advisors are almost always preferable to commission-based advisors. Don't be thrown off by charges that seem so visible, and perhaps appear high at first glance.

The services of a fee-only advisor may actually be less expensive than "free" services when you compare the fees with the commissions you would pay on investments recommended by a commission-based advisor.

A fee-only advisor's investment recommendations are not influenced by compensation arrangements. The advisor has no incentive to encourage frequent trading of securities, for example, or to favor load funds over no-load funds.

Fee-only advisors typically provide clients with a wider variety of choices because recommendations aren't limited to firms offering attractive commissions on their investment products.

## A Closer Look At Certain Commissions

As with fees, you should look closely at commissions charged for products you would purchase through the advisor. This is especially true for investments because their costs directly reduce returns that end up in your pocket. Because mutual funds are so widely held, we illustrate the point in the following examples of fund investments.

## Up-Front Commissions

A typical initial sales charge for a load mutual fund is about 5%, or $5,000 per $100,000 invested. This means, for example, that only $95,000 of $100,000 earmarked for a load mutual fund would be put to work for you.

Many annuities pay the salesperson commissions up to 10%, or $10,000 per $100,000 invested. Before purchasing an annuity ask them what percent commission the insurance company pays.

## 12b-1 Fees

All mutual funds have operating expenses, but the expense ratios of some funds are higher than others—and one reason may be that marketing (or 12b-1) fees are included in operating expenses. A portion of these fees may be used to pay commissions to financial advisors. The average expense ratio for funds that charge a 12b-1 fee is 1.21% (or $1,210 per $100,000), compared with 0.62% ($620 per $100,000) for funds without these fees.

## Different Share Classes

Because most investors hate to pay up-front sales charges, many fund families now offer different classes of shares within a fund. Investors can choose a class that carries an up-front sales charge that reduces the amount initially invested. Or, investors can choose to invest the full amount and pay a higher annual expense ratio that is designed to provide commissions to the advisor year after year.

Do your homework first. Many fund companies now offer up to five different classes of funds (A, B, C, D, Y, etc.). Make sure the advisor fully explains which class of fund they recommend and their reason.

Of course, many advisors recommend no-load funds—such as Vanguard, Janus, Invesco, etc. that have low expense ratios. This choice allows you to keep more of a fund's returns. Indeed, the combined cost of the advisor's fee and a low-cost fund's operating expenses could quite easily be lower than the ongoing operating costs of the average mutual fund alone. So keep no-load and low-cost funds in mind as you discuss investment options with your advisor.

# Narrowing The Field

As you identify candidates, gather enough information about each one to develop a short list of advisors who you believe merit an in-depth review. This preliminary screening is typically done by telephone.

Confirm that the advisor can provide the services you want, including any that may require special expertise. Some financial planners, for example, may specialize in a particular client profile, such as family business owners, doctors, executives, or professional athletes. Ask for a description of typical clients to see whether their assets, income, and financial circumstances resemble yours.

Obtain personal and professional background information such as the advisor's education, years of experience, prior jobs, and credentials. Determine whether the advisor is compensated by fees or commissions, then review the fee or commission schedule, including any minimum fees. If an advisor earns both, ask about the percentage of income he or she earns from each source.

## Interviewing The Final Candidates

Interview your financial experts with the same care and attention you would if you were talking to a doctor who was preparing to perform major surgery on you.

Reviewing the results of your preliminary screening will produce a short list of candidates to interview in depth, either in person or by telephone. Note that most reputable advisors won't charge for this initial meeting and you won't incur any obligation, but be sure to ask.

An efficient way to conduct this phase is to gather the same information on all your candidates. Asking the same questions of everyone makes it easier to compare answers after you complete the interviews. Although you should ask for client recommendations, an advisor may say 'no' for confidentiality reasons.

Your goal at this stage of the search is to become more familiar with the advisors' services and the way they work with their clients, and to see how comfortable you are with each advisor's personal and professional style. And for advisors who provide investment advice or portfolio management, you'll want to be sure you thoroughly understand their investment approach.

For example, will recommendations be based on a forecast of the economy, of interest rates, or of the financial markets? This approach may result in frequent portfolio adjustments—and possibly higher costs and tax effects—as forecasts change.

An alternate approach draws on a client's goals and risk tolerance to determine the proportion of funds to invest in different asset classes, such as stocks and bonds. The idea is to develop a diversified portfolio that requires only occasional adjustments, regardless of the ups and downs in the financial markets.

A good broker or investment advisor will welcome your questions, no matter how basic. Financial professionals know that an educated client is an asset, not a liability. They would rather answer questions before you invest, than confront your anger and confusion later.

## Documents To Request

Be sure to get in writing a description of the exact services you will receive and the total costs. Also request samples of the advisor's work, such as a typical financial plan, investment performance report, statement, or client newsletter. You'll want to evaluate these documents for how user-friendly they are.

If the advisor you're considering is a registered investment advisor, another important document to get is Form ADV. The form ADV is a valuable disclosure tool.

Request a copy of Part I of form ADV from the advisor. In it, you'll find any court or regulatory actions the advisor has been involved in. Part II—or a brochure that summarizes the information in Part II—must be given to new clients and offered to continuing clients each year. The disclosures encompass compensation arrangements, types of clients and investments, affiliations with financial services companies (a clue to potential conflicts of interest), and the education and business background of key staff members.

The complete form is available from the Securities and Exchange Commission for advisors who manage $30 million or more, and from state regulators for advisors who manage less than $30 million.

Never be ashamed of asking tough but polite questions. The people you are questioning typically will have more respect for you, not less. If they refuse to give you answers, leave in a hurry. If you do not understand their answers, ask for clarification.

## Choosing Your Financial Advisor

It's time to compare the information you've gathered from your candidate interviews.

Your final task is to conduct a background check—no matter how distinguished an advisor may seem. A background check can verify credentials and uncover complaints or public disciplinary actions. Professional organizations and regulatory agencies that provide this information without charge are listed in the table below.

### Organizations to Contact for Background Checks

| Organization | Contact to ... | Phone Number and Web Address |
|---|---|---|
| Association for Investment Management and Research | Verify CFA designations | 1-800-247-8132 |
| Certified Financial Planner Board of Standards | Verify CFP credentials and disciplinary history | 1-888-237-6275 www.cfp-board.org |
| National Association of Securities Dealers Regulation, Inc. | Check credentials and disciplinary history of brokerage firms, brokers, and other registered representatives | 1-800-289-9999 www.nasdr.com |
| Securities and Exchange Commission (or your state's securities commission) | Get registered investment advisors' Form ADV | 1-202-942-8090 |
| Your state's securities commission, insurance commission, or board of accountancy | Check on licensing and disciplinary actions | — |

## How To Work With Your Advisor

If you'll be relying on the advisor for investment suggestions, be sure the two of you share the same investment philosophy. Ask your advisors to walk you through their fund or stock-selection process, and to thoroughly explain what would make them sell a stock or fund.

The advisor you choose should develop a clearly written plan for you. The plan should be based on your financial objectives, and it should include explanations you can understand. If the advisor is to provide ongoing advice, agree beforehand how frequently he or she will monitor your financial plan and provide status reports. And if the advisor is to manage your investments, be sure to evaluate results objectively.

## Getting Off On The Right Foot

Here are some ways you can ensure a successful relationship with your advisor from the start:

1.  Be open and honest about your financial situation.

2.  Include your spouse, and other appropriate people, in all discussions and decisions.

3.  Be sure your goals are realistic. This includes planning over an appropriate time period—for instance, not using stocks (a long-term investment vehicle) to finance an immediate goal (because of stocks' potential short-term volatility).

4.  Review progress toward your goals regularly (annually at a minimum) and whenever a significant change occurs in your life.

5.  Monitor investment performance regularly, but don't be put off by short-term results. Less-than-stellar investment returns may simply reflect the state of the financial markets, not poor performance by your advisor. Allow adequate time to fairly evaluate your advisor, generally one to two years.

6.  Understand the pros and cons of giving your advisor discretionary control over investment assets.

## Evaluating Performance Objectively

You should carefully review the periodic performance reports you receive from your advisor, but don't succumb to the temptation to alter your investment plans because of short-term market swings.

What counts is performance over the long term. In addition, you should:

1.  Expect personalized performance to be presented over several time periods.

2.  Compare investment results with relevant market indexes. A fund with a 20% gain could actually be under-performing if, for example, its benchmark appreciated by 30%. Similarly, a 5%

234

loss would be very good if the benchmark (usually the S&P 500 index) fell by 10%.

3.  Make sure that performance information provided on your statement is shown before and after all money management and transaction fees have been deducted.

## Considering A Discretionary Account?

Many people give their advisors the right to buy and sell securities for them in what's known as a "discretionary" account. They do so for two reasons: to take advantage of professional management and to reduce the time they have to spend on their investments.

You should understand, however, the exact nature of the authority you're granting to the advisor.

Give your advisor authority to trade securities for you only if:

1.  Your advisor is paid by fees. This avoids conflicts of interest.

2.  You monitor your advisor to make sure that he or she doesn't depart from the agreed-upon investment plan. A good advisor will alert you if there are significant changes and will explain them to you.

3.  The exact nature of the authority you're granting is clearly stated in a contract between you and the advisor. The discretionary authority should allow the advisor only to trade securities for you and not to withdraw funds.

## Closing Thoughts

As you work with your financial advisor, don't be afraid to ask questions—no matter how simple or tough they may seem. You're paying for the answers. And even if you've already paid for his or her services, don't be afraid to drop your advisor if you feel the relationship isn't working.

Remember: It's your money, and you're the boss.

# Chapter 13

---

# Final Thoughts

## The Million $ Mission

(We use this example when we teach high school students.)

Imagine you're sitting in a math class, minding your own business, when in walks a Bill Gates kind of guy—a very successful businessman. He's made it big, and now he has a job offer for you.

He doesn't give too many details except that it's dangerous and he would like to hire you for a month, and you'll have to miss school (darn!). He said you will get paid for this job. However, he said he will give a choice of two payment options—either:

1) One cent on the first day, two cents on the second day, and double your salary every day thereafter for the thirty days;

or

2) Exactly $1,000,000. (That's one million dollars!)

You jump up out of your seat at that. You've got your man, Bill, right here. I'll take that million. I'm out of here. And off you go on this dangerous million-dollar mission.

So how smart was this decision?

Did you make the best choice?

Sounds like it at first, but before we decide for sure, let's investigate the first payment option. Complete a table like this for the first week's work.

### Pay With First Option – Week 1

| Day # | Pay for that Day | Total Pay (In Dollars) |
|-------|------------------|------------------------|
| 1 | $0.01 | $0.01 |
| 2 | $0.02 | $0.03 |
| 3 | $0.04 | $0.07 |
| 4 | $0.08 | $0.15 |
| 5 | $0.16 | $0.31 |
| 6 | $0.32 | $0.63 |
| 7 | $0.64 | $1.27 |

So you've worked a whole week and only made $1.27. That's pretty awful, all right. There's no way to make a million in a month at this rate. Right? Let's check out the second week. Fill out the second table.

### Pay with First Option - Week 2

| Day # | Pay for that Day | Total Pay (In Dollars) |
|-------|------------------|------------------------|
| 8 | $1.28 | $2.55 |
| 9 | $2.56 | $5.11 |
| 10 | $5.12 | $10.23 |
| 11 | $10.24 | $20.47 |
| 12 | $20.48 | $40.95 |
| 13 | $40.96 | $81.91 |
| 14 | $81.92 | $163.83 |

Well, you would make a little more the second week, at least your over $100. But there's still a big difference between $163.83 and $1,000,000. Want to see the third week?

### Pay with First Option - Week 3

| Day # | Pay for that Day | Total Pay (In Dollars) |
|-------|------------------|------------------------|
| 15 | $163.84 | $327.67 |
| 16 | $327.68 | $655.35 |
| 17 | $655.36 | $1,310.71 |
| 18 | $1,310.72 | $2,621.43 |
| 19 | $2,621.44 | $5,242.87 |
| 20 | $5,242.88 | $10,485.75 |
| 21 | $10,485.76 | $20,971.51 |

We're getting into some serious money here now, over $20,000, but still nowhere even close to a million. And there are only 10 days left. So it looks like the million dollars is the best deal. Of course, we suspected that all along.

### Pay with First Option - Week 4

| Day # | Pay for that Day | Total Pay (In Dollars) |
|-------|------------------|------------------------|
| 22 | $20,971.51 | $41,943.03 |
| 23 | $41,943.04 | $83,886.07 |
| 24 | $83,886.08 | $167,772.15 |
| 25 | $167,772.16 | $335,544.31 |
| 26 | $335,544.32 | $671,088.63 |
| 27 | $671,088.64 | $1,342,177.27 |
| 28 | $1,342,177.28 | $2,684,354.55 |

Hold it! Look what has happened. What's going on here? We went from $21,000 to over a million in 6 days. This can't be right. Let me check the calculations. No, I can't find any mistakes. This is amazing. Look how fast this pay is growing. Let's keep going. I can't wait to see what the total will be.

### Pay with First Option

| Day # | Pay for that Day | Total Pay (In Dollars) |
|-------|------------------|------------------------|
| 29 | $2,684,354.56 | $5,368,709.11 |
| 30 | $5,368,709.12 | $10,737,418.23 |

In 30 days, it increases from 1 penny to over 10 million dollars. That is absolutely amazing.

Oh, well, at least you have a million dollars!

Even though this book is about money and how to manage it, its not everything in life. The statement below is food for thought.

MONEY

| | |
|---|---|
| Money can buy a bed | But not sleep. |
| Money can buy you a house | But not a home. |
| It can buy you a clock | But not time. |
| It can buy you a book | But not knowledge. |
| It can buy you a position | But not respect. |
| It can buy you medicine | But not health. |
| It can buy you blood | But not life. |
| It can buy you sex | But not love. |

So you see, money isn't everything. The best things in life can't be bought, and often we destroy ourselves trying!

# Glossary

## [ A ]

### AARP
The American Association of Retired Persons. This large organization also offers great deals and discounts for senior members.

### ABA
The American Bankers Association. The letters also represent the American Bar Association.

### A-B Trusts
Before the adoption of the unlimited marital deduction and while the marital deduction was limited to 50% of an individual's adjusted gross estate, it was common to create two trusts for the benefit of an individual's spouse, one which qualified for the marital deduction and one which did not. These were frequently referred to as A-B Trusts.

### Abandon
Refers to the decision not to exercise an option or, sometimes, a clause. It may also refer to the intentional or unintentional lack of use, maintenance, or affirmation process about assets. These assets may include securities, bank accounts, refunds, trademarks, and so on. In such cases the property can go to a jurisdiction such as a state or federal government.

### ACATS
The Automated Customer Account Transfer Service. This usually happens when an account is transferred between brokerage houses.

### Accelerated Depreciation
An accounting technique which provides larger than straight-line depreciation amounts in the early years and smaller than straight-line depreciation amounts in the later years.

## Account Executive

The party who acts as an agent for his customer. The broker receives a commission as compensation. This person may also participate in spreads or other fees which generate revenue for the firm. This person is also known as an Associated Person (AP), Investment Executive (IE), Registered Representative (RR), Registered Customer Support Person or Securities Salesman. Brokers are required to be licensed according to product lines and states when required.

## Accrued Interest

The amount of interest that has accumulated since the last coupon interest payment for a bond. It is the amount of interest to which the holder is entitled but is not due until the payment date. The buyer pays the seller of the bond the accrued interest.

## Accumulated Depreciation

The amount of depreciation already taken against an asset.

Assume that a computer costs $6,000 and has an expected life of five years and no residual value. After three years the accumulated depreciation would be $3,600 (3 x $1,200 annual depreciation).

## Accumulation

Refers to buying, often coincident with market bottoms or consolidations. It also refers to purchases by insiders, control people, or major investors.

## ACH

Automated Clearing House is a secure payment transfer system that connects all U.S. financial institutions. The ACH network acts as the central clearing facility for all Electronic Fund Transfer (EFT) transactions that occur nationwide, representing a crucial link in the national banking system. It is here that payments linger in something akin to a holding pattern while awaiting clearance for their final banking destination. Scores of financial institutions transmit or receive ACH entries through ACH operators such as the American Clearing House Association, the Federal Reserve, the Electronic Payments Network, and Visa.

## Acid Test Ratio

This is another term to describe the Quick Asset Ratio. It measures an organization's liquidity by adjusting current assets by subtracting inventories and then dividing by the current liabilities.

## Actual Hedging

The risk management of a position when a hedger has a bona fide long or short actual position and is involved in an offsetting transaction. This offset is usually in the derivatives market.

## Actual or Observed

The real or reported price, data, or event. It compares to the theoretical, implied or hypothetical price, data, or event. The actual or observed data describe or define the underlying process or condition.

## Actuals

The real or underlying asset for a derivative product or commodity market.

## Adjustable Rate Mortgage (ARM)

A loan which has a coupon or interest rate that is subject to change on predetermined reset dates. These loans use interest rate indices as the benchmark rate. Adjustable Rate Mortgages come in many variations. Typically, the reset dates recur every one, three, or five years; but there are other periods used as well. These loans may have cap and floor features that constrain each reset change in interest rates. There may also be lifetime cap and floor features. Adjustable Rate Mortgages may be strictly amortizing though some have negative amortization features.

## ADP

The Alternative Delivery Procedure at the New York Mercantile Exchange. It provides for longs and shorts to make and take delivery under terms which differ from those specified as good delivery for the contract. These transactions can occur at any time during a delivery period.

## Ad Valorem Tax

A tax placed on real property. This is a primary revenue source for many municipalities.

## Advanced Refunding

The technique of replacing one bond issue by another. This typically occurs when a municipality can borrow at more favorable terms than the outstanding issue. The new issue's proceeds are used to purchase government obligations which are held in escrow. The income and/or appreciation of these government securities is then used to service the outstanding debt. The escrow may be held until the first call date or maturity of the initial bond issue. If the escrowed funds retire the original issue at the first call date then the issue is pre-refunded. This retirement and replacement process of debt is also known as defeasance.

## Advance-Decline (A/D) Line
A measurement of market breadth. It is calculated by subtracting the number of stocks that decline in price over a given period (weekly or daily) from the number that advance, and accumulating the differences. When advancing issues outnumber declining issues, the A/D line moves upward. Conversely, if the majority of issues fall in price the line trends downward. The basic calculation should be adjusted slightly to facilitate historical comparability. Each week (assuming a weekly A/D line) divide the difference of advances minus declines by the total number of issues changing in price. For example, if there were 6,000 advancers and 4,000 decliners the ratio would be (6,000-4,000)/10,000, or 0.20. Then accumulate the weekly ratio readings. Without this adjustment, the A/D line exhibits a bullish bias given the long-term increase in the number of issues traded. When this adjusted A/D line is in a uptrend, the odds are that stocks are in a bull market. If the adjusted A/D line is falling, the likelihood of a major downtrend increases. The A/D line is in an established uptrend when the current weekly figure is above the average A/D line reading of the last 52 weeks. A downtrend is established when the current A/D line reading is below the average A/D line reading of the last 52 weeks.

## Aftermarket
Trading in the secondary market following a new securities issuance.

## Against Actuals
A commodity market transaction whereby futures are exchanged or transferred against a cash position.

## Agency Bonds
A security issued by a government organization but not the treasury. These organizations include: the Federal Home Loan Mortgage Corporation (FHLMC or Freddie Mac), the Federal National Mortgage Association (FNMA or Fannie Mae), and the Government National Mortgage Association (GNMA or Ginnie Mae).

## Agent
A party who acts on the behalf of another. This occurs when a broker executes a trade for the benefit of the customer. Here, the broker receives a commission. This compares to a dealer transaction.

## AGI

Adjusted Gross Income, which is your gross, or total, income from taxable sources minus certain deductions, such as medical expenses, alimony and IRA contributions.

## Aging

The concept which assumes that newly-issued mortgages tend to prepay slower than mortgages which are older or seasoned. This aging refers to the underlying collateral and not the securities created upon that collateral.

## AICPA

The American Institute of Certified Public Accountants.

## Alaska Trusts

These trusts, available in certain states, combine the benefits of multigenerational planning with an attempt at protection from the grantor's creditors. They have risks which must be carefully considered.

## Alpha

A measure of the incremental reward (or loss) that an investor gained in relation to the market. Typically, this is measured as performance of a selected portfolio relative to a market benchmark. An enhanced S&P 500 portfolio might have an alpha of .25, which means that the pickup was .25% or a quarter point better than the standard.

## Alternative Investments

Usually investments other than mutual funds, certificates of deposit, or direct investments in equities and bonds. Some of these alternatives are: art, collectibles, commodities, commodity funds, commodity pools, derivatives, foreign exchange, hedge funds, oil and gas, precious metals, and real estate ventures.

## American Depositary Receipt (ADR)

A tool for allowing American investors to buy shares of foreign-based corporations in the U.S. rather than in overseas markets. ADRs are receipts for the shares of a foreign-based corporation held in the vault of a U.S. bank which entitles the shareholders to all dividends and capital gains. ADS (American Depository Share—a term often used interchangeably with ADR) is the share representing the underlying ordinary share which trades in the issuer's home market. Technically, ADS is the instrument which actually trades, while ADR is the certificate that represents a number of ADSs.

## American Stock Exchange (AMEX)

The second-largest floor-based stock exchange in the US after the New York Stock Exchange (NYSE). The (AMEX) operates a central auction market in stocks and derivatives, including options on many NYSE-traded and over-the-counter stocks.

Although AMEX merged with the electronic NASDAQ Stock Market Group, the exchange continues to operate independently.

## Amex Index

Composite index of shares listed on the American Stock Exchange.

## Amortization

The periodic pay-down of principal. This is a common feature of most mortgages. Amortize also refers to the accounting write-down or reduction in an intangible asset. This creates a charge against income. Amortization can also refer to the reduction in the cost basis of a bond purchased at a premium to par. Sometimes, amortization is used as a synonym for depreciation or other write down of an asset or liability. In the later capacity it tends to apply to intangible assets.

## Annual Report

The yearly statement of financial condition for a financial organization. It includes balance sheet and income statement items. It may also include a descriptive synopsis of organizational highlights.

By law, each publicly-held corporation must provide its shareholders with an annual report showing its income and balance sheet. In most cases, it contains not only financial details but a message from the chairman, a description of the company's operations, and an overview of its achievements.

Most annual reports serve as marketing pieces. Copies are generally available from the company or they may appear on the company's website. The company's 10-k report is a more comprehensive look at its finances.

## Annuitant

The party receiving annuity payments. Many times the annuitant is also the owner of the policy, but not always.

## Annuity

An insurance product which comes in two basic forms: fixed and variable. The fixed version can make a lump sum or periodic lifetime payments to the annuitant. The variable version has a separate account attached to the annuity contract. This type of contract is considered a security because it is dependent on equities and its total value is subject to fluctuate due to market risk.

There are many annuity varieties. Some are: Annuity Certain, Annuity Due, Deferred Annuity, Fixed Annuity, Life Annuity, Ordinary Annuity, Perpetuity, and Variable Annuity.

## Anticipatory Hedging
Refers to the placement of a hedge prior to placement of the actual position. Sometimes this occurs when a firm knows that it will receive investment funds later that day or week and prefers to hedge numerous potential risks at the earlier date. Similarly, a commodity producer may prefer to hedge prior to the harvest of a crop, production of an energy product, or processing a raw material into a deliverable lot.

## Appraisal
An expert evaluation of the current, probable market value of a property. It is not necessarily the market value or transaction price.

## APR
The Annual Percentage Rate of Interest.

## APY
The Annual Percentage Yield of Interest.

## Arbitrage
The simultaneous purchase of a security at a lower price in one market and selling it at a higher price in another to make a profit on the spread between the prices. Although the price difference may be very small, the arbitrageurs trade large amounts at a time so they can make a sizeable profit.

## Arbitration
A process to resolve disputes for securities and futures markets. It can involve broker/dealers, clients, and employees of broker/dealers. There are different forums such as the NASD and NYSE.

## Arbitration Panel
The group of Arbitrators selected to resolve a dispute.

## Arbitrator

A person who is selected to resolve a dispute in the financial industry. Usually there are three arbitrators on a panel. The composition of the arbitrators is from a pool of candidates viewed either as "Public" or "Industry."

## Arms Index

Also known as the short-term trading index. It is the average volume of declining issues divided by the average volume of advancing issues.

## Ask

The stock price requested, at the minimum, for an order to be acceptable and executed for the seller.

## Assessed Value

The taxable basis of a property. It is imposed by the municipality. Often it is at a fraction of the market value. Equally as important is the rate of taxation on that assessed value. Assessed values may differ substantially from market values and appraised values.

## Asset and Liability Management

The process for financial institutions and corporations to adjust their funding and usage of funds. Some approaches are the Bucket, GAP, Hedging, Matched Book, Matched Funding, Financial Swaps, and Structured Products. With the lowering of various insurance, investment and commercial banking barriers, the definition is now more inclusive. Previously, it tended to be reserved for non-investment banking and brokerage operations. Broker/dealer institutions tended to describe their hedging activities as risk management.

## Asset Backed Securities

A security backed by notes or receivables against assets other than real estate. Some examples are autos, credit cards, and royalties.

## Assets

Properties owned by or are due to a person or organization. Assets are typically viewed in three categories: Current, Fixed or Long-term, and Intangible.

## Associated Person

The registered person who handles orders in the commodities and futures business. Here, registration is at the National Level.

## ATM

An Automated Teller Machine. It also refers to an At-the-Money option (see below).

## At-The-Money

An option which has an exercise or strike price that is the same as the underlying instrument at current market valuations.

## Authorized Shares

The number of shares that a corporation may issue. They represent the maximum shares that can be outstanding.

## Automatic Exercise

Occurs after an option expires. Each exchange and its clearinghouse has rules which govern this exercise. There are minimum in-the-money requirements. A holder of an option must inform the clearinghouse not to automatically exercise an option. These instructions not to exercise may be due to relatively high transaction costs, increases in position limits, or unacceptable alterations in position profiles. Also, after hours trading indications may suggest dramatically different prices than those used to determine the automatic exercise in-the-money amounts.

## Averaging Down

Buying shares of the same security at successively lower prices in order to reduce the average purchasing price.

## Await Instructions

The designation for a special pairing or matching of transactions. It also refers to additional handling instructions for a transaction for a specific account. These instructions supercede the standard or default instructions.

## Award

The decision of an Arbitration Panel.

# [ B ]

## Balance Sheet

The summary of a company's assets, liabilities, and shareholders' equity. Since balance sheets do not list items at their current monetary value, they may overstate or understate the real value of certain corporate assets and liabilities. Also called the statement of financial condition.

## Basis Point

One one-hundredth of one percent (1/100 of 1%). For example, one hundred basis points equals 1%. Basis point is used for investment costs, fees, and performance.

## Bearer Bond

A certificate that states the security's par value and rate at which its interest will be paid. A bearer bond isn't registered, and there's no record of ownership, which means it can be sold or redeemed by the person who holds it.

## Bear Market

An extended period of general price declines in the financial markets, when prices fall by 15% or more. A bear market in stocks occurs when investors sell off shares because they anticipate worsening economic conditions and falling prices.

## Benchmark

An index or average whose movement is considered a general indicator of the direction of the overall market, against which investors and financial professionals often gauge their market expectations and judge the performance of individual stocks or market sectors. For example, the Standard and Poor's 500-stock Index (S&P 500) and the Dow Jones Industrial Average (DJIA) are the most widely followed benchmarks, or indicators of the US market.

## Beta

A measure of an investment's relative volatility. The higher the beta, the more sharply the value of the investment can be expected to fluctuate in relation to a market index.

## Big Board

The nickname of the New York Stock Exchange.

## Blind Trust

A trust, often created by a politician after election to office, pursuant to which certain assets of the grantor are managed by one or more trustees without the grantor being advised of (or having any continued input as to) what is taking place. The assets, however, are managed for the benefit of the grantor of the trust.

## Block Trade

A trade of 10,000 shares of stock or more.

## Blue Chip Stocks

Nationally known companies which usually have large-capitalization and long records of profitable growth and dividend payments. Examples include General Motors, 3M, Coca Cola, and IBM. Blue chip stocks are generally considered less risky than small-cap companies but have less potential for large short-term gains.

## Blue Sky Laws

State regulations covering the offering and sale of securities within state boundaries.

## Book-To-Bill Ratio

A measure of sales trends particularly watched in the semiconductor industry. A number over 1.0 indicates an expanding market, while a number below 1.0 indicates a contracting market. A ratio of 1.10 means that for every $100 of products shipped, $110 of new orders was received. However, as with every ratio, it is important to look at the underlying numbers for trends which a ratio might conceal.

## Book Value

Often used as an indicator for selecting undervalued stocks. It is also used to determine the ultimate value of securities in a liquidation. Book value is calculated by the following: total assets minus intangible assets (goodwill, patents etc) minus any long-term liabilities = total net assets. This figure, divided by the number of shares of preferred and/or common stock, gives the Net Asset Value—or Book Value—per share of preferred or common stock.

## Breadth Of The Market

The percentage of stocks participating in a particular market move. If two-thirds of the stocks listed on an exchange rise during a given trading day, it is generally considered good breadth. Analysts look to this as an indicator that the trend is probably more significant and longer-lasting than one with limited breadth.

## Breakout

The advance of a stock price above a resistance level, or the fall of a stock price below a support level. If a stock experiences a breakout on heavy volume, it indicates to market technicians that the stock is about to engage in a major price move in the direction of the breakout.

## Bull Market

An extended period of generally rising prices in an individual item (a stock), group of items (an industry group), or the market as a whole.

## Bypass Trust

This trust is customarily designed to receive the maximum amount which can pass free of Federal estate tax upon the death of the first of two spouses to die. It has numerous variations. Frequently the terms of the trust provide that all of its income will be payable to the surviving spouse for life, with the assets then passing to, or in trust for, one or more others upon the surviving spouse's death.

# [ C ]

## Call

An issuer's right to redeem bonds it has sold before the date they mature. Some bonds are sold with call protection. This can be useful when interest rates are dropping thus allowing the holder to keep the higher bonds when others are selling at lower rates.

## Call Option

An option that permits the owner (option holder) to purchase a specific asset at a predetermined price until a certain date.

## Capital Appreciation

An increase in an asset's fair market value. If a stock increases from $10 a share to $20 a share, it shows capital appreciation.

## Capitalization

A term usually referring to Market Capitalization which is the value of a company as determined by the most recent stock price multiplied by the number of shares outstanding.

## Capital Gains

Difference between the price at which a financial asset is sold and its original cost (assuming the price has gone up). Long-term capital gains are taxed at a lower rate than your income.

## Cash Flow

Cash flow is an important aspect of a company's performance. It is an analysis of all the changes affecting cash in the categories of operations, investments, and financing. A positive cash flow means that more cash is taken in than is paid out, and the opposite is a negative cash flow. A company might be forced into bankruptcy, even with assets well in excess of liabilities, if it does not have enough cash to meet current obligations.

## Cemetery Trust

Typically a trust for the purpose of maintaining one or more graves or grave sites in a cemetery.

## Charitable Lead Trust

A trust pursuant to which a specified sum (expressed as a fixed percentage of the value of the trust at inception [in effect, an annuity] or as a fixed percentage of the value of the net assets of the trust, calculated annually) is to be paid to a charity at least annually, for a specified period, with the remainder then passing to one or more individuals. If an annuity is utilized, it is a Charitable Lead Annuity Trust (a CLAT); if a percentage of the net assets valued annually is utilized, the trust is a Charitable Lead Unitrust (a CLUT). Such trusts may save estate, gift, and income taxes.

## Charitable Remainder Trust

A trust pursuant to which one or more individuals receive, at least annually, either a sum equal to a fixed percentage of the assets valued at the trust's inception (in effect, an annuity) or a sum equal to a fixed percentage of the net assets of the trust valued annually, either for a set number of years or for one or more lifetimes. If an annuity is utilized, the trust is a Charitable Remainder Annuity Trust (a CRAT); if a percentage of the net assets valued annually is utilized, the trust is a Charitable Remainder Unitrust (a CRUT). Such trusts may save estate, gift, income, and/or capital gains taxes.

## Chicago Board of Trade (CBT)

An exchange that trades grains, bonds, and short-term interest rates.

## Chicago Mercantile Exchange (CME)

An exchange that trades livestock, currencies, and stock index futures.

## Clifford Trust

This type of trust, no longer being created (although some previously created ones still exist), provided that its assets were to be held for a period of at least ten years, with the income payable to a person other than the grantor, and with the assets reverting to the grantor at the end of the term of the trust. Its purpose was to shift income and reduce income tax liability. Tax law changes have eliminated its usefulness.

## Closed-End Mutual Fund

A closed-end mutual fund raises capital only once by issuing a fixed number of shares. They are traded on an exchange, and their prices fluctuate based on supply and demand as well as on changes in the value of their underlying holdings.

## Commercial Paper
Issued by banks and corporations to help meet their immediate needs for cash. Commercial paper is an unsecured short-term debt instrument.

## Commission
Securities brokers and other sales agents charge a commission, which is a sales charge on each transaction. A mutual fund can pay the agent as much as 5½ % commission. The incentive for commissioned brokers is to trade your account often.

A fee-only advisor, on the other hand, usually charges a percentage of assets under management. The fee-only advisor isn't compensated for transactions, instead they are motivated to manage and grow the account.

## Commodity
Are bulk goods and raw materials, such as livestock, grains, oil, coffee, sugar, metals, that are used to produce consumer products. The term also describes financial products, such as currency or stock and bond indexes, that are the raw materials of trade.

Commodities are bought and sold on the cash market, and they are traded on the futures exchanges in the form of futures contracts.

## Common Stock
Often called Capital Stock, it is units of ownership in a public corporation which typically entitles the holder to vote on the selection of directors and receive dividends. In the event of a liquidation, claims of secured and unsecured creditors, and bond and preferred stock holders take precedence over common stock holders.

## Constructive Trust
This trust is created by law. No trust documents are involved. If a person receives assets he or she should not have received he or she may be deemed by law to be holding those assets for someone else in a Constructive Trust.

## Consumer Price Index
The Consumer Price Index, or CPI, measures the monthly change in prices of goods and services that the spending habits of the average American. The changes are measured against an index established in 1982.

The CPI is used as a benchmark to measure inflation in order to adjust increases in Social Security benefits.

## Contingent Trust
This trust which comes into being only in the event a contingency occurs. For example, a document may provide that if any assets are distributable to a person under the age of 21 years, those assets are held in a Contingent Trust for the benefit of that person until that person attains 21 years of age.

## Cost Of Goods Sold
The expenses directly associated with the production of goods or services the company sells (such as material, labor, and overhead) excluding depreciation, depletion, and amortization.

## Credit Shelter Trust
A trust customarily designed to receive the maximum amount that can pass free of Federal estate tax upon the death of the first of two spouses to die. It has numerous variations. Frequently the terms of the trust provide that all of its income will be payable to the surviving spouse for life, with the assets then passing to, or in trust for, one or more others upon the surviving spouse's death.

## Crummey Trust
A trust which permits one or more individuals to withdraw a limited amount from the assets added to the trust in a specified manner during a specified period. Its purpose is to avoid gift taxes with respect to assets placed in the trust. Insurance Trusts are often designed as Crummey Trusts.

## Current Yield
A measure of an investor's return on a bond calculated by dividing the annual interest on the bond by the market price. It is the actual income rate or the yield to maturity as opposed to the coupon rate (the two would be the same if a bond was purchased at par). For example, a 10% (coupon rate) bond with a face value (par) of $1,000 is bought at a market price of $800. The annual income on the bond is $100, but since $800 was paid for the bond, the current yield is $100 divided by $800 or 12½%.

# [ D ]

## Debenture
An unsecured bond issued usually by large corporations which are backed by the corporation's reputation rather than secured by collateral.

## Debt-To-Asset Ratio
A coverage ratio that measures the amount of debt a company has in relation to its assets. It is calculated by dividing total debt by total assets. The amount of debt to asset may vary from industry to industry and should be compared as such.

## Debt-To-Equity Ratio
A measurement of financial leverage—the use of borrowed money to enhance the return on owner's equity. It is calculated by long-term debt divided by common stockholders equity. The higher the ratio, the greater the leverage.

## Default
Failure to pay back a debt.

## Defective Grantor Trust
A type of trust purposely made "defective" so as to be a Grantor Trust for income tax purposes but an Irrevocable Trust for estate and gift tax purposes. It may result in increased tax savings.

## Defined Benefit Plan
A defined benefit plan is also known as a pension which provides income for retirees. The amount you receive usually depends on age when you retire, final salary, and the numbers of years of employment. Today most employers offer defined contribution plans.

## Delaware Business Trust
Similar to a family limited partnership or limited liability company, as opposed to a traditional trust. A Delaware Business Trust is a way to hold and invest assets, possibly including life insurance, with greater flexibility than most trusts allow, with the grantor of the trust retaining far more control than the tax laws permit as to traditional trusts, and with opportunities for limited liability, creditor protection, and valuation discounts.

## Depreciation

An accounting method to amortize fixed assets, such as plant and equipment, so as to allocate the cost over their depreciable life. Depreciation reduces taxable income but does not reduce cash. The most common methods are accelerated depreciation and straight-line depreciation.

## Derivative

Are hybrid investments such as futures contracts, options, and mortgage-backed securities, whose value is based on the value of an underlying investment. For example, the changing value of natural gas futures contract depends on the upward or downward movement of natural gas prices.

Certain investors, called hedgers, are interested in the underlying investment. For example, a baking company might buy wheat futures to help estimate the cost of producing its bread in the months to come.

## Devaluation

The lowering of the value of a country's currency relative to gold and/or the currencies of other nations. When a currency is devalued, imported goods become more expensive, while its exports become less expensive.

## Disclaimer Trust

This trust is meant to receive property that is disclaimed (renounced) by a beneficiary. For example, if a husband writes a will and wants to provide that all of his assets are to benefit his wife, but he is not sure whether he has sufficient assets so he would want to utilize a Credit Shelter Trust, he may provide in his will that any assets disclaimed by his wife pass to a trust for her benefit. This gives his wife the option of either taking the assets outright or disclaiming some, such as the maximum amount that can pass free of Federal estate tax, with the disclaimed assets to pass into the Disclaimer Trust from which the surviving spouse herself may receive the net income. Note that such an arrangement is only possible with respect to a spouse.

## Discount Rate

The interest rate that the Federal Reserve charges member banks for loans, using government securities as collateral. This provides a floor for interest rates since banks set their loan rates a notch above the discount rate. The discount rate is also used in determining the present value of future cash flows.

## Discretionary Order
A market order that allows the broker to decide when to trade a security.


## Discretionary Trust
Any trust in which the trustees have discretion to distribute (or not distribute) income and/or principal to or among one or more beneficiaries. The discretion may apply to income, principal, or both. The trustees may have the right to give or not give income or principal to a single beneficiary, or to distribute some or all of the income or principal among members of a group, excluding one or more members if desired.


## Dividends
A distribution of a company's earnings to shareholders, prorated by class of security and usually paid in the form of cash or stock. The amount is decided by the Board of Directors and is usually paid quarterly.


## Dow Jones Composite Average
Tracks the stock performance of the 65 stocks which comprise the three averages below: Industrial, Transportation, and Utility.


## Dow Jones Industrial Average
The best known of all U.S. stock indices, the Dow as it is often called, contains 30 stocks that trade on the NYSE (New York Stock Exchange) and is a general indicator of how shares of the largest U.S. companies are trading.


## Dow Jones Transportation Average
The DJIA monitors the stock performance of 20 airlines, railroads, and trucking companies.


## Dow Jones Utility Average
The DJUA monitors the stock performance of 15 gas, electric, and power companies.


## Dry Trust
This trust has no assets. A Dry Trust is usually created either to receive assets upon the death of an individual, such as a pour-over under the individual's will, or to receive assets transferred to the trust via a power of attorney in the event of an individual's incapacity.

## Dynasty Trust

This is a name customarily used for a Generation-Skipping Trust that continues for an extended period of time, such as for multiple generations, limited only by the applicable Rule Against Perpetuities, if any. In certain states such a trust may run for a very extended period of time. Its purpose is to avoid estate taxation for several generations, and to provide for an individual's descendants (or equivalent) for a very long period.

## [ E ]

### Earnings

A generalized term referring to corporate profits. Profits can be calculated in different ways depending upon the industry and accounting practices. Earnings is one of the frequently used measures of a company's financial condition. It is commonly used to determine the risk/reward profile of a given security—the ratio of stock price to earnings (see P/E Ratio).

### Earnings per Share

The dollars of profit generated for each share of common stock. A company that earned $1 million last year and has 1 million shares outstanding would report earnings per share of $1.00. The figure is calculated after paying preferred shareholders, bond holders, and taxes.

### Earnings Report

An official quarterly or annual financial document published by a public company, showing earnings, expenses, and net profit. Also called income statement or profit and loss statement.

### EBIT

Earnings Before Interest and Taxes.

### EBITDA

Earnings Before Interest, Taxes, Depreciation, and Amortization.

### Education IRA

A relatively new type of tax-deferred financial planning vehicle, which enables a person to save money for future education-related expenses.

## Education Trust

A trust for a minor (actually a person under the age of 21 years), designed to receive the annual gift tax exclusion for gifts on behalf of the minor. Education Trusts are an alternative to the use of the Uniform Gifts (or Transfers) to Minors Act and are often a better way of planning with respect to gifts to children, particularly if under the age of 14 years, whose parents are in a high income tax bracket. An Education Trust can have provisions allowing more flexibility than is available under the Uniform Gifts (or Transfers) to Minors Act. Variations of this trust permit the trust to continue beyond the date on which the beneficiary attains the age of 21 years.

## Effective Date

In the securities industry, the date when an offering filed with the Securities and Exchange Commission may commence—usually 20 days after the filing of the registration statement.

## Efficient Portfolio

A portfolio that provides the greatest expected return for a given level of risk, or equivalently, the lowest risk for a given expected return.

## Employee Stock Ownership Plan (ESOP)

A trust established by a corporation for the allocation of some of its stock to its employees over time, intended to motivate employees, and often providing tax benefits to the company.

## Employee Stock Purchase Plan (ESPP)

A program that allows employees to purchase company stock at a discount to its fair market value.

## Estate Trust

This type of Marital Deduction Trust provides that, upon the death of the surviving spouse, the assets in the trust, or at least the accumulated income of the trust, are payable to his or her estate.

## Eurodollars

Dollar-denominated deposits in banks outside the United States.

# [ F ]

## Face Value

The value of a bond which appears on the face of the bond, unless the value is otherwise specified by the issuing company. Face value is ordinarily the amount the issuing company promises to pay at maturity.

Face value is not an indication of market value. Sometimes referred to as par value.

## Fannie Mae (Federal National Mortgage Association)
Publicly-owned, Government-sponsored corporation, established in 1938 to purchase both government-backed and conventional mortgages from lenders and securitize them. Its objective is to increase the affordability of home mortgage funds for low to middle income home buyers. It is the largest source of home mortgage funds in the U.S. and a large issuer of debt securities which are used to finance its activities. Equity shares of Fannie Mae trade on the NYSE.

## Federal Home Loan Mortgage Corp (FHLMC or Freddie Mac)
Government-chartered corporation which buys qualified mortgage loans from the financial institutions that originate them, securitizes the loans, and distributes the securities through the dealer community. The securities are not backed by the U.S. Government. The market value of these securities prior to maturity is not guaranteed and will fluctuate.

## Federal Funds Rate
The interest rate banks charge on overnight loans to other banks in need of funds in order to meet reserve requirements. The rate is set by the Federal Reserve.

## Financial Futures
Legally binding agreements to buy or sell financial instruments at a future date (for example, stocks, treasury bonds, foreign currency).

## Fixed Exchange Rate
A set rate of exchange between currencies determined by agreement.

## Floating Exchange Rate
Rates determined by the response of the currencies to market forces.

## Fundamental Research
Analysis of industries and companies based on such factors as sales, assets, earnings, products or services, markets, and management. As applied to the economy, fundamental research includes consideration of gross national product, interest rates, unemployment, inventories, savings, etc.

## Futures Contract
An agreement to buy or sell a specific amount of a commodity or financial instrument at a particular price on a stipulated date. The price is

established between the buyer and seller on the floor of an exchange. A contract obligates the buyer to purchase an underlying commodity and the seller to sell it, unless the contract is sold to another before the settlement date. This contrasts with options trading, in which the option buyer may choose whether or not to exercise the option by the exercise date.

# [ G ]

## General Mortgage Bond
A bond secured by a blanket mortgage on the company's property but may be outranked by one or more other mortgages.

## Generation-Skipping Trust (GST Trust)
This trust either skips over an entire generation or provides for members of more than one generation—normally geared to utilize the exemption from the tax on generation-skipping transfers. Under Federal law this exemption may be as much as $1,000,000 per trust creator (not per trust and not per grandchild).

## Good 'Til Canceled (GTC) or Open Order
An order to buy or sell that remains in effect until it is either executed or canceled.

## Goodwill
In accounting, goodwill is any advantage, such as brand names, that enables a business to earn higher profits than its competitors.

## Grantor Retained Annuity Trust (GRAT)
An irrevocable trust created by an individual (the grantor) which provides for the payment to the grantor, at least annually, of a sum equal to a fixed percentage of the value of the assets placed in the trust (in effect, an annuity) for a fixed period of time, or until the grantor's death, if sooner. Upon its termination, the balance in the trust usually passes to the grantor's estate if the grantor does not survive the term of the trust, or to (or in trust for) another individual(s) if the grantor survives the term of the trust.

Its purpose is to reduce gift and estate taxes. It serves little, if any, tax purpose if the grantor dies during the term of the trust. Note, also, that it does not yield a step-up in basis of the assets of the trust if the trust terminates during the grantor's lifetime, and it is possible for the gift tax and resulting capital gains tax (assuming the assets are then sold) to exceed the tax saving resulting from the creation of the trust.

## Grantor Retained Income Trust (GRIT)

This trust, now only used in limited situations, is an irrevocable trust where the grantor retains the right to income for a fixed period of years geared to end before the grantor's death. Upon termination of the trust, the assets in the trust pass to another. The main purpose of such a trust is to reduce the gift tax value of the transfer, because the value today of a gift of an asset in the future is less than the present value of that asset. Grantor Retained Income Trusts are now used for gifts to nonimmediate family members (e.g., nieces or nephews). Such a trust serves little or no tax purpose if the grantor dies before it terminates.

## Grantor Retained Unitrust (GRUT)

Very similar to a Grantor Retained Annuity Trust (see above), except that, rather than a fixed sum (a percentage of the assets of the trust valued at the creation of the trust), the grantor is to receive an annual (or more frequent) payment equal to a fixed percentage of the value of the net assets of the trust valued annually during the term of the trust.

## Grantor Trust

A type of trust the income and capital gains of which are taxed to the grantor even if not payable to him.

## Gross Domestic Product

GDP is the total value of goods and services produced by a nation.

## Gross National Product

GNP is the dollar value of all goods and services produced in a nation's economy, including goods and services produced abroad.

## Growth Stock

Stock of a corporation that has exhibited faster-than-average gains in earnings over the last few years and is expected to continue to show high levels of profit growth. Over the long run, growth stocks tend to outperform slower-growing stocks but they also tend to have higher price/earnings ratios and are consequently, riskier investments.

## Group of Eight (G8)

An organization of the eight major industrialized nations including the U.S., Canada, Britain, France, Italy, Germany, Japan, and recently they have included Russia.

# [ H ]

## Hedge Fund
Investment vehicles, much like mutual funds, which are generally structured as partnerships wherein the number of investors is limited and whose general partner has made a substantial personal investment in the fund.

The offering of most hedge funds allows them to use a combination of sophisticated investment strategies such as taking both long and short positions, using leverage and derivatives, and investing in many markets. The funds usually require investors to make a large fixed investment (i.e., $100,000) and only allows withdrawals at certain times of the year. Because hedge funds move billions of dollars in and out of markets quickly, they can have a significant impact on the day-to-day trading developments in the stock, bond, and futures markets.

## Hedging
Hedging is an investment strategy most often used to offset potential risk, although it can be used as a speculative investment in and of itself. Widely used hedging techniques include buying or selling Put or Call Options, Selling Short, and buying or selling the Futures market.

## Holding Company
A corporation that owns the securities of another, in most cases with voting control.

# [ I ]

## Income Bond
Generally income bonds promise to repay principal but to pay interest only when earned. In some cases, unpaid interest on an income bond may accumulate as a claim against the corporation when the bond becomes due. An income bond may also be issued in lieu of preferred stock.

## Indenture
A written agreement under which bonds and debentures are issued, setting forth maturity date, interest rate, and other terms.

## Index
A statistical composite used to indicate the performance of a market or a market sector over various time periods. A variety of indices are used to gauge the performance of stocks and other securities such as the Dow

Jones Industrial Average, The Standard and Poors 500 index, The Russell 2000, and many more.

## Initial Public Offering (IPO)
A corporation first offering of stock to the public. The share prices of IPOs can fluctuate wildly, with what seems to be little regard for the current value of the underlying company.

## Insider Trading
When the management of a publicly held company, or members of its board of directors, or anyone else who holds more than 10% of the company, buys or sells its shares, the transaction is considered insider trading.

This type of trading is perfectly legal, provided it's based on information available to the public. But insider trading is illegal if the buy or sell decision is based on knowledge of corporate developments—such as a change in corporate earnings, or a merger.

## Institutional Investors
Holdings by organizations that trade large volumes of securities such as banks, mutual funds, insurance companies, pension funds, college endowment funds, etc.

## Insurance Trust
A trust, generally irrevocable, meant to own insurance on the life or lives of one or more individuals and to provide for the disposition of the proceeds of such insurance. Unless irrevocable, an Insurance Trust serves no tax purpose whatsoever.

## Interest Rate Swap
A derivative in which a party agrees to pay a fixed interest rate in return for receiving a floating interest rate from another party.

## Interest Sensitive Stock
Stock of a company whose earnings change when interest rates move, such as a bank or utility. These stocks tend to go up or down on news of interest rate changes.

## Inter Vivos Trust
Any trust created during the lifetime of the person creating the trust.

## Investment Banker
Also known as an underwriter. The "middleman" between the corporation issuing new securities and the public. The usual practice is for one or more investment bankers to buy a new issue of stocks or bonds outright from a corporation. The group forms a syndicate to sell the securities to individuals and institutions. Investment bankers also distribute very large blocks of stocks or bonds—perhaps held by an estate.

## Investment Company
A company or trust that uses its capital to invest in other companies. There are two principal types: the closed-end and the open-end or mutual fund. Shares in closed-end investment companies, some of which are listed on the New York Stock Exchange, are readily transferable in the open market and are bought and sold like other shares. Capitalization of these companies remains the same unless action is taken to change, which is seldom. Open-end funds sell their own shares to investors, stand ready to buy back their old shares, and are not listed. Open-end funds are so called because their capitalization is not fixed; they issue more shares as people want them.

## IRA
Individual Retirement Account. A pension plan with tax advantages. IRA permits investment through intermediaries like mutual funds, insurance companies and banks or directly in stocks and bonds through stockbrokers.

## IRA QTIP
A type of QTIP Trust specifically designed to receive the proceeds of an IRA. It requires specific provisions in the IRA and in the IRA QTIP Trust to qualify for the marital deduction and to avoid adverse income tax consequences.

## Irrevocable Trust
Any trust that may not be amended or revoked by the grantor. Transfers to such a trust may be subject to gift tax.

# [ K ]

## Keogh Plan
Tax advantaged personal retirement program that can be established by a self-employed individual.

# [ L ]

### Lehman Brothers Treasury Bond Index
An index of prices of long-term treasury bonds.

### Leverage Buyout
The purchase of a company by a small group of investors largely financed by debt. Most often, the target company's assets serve as security for the loans taken out by the acquiring firm, which repays the loan out of cash flow of the acquired company. When a company that has gone private in a leveraged buyout offers shares to the public again, it is called a Reverse Leveraged Buyout.

### LIBOR
London Interbank Offered Rate—rate that the most creditworthy international banks dealing in Eurodollars charge each other for large loans. It is usually a basis for other large Eurodollar loans to less creditworthy corporate and government borrowers. For example, a Third World country may have to pay a point over LIBOR when it borrows money.

### Limit Order
A market order that specifies the highest or lowest price at which the customer is willing to trade securities.

For example: "Buy 100 shares of IBM at $100.00."

### Liquidation
The process of converting securities or other property into cash. The dissolution of a company, with cash remaining after sale of its assets and payment of all indebtedness being distributed to the shareholders.

### Liquidity
The ability of the market in a particular security to absorb a reasonable amount of buying or selling at reasonable price changes. Liquidity is one of the most important characteristics of a good market.

### Living Trust.
Any trust created during the lifetime of the person creating the trust. In many instances the term "Living Trust" is used to refer to a Revocable Living Trust.

## Load

The portion of the offering price of shares of open-end investment companies in excess of the value of the underlying assets. Covers sales commissions and all other costs of distribution. The load is usually incurred only on purchase, there being, in most cases, no charge when the shares are sold (redeemed).

## Long Position

Having a long position when you own a stock or bond means you have the right to collect the dividends or interest it pays, the right to sell it or give it away when you wish, and the right to keep any profits if you do sell.

## Loving Trust

This is the name given by some trust salesmen to Living Trusts.

# [ M ]

## Margin Account

A brokerage account allowing customers to buy securities with money borrowed from the brokerage firm. Margin accounts are governed by Regulation T, the NASD, the NYSE, and the firm's house rules. Margin requirements can be met with cash or eligible securities. Under Federal Reserve Board regulation, the initial margin required since 1945 has ranged from 50 to 100 percent of the security's purchase price.

## Margin Call

A demand upon a customer to put up money or securities with the broker. The call is made when a purchase is made; also if a customer's account declines below a minimum standard set by the Exchange or by the firm.

## Marital Deduction Trust

Any trust that qualifies for the estate tax (or gift tax) marital deduction. A Marital Deduction Trust may provide, for example, that the individual's spouse receives all of the net income for life, with the assets remaining in the trust and passing to a specified other individual(s) upon the spouse's death. It may also provide that the net income is payable to the spouse for life, and give that spouse the right, either by will or by another specified instrument, to determine who receives the assets remaining in the trust upon that spouse's death.

## Market Order

Authorization for a broker to buy or sell securities at the best price that can be negotiated at the moment.

For example: "Buy 100 shares of IBM at Market."

## Market Price

The last reported price at which the stock or bond sold, or the current quote.

## Market Value

Market value is the current market price of a security, as indicated by the latest trade recorded.

## Massachusetts Trust

This is not a trust at all but, rather, a corporation-like arrangement customarily utilized only in Massachusetts.

## Medicaid Trust

Typically an Inter Vivos Trust created by an individual for him-or herself, or his or her spouse, for the purpose of protecting assets and permitting eligibility for Medicaid benefits. In most instances such a trust is ineffective in obtaining such benefits. Note, however, that a Testamentary Trust may provide the benefits being sought (after the death of the person under whose will it is created). See also Supplemental Needs Trust.

## Minority Trust

This is a trust geared to hold assets during an individual's minority, although it frequently runs until the individual attains the age of 21 years (the age of majority is generally 18).

## Momentum Investing

An investment style currently popular among investors. It involves targeting companies with rapidly growing earnings—i.e. a history of positive quarterly earning surprises. The strategy inevitably involves buying stocks with extremely high P/E ratios and carries a great deal of risk. Momentum investing is favored by aggressive managers of aggressive growth and capital appreciation mutual funds.

## Money Market Fund

A mutual fund whose investments are in high-yield money market instruments such as federal securities, CDs, and commercial paper. Its intent is to make such instruments, normally purchased in large denominations by institutions, available indirectly to individuals.

## Mortgage Backed Securities
Debt issues backed by a pool of mortgages. Investors receive payments from the interest and principal payment to the underlying mortgages.

## Mortgage Bond
A bond secured by a mortgage on a property. The value of the property may or may not equal the value of the bonds issued against it.

## Moving Average
A tool used in technical analysis and charts. It is the average prices of securities or commodities constructed over a given period and showing trends for the latest interval. For example, a thirty-day moving average includes yesterday's figures; tomorrow the same average will include today's figures and will no longer show those for the earliest date included in the average. Thus, every day the average includes figures for the latest day and drops figures for the earliest day.

## Municipal Bond
A bond issued by a state or a political subdivision, such as a county, city, town, or village. The term also designates bonds issued by state agencies and authorities. In general, interest paid on municipal bonds is exempt from federal income taxes and state and local taxes within the state of issue.

## Mutual Fund
A fund operated by an investment company that pools money from shareholders and invests in various instruments such as stocks, bonds, options, futures, currencies, or money market securities. Mutual funds vary in their focus—some invest solely in foreign securities, and some target capital appreciation, while others invest to generate income. Investors in mutual funds can more easily diversify their holdings and take advantage of a professional management team. Investors can expect to pay management fees for the service.

# [ N ]

## NASD
The National Association of Securities Dealers, an association of brokers and dealers in the over-the-counter securities business.

## NASDAQ Stock Market

Includes the NASDAQ Stock Market and NASDAQ National Market, or NNM. There is no physical exchange where stocks are traded. Instead, prices are determined and trades are made on computer screens at brokerages around the country. The NASDAQ National Market trades via a computerized system that provides brokers and dealers with price quotes.

The NASDAQ Stock Market is not synonymous with the over-the-counter (OTC) market. The more than 5,000 NASDAQ-listed companies trade in a highly structured environment which has listing standards, real-time trade reporting, corporate governance requirements, affirmative obligations for market makers, execution services, and automatic linkages with clearance and settlement facilities. This cannot be said of the approximately 5,000 OTC securities.

While companies have to meet certain requirements to be listed on the NASDAQ, NASDAQ stocks are usually small-cap companies without long histories of earnings and tend to be more volatile.

## NASDAQ Composite Index

A composite index of more that 3,000 companies listed on the Nasdaq stock exchange (also referred to as over-the-counter or OTC stocks). It is designed to indicate the stock performance of small-cap and technology stocks.

## Net Asset Value

Usually used in connection with investment companies to mean net asset value per share. An investment company computes its assets daily, or even twice daily, by totaling the market value of all securities owned. All liabilities are deducted, and the balance divided by the number of shares outstanding. The resulting figure is the net asset value per share.

## Net Income Makeup Charitable Remainder Unitrust

This type of Charitable Remainder Unitrust, often used to supplement a retirement plan, permits the trustee to invest for maximum growth of capital since only the net income of the trust need be distributed currently. In the future (e.g., at retirement), the trust investments are rearranged to increase the trust's income, and the "unpaid" past distributions may be made up.

## New York Stock Exchange

Founded in 1792, the NYSE is the oldest and largest stock exchange in the U.S. The Big Board, as it is known, lists more that 1,600 companies who meet stringent listing requirements. There are 1,366 seats on the NYSE, many of which are owned by partners or officers of securities firms, and which handle trades for the public.

## New York Stock Exchange Composite Index
A composite index of shares listed on the NYSE.

# [ O ]

## Odd Lots
Stocks sold in quantities of less than 100 shares. Generally, it costs less to trade in round lots (purchases of 100 or more shares).

## Offer
The price at which a person is ready to sell. Opposed to bid, the price at which one is ready to buy.

## Offshore Trust
A trust administered outside of the United States, frequently for the purpose of hiding funds from the grantor's creditors.

## Open Market Operation
One of the three means of conducting monetary policy used by the Federal Reserve. It involves the purchase and sale of Government securities by the Federal Reserve Bank of New York (as directed by the Federal Open Market Committee) in an effort to regulate the money supply. The actions of the New York Fed effectively alter bank reserves which, in turn, affects the supply of credit. This affect is realized throughout the economy.

## Open Order
A limit order that does not expire at the end of the trading day.

## Operating Income
Essentially, it is the income derived from a company's regular business, excluding all income or losses from other sources. Operating income is defined as the revenues of a business minus related costs and expenses. It excludes extraordinary items, such as all realized gains and losses on investments or discontinued operations, taxes, prior year adjustments, write-offs of intangibles, bonuses and other profit distributions to employees, sales of divisions, etc.

## Options
The right to buy or sell stock at a certain price before a specified date. If the buyer chooses not to exercise the option, the option expires and the

option buyer forfeits the money. The buyer hopes that the stock's price will go up (a call) or down (a put) by an amount sufficient to provide a profit when the option is sold. If the stock price holds steady or moves in the opposite direction, the price paid for the option is lost entirely. There are several other types of options available to the public but these are basically combinations of puts and calls. Individuals may write (sell) as well as purchase options. Options are also traded on stock indices, futures, and debt instruments.

## Overbought
An opinion as to price levels. May refer to a security that has had a sharp rise in price or to the market as a whole after a period of vigorous buying, which, it may be argued, has left prices "too high."

## Oversold
The reverse of overbought. A single security or a market which, it is believed, has declined to an unreasonable level.

## Over-The-Counter Stocks (OTC)
Stocks that are not listed and do not trade on an organized exchange, such as the NYSE or the AMEX. They are usually small-cap companies that do not meet the exchange requirements. Trading procedures are written and enforced by the National Association of Securities Dealers (NASD), a self-regulatory group. Transactions are conducted by phone and computer network which connect dealers and provide quotes. Some large companies (i.e. Intel and Microsoft) have chosen to remain as over-the-counter because they favor the system of multiple trading by many dealers over the centralized exchange system of specialists.

# [ P ]

## Par
The nominal or face values of a security. Bonds are issued at, and mature at, par which is usually $1,000 per bond. Prior to maturity, they trade at, above, or below par, depending on their coupon rate versus the current level of interest rates. Par value for common stocks is set by the issuing company and has no relation to market value. Par value is more important in the case of preferred stock, where dividends are often stated as a percentage of the par value of the preferred stock issue.

## Penny Stocks
Low-priced issues, often highly speculative, selling at less than $1 a share. Frequently used as a term of disparagement, although some penny stocks have developed into investment-caliber issues.

## Pour-Over Trust
A trust fed from another instrument. For example, in a person's will the executor may be instructed to transfer (pour over) all or a portion of the assets of the estate to a trust created under another instrument.

## Power Of Appointment Trust
A trust over which an individual has a power of appointment—being the right to designate who will receive some or all of the assets of the trust at a specified time(s). A power of appointment may be exercisable either during life (an "Inter Vivos Power") or by a will (a "Testamentary Power").

## Preferred Shares
A class of stock that normally pays dividends at a fixed rate and carries no voting rights. Preferred shareholders do, however, carry a preference over shareholders of Common Stock in the payment of dividends and liquidation of assets.

## Price-To-Book Value
Also called Multiple-to-Book Value, it is a measure of the relative risk/reward profile of a stock. It is calculated by dividing the latest stock price per share by the most recent per share value of stockholders equity (book value). A company with a stock price of $12 per share and a book value of $6 per share is trading at two times book value. Generally, the higher the multiple-to-book value, the riskier the stock is, however, it is important to know that multiples vary from industry to industry and should be considered as such.

## Price/Earnings Ratio (P/E)
A widely used valuation measure of the relationship between a stock's price and its earnings per share, it is also referred to as Multiple-to-Earnings or simply, The Multiple. Its formula is: current stock price per share divided by the most current earnings per share. It is an important tool for investors, as it indicates how much they are paying for a company's earning power. Stocks with low P/E multiples (those below 20, although relative multiples do vary from industry to industry) tend to be slow growth, steady, and perhaps mature companies. Those with higher P/E multiples are usually growth stocks and tend to be more risky. Trailing P/E multiples use last year's earnings and the current price.

## Prime Rate
The lowest interest rate charged by commercial banks to their most credit-worthy customers. Other interest rates, such as personal,

automobile, commercial, and financing loans are often pegged to the prime.

## Program Trading
Investment strategy that uses computers programmed to buy or sell large numbers of securities to take advantage of price discrepancies between stock index futures or options and the actual stocks represented in those averages.

## Profit-Taking
Selling stock which has appreciated in value since purchase, in order to realize the profit. The term is often used to explain a downturn in the market following a period of rising prices.

## Pro Forma
Latin for "as a matter of form. " Used on balance sheets and income statements to refer to data that is hypothetical. For example, if company A buys company B mid-year, the year-end financials of Company A might show the current earnings results and the year-ago results as Pro Forma—as if the two companies had been merged all along. This gives a more relevant earnings comparison, year over year.

## Prospectus
The official selling circular that must be given to purchasers of new securities registered with the Securities and Exchange Commission. It highlights the much longer Registration Statement file with the Commission.

## Proxy
Written authorization given by a shareholder to someone else to represent him or her and vote his or her shares at a shareholders' meeting.

## Put Option
An option that gives the owner (option holder) the right, but not the obligation, to sell a specific asset at a predetermined price until a certain date. Investors purchase put options in order to take advantage of a decline in the price of the asset.

# [ Q ]

## Qualified Domestic Trust (QDOT)
Trust very similar to a QTIP Trust, but is meant for a surviving spouse who is *not* a *citizen* of the United States. A Qualified Domestic Trust must have specific provisions regarding the distribution of income and

principal, dealing with who may be trustees and, unless an appropriate bank or trust company is a trustee, securing the IRS with respect to future taxes. It is subject to special tax rules applicable only to such trusts.

## Qualified Personal Residence Trust (QPRT)
Variation of a Grantor Retained Annuity Trust. It is a trust funded with the grantor's residence or vacation home. It provides that the grantor may reside in the residence (or in another purchased with the proceeds of the sale of the residence) for a specified number of years, at the end of which the property passes to or in trust for one or more other persons. Its purpose is to reduce the value of the property for transfer tax purposes.

## Qualified Terminable Interest Property Trust (QTIP)
One of several types of trusts designed to qualify for the estate or gift tax marital deduction. It provides that the grantor's spouse receives all of the net income for life. It may (but need not) provide for invasions of principal for the benefit of that spouse. Upon the death of the spouse for whose benefit the trust was created, the assets in the trust are includable in that spouse's estate for estate tax purposes and are distributed in accordance with the provisions of the trust.

## Quote
The highest bid to buy and the lowest offer to sell a security in a given market at a given time. If you ask your broker for a "quote" on a stock, he or she may come back with something like "45¼ to 45½." This means that $45.25 was the highest price any buyer wanted to pay at the time the quote was given on the floor of the Exchange and that $45.50 was the lowest price any seller would take at the same time.

# [ R ]

## Rabbi Trust
This is not a typical trust arrangement but, in fact, a type of retirement plan or deferred compensation arrangement. The first was created for a rabbi (thus its name).

## Rally
A brisk rise following a decline in the general price level of the market, or in an individual stock.

## Rate of Return
Percentage increase in the value of an investment.

## Real Estate Investment Trust (REIT)

Publicly-traded companies that manage portfolios of real estate to generate profits. The underlying assets are investments in shopping centers, medical facilities, office buildings, apartment complexes, hotels, and various other real estate holdings. One type of REIT takes equity positions in real estate and distributes the income from rents and capital gains (when properties are sold) to shareholders. Other REITs act as lenders to property developers and pass interest income on to shareholders. A third type of REIT combines equity and mortgage investments. To avoid taxation, REITs must distribute 95% of their taxable income to shareholders annually.

## Record Date

The date on which you must be registered as a shareholder of a company in order to receive a declared dividend or, among other things, to vote on company affairs.

## Redemption Price

The price at which a bond may be redeemed before maturity, at the option of the issuing company. Redemption value also applies to the price the company must pay to call in certain types of preferred stock.

## Registrar

Usually a trust company or bank charged with the responsibility of keeping record of the owners of a corporation's securities and preventing the issuance of more than the authorized amount.

## Residuary Trust

Any trust (there are numerous varieties) funded with the assets remaining (the residue) after the payment of all prior ("pre-residuary") bequests, as well as debts, expenses, etc. and, sometimes, taxes.

## Return on Equity (ROE)

A measure of return for each dollar of shareholder investment—in essence, it is how effectively the shareholder's investment is being employed. The percentages can be compared year over year and considered relative to industry composites, both to reveal trends and a company's position versus its competitors. ROE is calculated by dividing the annual earnings from operations (*see Operating Income*) by common shareholders equity (total assets minus total liabilities).

## Revocable Living Trust

A trust created during the grantor's life that may be revoked by the grantor. It is sometimes used to avoid probate, sometimes to provide management during the grantor's lifetime, sometimes to permit the administration, without additional ("ancillary") probate proceedings, of assets (e.g., real estate) located in a jurisdiction other than the one in which the grantor resides, and sometimes for other purposes. Such trusts save absolutely no income, gift, or estate taxes, as compared to wills, and may, or may not, reduce administration expenses and legal and accounting fees. Revocable Living Trusts must be executed in accordance with applicable state law. People often receive totally inaccurate information as to the benefits (and detriments) of Revocable Living Trusts.

## Rights Offering
An offering of common stock to existing shareholders who hold rights which entitle them to purchase the newly-issued shares at a discount to the market price.

## Round Lots
Stocks sold in 100-share quantities.

## Russell 2000 Index
A market capitalization weighted index published by Frank Russell of Tacoma, Washington. The Russell 2000 is one of the most widely regarded measures of the stock price performance of small companies. It is a part of the Russell 3000 Index, which consists of the 3,000 largest U.S. stocks in terms of market capitalization. The highest-ranking 1,000 stocks are in the Russell 1000 Index (which closely mirrors the S&P 500 Index). The remaining 2000 stocks, the Russell 2000 Index, represent approximately 11% of the Russell 3000 Index's total market capitalization.

# [ S ]

## S&P 500 Index
A broad-based measurement of changes in stock market conditions based on the average performance of 500 widely-held stocks including industrial, transportation, financial, and utility stocks. The composition of the 500 stocks is flexible and the number of issues in each sector varies over time.

## S.E.C.
The Securities and Exchange Commission, established by Congress to help protect investors. The SEC administers the Securities Act of 1933, the Securities Exchange Act of 1934, the Securities Act Amendments of

1975, the Trust Indenture Act, the Investment Company Act, the Investment Advisers Act, and the Public Utility Holding Company Act.

## Second-To-Die Insurance Trust
A type of Insurance Trust geared to own one or more second-to-die (also called Survivorship or Last-to-Die) life insurance policies insuring the lives of two (generally) people, who may (but need not) be husband and wife.

## Section 2503(c) Trust
A trust for a minor (actually a person under the age of 21 years) designed to receive the annual gift tax exclusion for gifts on behalf of the minor. Section 2503(c) trusts are an alternative to the use of the Uniform Gifts (or Transfers) to Minors Act and are often a better way of planning with respect to gifts to children, particularly if under the age of 14 years, whose parents are in a high income tax bracket. A Section 2503(c) trust can have provisions allowing more flexibility than is available under the Uniform Gifts (or Transfers) to Minors Act. Variations of this trust permit the trust to continue beyond the date on which the beneficiary attains the age of 21 years.

## Securities
Documents proving debt or ownership that may be bought or sold.

## Selling Short
Selling a security or a futures contract which the seller does not own. It is a strategy used to take advantage of an anticipated decline in price or to protect a long position. In the case of stocks, the seller borrows the stock for delivery, betting that the market price will drop and that the stock can be bought later at a lower price. If a stock is sold short at $20 per share and the price of that stock drops to $15, then the seller can buy the shares at $15, making a profit of $5 per share. Short sellers can face a substantial loss if the stock price rises. They may be forced to buy back the stock at prices much higher than when they were originally sold.

## Shareholders Equity
Also called Stockholder's Equity and Net Worth, it is Total Assets minus Total Liabilities of a corporation.

## SIPC
Securities Investor Protection Corporation, which provides funds for use, if necessary, to protect customers' cash and securities that may be on deposit with a SIPC member firm in the event the firm fails and is liquidated under the provisions of the SIPC Act. SIPC is not a

government agency, however, it is a non-profit membership corporation created by an act of Congress.

## Speculators
Investors who seek large capital gains through relatively risky investments.

## Spill-Over Trust
A trust fed from another instrument. For example, in a person's will the executor may be instructed to transfer (spill over) all or a portion of the assets of the estate to a trust created under another instrument.

## Spot Trading
Trading in commodities that will be delivered immediately (also called cash trading).

## Sprinkling Trust
A discretionary trust for the benefit of the members of a specified group, such as the grantor's spouse and descendants.

## Standby Trust
A trust created during life that is normally unfunded until assets are added to it via a power of attorney upon the incapacity of the grantor of the trust.

## Stock Split
Authorized by a company's Board of Directors, splits have the effect of increasing the number of shares outstanding without changing the total market value of the company or diluting a shareholder's percentage stake in the company. The theory behind splits is to lower the stock price so as to make investment in the company available to a broad base on investors. A 2-for-1 split, for example, would give a stockholder of 100 shares trading at $50 per share ownership of 200 shares trading at $25 per share.

## Stop Order
An order to buy at a price above or sell at a price below the current market. Stop buy orders are generally used to limit loss or protect unrealized profits on a short sale. Stop sell orders are generally used to protect unrealized profits or limit loss on a holding. A stop order becomes a market order when the stock sells at or beyond the specified price and, thus, may not necessarily be executed at that price.

## Strike Price
Exercise price at which the owner of a call option can purchase the underlying stock or the owner of a put option can sell the underlying stock. The strike price is set by the exchange.

## Supplemental Needs Trust
A trust for the benefit of an incapacitated person. It typically provides that its assets are available to be used for the benefit of that person, but the trustees are not to use trust assets to the extent the incapacitated person would otherwise be receiving governmental benefits. Accordingly it is possible, for example, for a parent to create a Supplemental Needs Trust for an incapacitated child without interfering with the child's Medicaid benefits. Supplemental Needs Trusts often provide care for the beneficiary in addition to what Medicaid provides and deal with a beneficiary's nonessentials, such as paying for a vacation, a television set, etc. The use of Supplemental Needs Trusts was expanded under provisions of the tax law enacted by Congress in 1993, but such trusts can be used only for certain beneficiaries and only under certain circumstances.

# [ T ]

## Technical Research
Analysis of the market and stocks based on supply and demand. The technician studies price movements, volume, trends, and patterns, which are revealed by charting these factors, and attempts to assess the possible affect of current market action on future supply and demand for securities and individual issues.

## Testamentary Trust
Any trust created under a Last Will and Testament.

## Ticker
A telegraphic system that continuously provides the last sale prices and volume of securities transactions on exchanges. Information is either printed or displayed on a moving tape after each trade.

## Ticker Symbol
The abbreviation used to identify a company's securities for trading purposes, such as IBM for International Business Machines, and KO for Coca-Cola.

## Total Return
Stocks: The annual increase or decrease in the investment including appreciation, dividends, and interest. the value of a security.

Bonds: Held to maturity, it is the Yield to Maturity.

Mutual Funds: The net asset value plus any capital gains and income distribution.

## Totten Trust
This name is given to a permitted asset (not a trust) titled so that, upon the death of that person, it passes to one or more other named persons without going through probate.

## Treasury Bills, Notes, Bonds
Negotiable debt obligations of the U.S. Government. Auctions take place frequently and yields are watched closely in the money markets for signs of interest rate tends. T-Bills are short-term instruments with maturities of one year or less, issued at a discount from face value. T-Notes are intermediate securities with maturities of one to 10 years. T-Bonds are long-term debt instruments with maturities of 10 years or longer.

## Treasury Stock
Stock issued by a company but later reacquired. It may be held in the company's treasury indefinitely, reissued to the public, or retired. Treasury stock receives no dividends and has no vote while held by the company.

## Triple Witching Hour
Term for the simultaneous expiration each quarter of stock-index futures, options on individual stocks, and stock-index options. The markets tend to be volatile on those days (the third Friday in March, June, September, and December) as there may be massive trades by hedge strategists, arbitrageurs, and other investors.

## Turnover Rate
The volume of shares traded in a year as a percentage of total shares listed on an Exchange, outstanding for an individual issue, or held in an institutional portfolio.

# [ U ]

## Undervalued Security

A stock selling below its liquidation value or below the market value that analysts believe it deserves. Undervalued stocks are sought after for investment before the stock price rises and they become fully valued. Undervalued companies are often the target of take-over attempts.

## Unified Credit Trust

A trust customarily designed to receive the maximum amount which can pass free of Federal estate tax upon the death of the first of two spouses to die. It has numerous variations. Frequently the terms of the trust provide that all of its income will be payable to the surviving spouse for life, with the assets then passing to or in trust for one or more others upon the surviving spouse's death.

## Unlisted Stock

A security not listed on a stock exchange.

# [ V ]

## Value Line Composite Index

An equal-weighted index which averages the price change from the previous day's close in each of the index's approximately 1,700 component stocks. Smaller, more volatile stocks have the same impact on the index value as large-cap less volatile stocks, therefore, the index is more sensitive to economic changes than a broad-based index.

## Variable Annuity

A life insurance policy where the annuity premium (a set amount of dollars) is immediately turned into units of a portfolio of stocks. Upon retirement, the policyholder is paid according to accumulated units, the dollar value of which varies according to the performance of the stock portfolio. Its objective is to preserve, through stock investment, the purchasing value of the annuity which otherwise is subject to erosion through inflation.

## Volume

In the case of the exchanges, it is the total number of stock shares listed on a particular exchange that traded. It is usually measured on a daily basis. In the case of a particular stock, it is the number of shares of that security which traded on a given day.

## Voting Right

The common stockholders' right to vote their stock in affairs of a company. Preferred stock usually has the right to vote when preferred dividends are in default for a specified period. The right to vote may be delegated by the stockholder to another person (proxy).

## Voting Trust

An arrangement for a specified, limited period by which one or more individuals authorize one or more other individuals to vote the shares of stock owned by the individual(s) creating the Voting Trust. It has no other typical trust attributes.

# [ W ]

## Warrant

A certificate giving the holder the right to purchase securities at a stipulated price within a specified time limit or perpetually. Sometimes a warrant is offered with securities as an inducement to buy.

## Wealth Replacement Trust

The name given to a type of insurance trust the purpose of which is to hold insurance on the life of an individual, or an individual and his spouse, and to utilize the proceeds of that insurance to replace assets passing to charity, such as upon the termination of a Charitable Remainder Trust.

## Wilshire 5000 Index

A widely-watched "total market" index that attempts to track the direction of most of the widely-traded shares on U.S. exchanges including small-, mid-, and large-cap issues.

## Working Control

Theoretically, ownership of 51 percent of a company's voting stock is necessary to exercise control. In practice—and this is particularly true in the case of a large corporation—effective control sometimes can be exerted through ownership, individually or by a group acting in concert, of less than 50 percent.

# [ Y ]

## Yield

Also known as return. The dividends or interest paid by a company expressed as a percentage of the current price. A stock with a current market value of $40 a share paying dividends at the rate of $3.20 is said to return 8 percent ($3.20 / $40.00). The current yield on a bond is figured the same way.

## Yield Curve
A graph plotting the yields of all bonds of the same quality with maturities ranging from the shortest to the longest available. The resulting curve shows if short-term interest rates are higher or lower than long-term rates. It is used as a tool by analysts to help determine the direction of interest rates. A Flat Yield Curve results when there is little difference between short-term and long-term rates. When short-term rates are lower than long-term rates, it is called a Positive Yield Curve. Conversely, it is called a Negative Yield Curve if short-term rates are higher than long-term rates.

## Yield to Maturity (YTM)
The rate of return yielded by a debt security that is held to maturity when both interest payments and the investor's capital gain or loss on the security are taken into account.

# [ Z ]

## Zero Coupon Bond
A bond which pays no interest but is priced, at issue, at a discount from its redemption price.

# Book Order Form

**TELEPHONE ORDERS:**    970-249-9900

**MAIL ORDERS:**    ElderAdo Financial Publishing
1100 S. Townsend Ave
Montrose, CO 81401

**EMAIL ORDERS:**    info@ElderAdoFinancial.com

Please send me _____ copies of WealthCare

@ $19.95 per book    _____

Colorado Residents add $ .70 per book sales tax    _____

Shipping:    $2.00 for first book;
$1.00 for each additional book    _____

    TOTAL    _____

Ship to:

Name _____
Address _____
City / State / Zip _____
Telephone ( ) _____

Make checks payable to:

ElderAdo Financial Publishing
1100 S. Townsend Ave
Montrose, CO 81401

(*Please allow 2 to 4 weeks for delivery*)